우루과이라운드

서비스 분야 양허 협상 1

우루과이라운드

서비스 분야 양허
협상 1

| 머리말

    우루과이라운드는 국제적 교역 질서를 수립하려는 다각적 무역 교섭으로서, 각국의 보호무역 추세를 보다 완화하고 다자무역체제를 강화하기 위해 출범되었다. 1986년 9월 개시가 선언되었으며, 15개 분야의 교섭을 1990년 말까지 진행하기로 했다. 그러나 각 분야의 중간 교섭이 이루어진 1989년 이후에도 농산물, 지적소유권, 서비스무역, 섬유, 긴급수입제한 등 많은 분야에서 대립하며 1992년이 돼서야 타결에 이를 수 있었다. 한국은 특히 농산물 분야에서 기존 수입 제한 품목 대부분을 개방해야 했기에 큰 경쟁력 하락을 겪었고, 관세와 기술 장벽 완화, 보조금 및 수입 규제 정책의 변화로 제조업 수출입에도 많은 변화가 있었다.

    본 총서는 우루과이라운드 협상이 막바지에 다다랐던 1991~1992년 사이 외교부에서 작성한 관련 자료를 담고 있다. 관련 협상의 치열했던 후반기 동향과 관계부처회의, 무역협상위원회 회의, 실무대책회의, 규범 및 제도, 투자회의, 특히나 가장 많은 논란이 있었던 농산물과 서비스 분야 협상 등의 자료를 포함해 총 28권으로 구성되었다. 전체 분량은 약 1만 3천여 쪽에 이른다.

2024년 3월
한국학술정보(주)

| 일러두기

· 본 총서에 실린 자료는 2022년 4월과 2023년 4월에 각각 공개한 외교문서 4,827권, 76만여 쪽 가운데 일부를 발췌한 것이다.

· 각 권의 제목과 순서는 공개된 원본을 최대한 반영하였으나, 주제에 따라 일부는 적절히 변경하였다.

· 원본 자료는 A4 판형에 맞게 축소하거나 원본 비율을 유지한 채 A4 페이지 안에 삽입하였다. 또한 현재 시점에선 공개되지 않아 '공란'이란 표기만 있는 페이지 역시 그대로 실었다.

· 외교부가 공개한 문서 각 권의 첫 페이지에는 '정리 보존 문서 목록'이란 이름으로 기록물 종류, 일자, 명칭, 간단한 내용 등의 정보가 수록되어 있으며, 이를 기준으로 0001번부터 번호가 매겨져 있다. 이는 삭제하지 않고 총서에 그대로 수록하였다.

· 보고서 내용에 관한 더 자세한 정보가 필요하다면, 외교부가 온라인상에 제공하는 『대한민국 외교사료요약집』 1991년과 1992년 자료를 참조할 수 있다.

| 차례

머리말 4

일러두기 5

UR(우루과이라운드)-서비스 분야 양허협상, 1992. 전6권(V.1 1-2월) 7

UR(우루과이라운드)-서비스 분야 양허협상, 1992. 전6권(V.2 3-5월) 233

0001

외 무 부

종 별 : 지 급

번 호 : GVW-0048

일 시 : 92 0109 2000

수 신 : 장관(수신처참조)

발 신 : 주제네바차석대사

제 목 : UR/GNS 협상

　　1.9(목) USTR 제네바 사무소에서는 1.20(월) 오후한.미간 서비스 양자 협상 개최를 요청하여왔는바, 동 서한을 별첨 송부하니 지급 검토 방침통보 바람. 첨부: USTR측 서한 1부(GVW(F)-0008)

　　수신처:통기, 경기원, 재무부, 법무부, 농림수산부, 문화부, 상공부, 건설부, 보사부, 노동부 ,교통부, 체신부, 과기처, 공보처, 항만청)

　　(차석대사 김삼훈-국장)

통상국	2차보	구주국	법무부	보사부	문화부	교통부	체신부	경기원
재무부	농수부	상공부	건설부	노동부	과기처	해항정	공보처	

PAGE 1

92.01.10　06:03 BU

외신 1과 통제관

0002

주 제 네 바 대 표 부

번 호 : GVW(F) - 0008   년월일 : 20/08   시간 : 2007

수 신 : 장   관(통기.경기원. 재부. 법무부. 농수산부. 문화부. 상공부. 건설부. 보사부

발 신 : 주 제네바대사   노동부. 근로부. 해사부. 차기처. 공보처.행만힘)

제 목 :

보 안
봉 제

외신과
봉 제

총   2   매(표지포함)

UNITED STATES TRADE REPRESENTATIVE

1-3 AVENUE DE LA PAIX
1202 GENEVA, SWITZERLAND
TELEPHONE: 732 09 70

9 January 1992

Dear Mr. Han,

Happy New Year!

Washington will be sending a team of experts to Geneva to conduct bilateral access negotiations for services. USTR Director for Services and coordinator of these negotiations, Ms. Bonnie Richardson, would like to meet with your delegation at USTR/Geneva, 1-3 Avenue de la Paix at <u>2:00 - 6:00 on Monday, 20 January</u>.

We would appreciate confirmation of this suggested time as soon as possible. Please contact me (749-5310) or my secretary, Ms. Brita Lineburger (749-5280). In the event you cannot reach either of us, USTR's fax number is 749-4885.

For your information, we expect to have a revised services offer ready for circulation on January 13. I will forward the offer as soon as I receive it from Washington.

Thank you for your consideration.

Sincerely,

Christina Lund
Attache, USTR/Geneva

0004

과 학 기 술 처

우 427-760 경기 과천 중앙 1, 정부 제2종합청사내 / (02)503-7659 / 전송

문서번호 기용16333-43

시행일자 1992. 1. 10.

(경유)

수신 수신처참조

참조

선결			지시		
접수	일자시간	92.1.17	결재·공람		
	번호	1282			
처리과					
담당자					

제목 UR협상 자료송부

　　　1. UR협상을 통해 스웨텐정부는 우리처에서 개정예정인 엔지니어링 진흥법에 대한 요지를 제출토록 요청하여온바 UR협상과 직접 관련된 조항을 발췌하여 송부하오니 스웨텐 UR협상 대표자에게 제출하여 주시기 바랍니다.

첨부 관련자료 1건.　　끝.

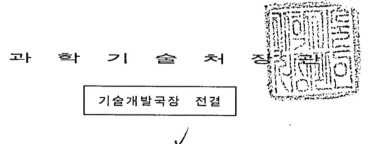

과 학 기 술 처 장

기술개발국장 전결

수신처 경제기획원장관(통상조정3과장), 외무부장관(통상기구과장)

기술용역육성법 비교 (신구대비표) - 요약

==

- UR협상과 관련된 쟁점 조항에 한함 -

현 안	개 정(안)
기술용역육성법	엔지니어링기술진흥법
제 1조 (목적) · 국내 기술용역업체의 건전한 육성과 국내 기술수준의 향상을 도모함으로써 국민 경제발전에 기여	제 1조 (목적) · 엔지니어링 활동주체의 기술집약화를 촉진함으로써 국민 경제발전에 기여
제 2조 (정의) · 생략	제 2조 (정의) · 생략
제 3조 (등록) · 용역의 종류별로 과기처에 등록	제 3조 (지원시책의 강구) · 정부는 엔지니어링기술의 진흥을 위해 지원시책강구
	제 4조 (엔지니어링 활동주체의 신고) · 엔지니어링 활동주체는 과기처에 등록)
	제 5조 (엔지니어링 사업평가) · 발주자는 입찰자의 기술,경영,실적등에 대하여 평가할수 있슴
	제 6조 (핵심엔지니어링 기술의 개발지원) · 정부는 엔지니어링기술을 개발 보급할 수 있슴
제 4조 (용역의 수행) ① 국내업자는 주계약자 또는 사업관리 대행자야 한다 ② 국내용역업자가 수행할수 없는 용역업무만을 외국용역업자가 수행가능 - 외국환 관리법에 따라 처리 ③ 국내기술로서 수행할수 없는 부분에 대하여 과기처장관의 승인하에 외국용역업자에게 수행가능 - 제1항과 관련 ④ 외자도입법에 의하여 외국용역업자에게 수행하게 하여야 할 특별한 사정이 있는 경우 - 과기처장관의 승인하에 외국용역가능	제 7조 (엔지니어링 기술도입 계획의 신고 등) · 외국기술을 도입코자 하는자는 계약체결전에 과기처에 신고 제 8조 (엔지니어링 기술도입 계약의 신고 등) ① 외국도입계약 체결자는 계약발효전에 과기처에 신고 ② 신고된 사항에 대해서는 외환관리법에 따라 외환추천 제 9조 (엔지니어링 기술수출 계획의 신고 등) ① 외국에 기술을 수출코자 하는자는 과기처에 신고

0006

The Comparison of existing Engineering Service Promotion Law (ESPL) and new the Law, which will be revised in the future

Excerpt from existing ESPL	Excerpt from new ESPL
Article 1 (Purpose) -The purpose of this law is to promote the steady growth of the nation's consulting engineering profession and to improve its engineering capability. thereby contributing to the development of national economy	Article 1 (Purpose) -The purpose of this law is to contribute the development of the national economy by promoting the engineering activities of the nation's consulting engineering firms.
Article 2 (Definition) - Omitted	Article 2 (Definition) - Omitted
Article 3 (Registration) -① Persons intending to providing services shall <u>register</u> with the Ministry of Science & Technology(MOST) by the classification of engineering practice prescribed in the Presidential Decree	Article 3 (Promotion policy) - The Government(MOST) may set up a policy to promote the national engineering industry
	Article 4 (Declaration) -① Engineering firms or Engineering units intending to provide services shall file a <u>declaration</u> with MOST by the classification of engineering activities prescribed in the Presidential Decree.
	Article 5 (Assessment of project implementation) -① The bidder may assess technical and managerial capabilities and past performance of tender to achieve optimal engineering performance.
	Article 6 (Development of core enginnering technology) -① The Government may provide to develop core engineering technolgy
Article 4 (Engineering Services Practice) -① All engineering projects in Korea shall be undertaken by native engineers, either as prime contractors or as project management agents -② Where the native engineers are in capable of providing a certain service, such assignment may be undertaken in accordance with the provisions of the Foreign Exchange Control Act, by foreign consulting engineers with Prior approval from MOST	Article 7 (Declaration of import plan of foreign engineering service) -① Persons intending to import foreign engineering practices shall declare their engineering practices import plan to MOST before they make contracts with foreign engineering services suppliers

0007

Excerpt from existing ESPL	Excerpt from new ESPL
-③ Native engineers, who secured the contracts and found parts of assignments beyond their own capabilities, may engage foreign engineers to carry out such portions with prior approval of MOST -④ Where the special cases under the Foreign Capital Inducement Law require the participation of foreign engineering service, it may be executed with prior approval from MOST Article 5 to Article 17 are omitted	Article 8 (Declaration of foreign Engineering Services Agreement) ① Persons who make agreements for foreign engineering services with foreign consulting engineers or firms shall declare their agreements to the MOST before their agreements enter into force. ② MOST shall make the necessary arrangements to send the services fee in compliance with the provision of the Foreign Exchange Control Act Article 9 (Engineering Services Export) ① Persons who intend to export their engineering services shall complete the declaration with MOST Article 10 to Article 37 are omitted

경 제 기 획 원

우 427-760 / 경기도 과천시 중앙동1 정부제2청사 / 전화 503-9149 / 전송 503-9141

문서번호 통조삼 10502-7

시행일자 1992. 1. 10.

(경유)

수신 수신처참조

참조

선결			지시		
접수	일자 시간	92: 1. 13	결재·공람		
	번호	1406			
	처리과				
	담당자				

제목 UR/서비스 협상대책 추진

1. 지난해 12월 20일 개최된 TNC회의에서 UR서비스협상그룹의장이 자신의 책임하에 제시한 UR서비스 일반협정문(안)을 송부하니 협상대책추진에 활용하시고 소관사항에 대하여 의견이 있는 경우 당원(통상조정3과)에 즉시 통보해 주기 바랍니다.

2. 현 단계에서 서비스 일반협정 제정을 위한 협상은 해운부속서를 제외하고는 거의 마무리가 된 상태이며 향후 UR/서비스협상은 전반적인 UR협상의 진전이 순조로울 경우 3월말까지 두세차례의 양허협상을 하여 국내서비스시장의 개방수준을 확정할 것으로 전망됩니다.

3. 이와 관련하여 아직 분야별 수정 Offer를 제출하지 않은 관계부처는 즉시 제출해 주시고 향후 각부처는 Offer 수정작업과 양허협상 대응작업에 적극 참여해 주기 바랍니다. Offer 수정작업은 1월말까지 완료하되 제출시기는 다른국가의 제출동향을 감안하여 UR대책 실무위원회에서 추후 결정할 예정입니다.

첨부 : UR/서비스 일반협정문(안)의 주요내용 1부. 끝.

경 제 기 획 원

대리경제 조정신장 전결

수신처 : 외무부장관, 내무부장관, 재무부장관, 법무부장관, 교육부장관, 문화부장관, 농림수산부장관, 상공부장관, 보건사회부장관, 건설부장관, 교통부장관, 노동부장관, 동자부장관, 체신부장관, 체육청소년부장관, 과학기술처장관, 환경처장관, 공보처장관, 경찰청장, 특허청장, 해운항만청장, 대외경제정책연구원장, 한국개발연구원장

0009

전 언 통 신 문

국금 22251-38

수신 외무부장관

발신 재무부장관

제목 UR/금융서비스 협상

1. USW-0663과 관련입니다.

2. UR 금융분야 수정 Offer List 진행사항과 관련한 미 재무성 Lundsager
한국과장의 문의와 관련 아국의 입장을 미 재무성에 긴급히 전달될 수 있도록
협조하여 주시기 바랍니다.

- 다   음 -

가. 현재 우리의 수정 Offer List 작성은 2.15까지 국내절차를 거친후
   2.17경 GATT에 정식 제출될 예정임.
나. 금융분야 수정 Offer List등 금융분야 양자협상은 당부 협상 대표인
   국제금융과장의 제10차 한.미 경제협의(2.24) 참석 일정상 제네바에서
   2.26-28이 적절함.

3. UR 금융분야 수정 Offer List 및 금융분야 양자협상을 위한 미국, EC등
주요 선진국가의 양자협의가 2.26-28동안 진행될 수 있도록 주 제네바 대표부
관계자들과 협의하여 주시기 바랍니다.   끝.

수 화 자 : 이 영 심

송 화 자 : 전 원 호

통화일시 : 1992. 1. 14. 14:15

0010

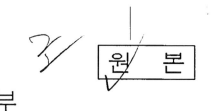

외 무 부

종 별 :

번 호 : GVW-0108   일 시 : 92 0116 1820

수 신 : 장 관(수신처 참조)

발 신 : 주 제네바대사

제 목 : UR/GNS 협상

1. 표제협상 관련 3월까지의 INITIAL COMMITMENT에 대한 양자협상 일정은 아래와 같음.

   O 1.20-1.31

   O 2.17-2.28

   O 3.9-3.20

   O 필요시 상기 주간사이에 INITIAL COMMITMENTS 관련미결 과제에 대하여 논의

2. 1월중 아국의 양자 협상 일정은 추보예정임. 끝

수신처:통기, 경기원, 재무부, 법무부, 농림수산부, 문화부, 상공부, 건설부, 보사부, 노동부, 교통부, 체신부, 과기처, 공보처, 항만청

(대사 박수길-국장)

통상국	법무부	문화부	교통부	체신부	경기원	재무부	농수부	상공부
동자부	건설부	노동부	과기처	해항청	공보처			

외 무 부

종 별 :

번 호 : GVW-0119   일 시 : 92 0117 1820

수 신 : 장 관(수신처참조)

발 신 : 주 제네바대사

제 목 : UR/GNS@양자협상

연: GVW-0108

1. 연호 서비스분야 INITIAL COMMITMENTS 협상관련 현재까지 협의된 아국의
양자협상일정을 하기보고함.

　　1. 1.28(화) 09:00 : EC (금융,통신 포함 전분야)

　　15:00 : 스웨덴 (상동)

　　0 1.29(수) 14:00 : 미국(통신포함 전분야, 금융분야포함 여부 미정)

　　0 1.30(목) 16:00 : 뉴질랜드 (금융, 통신포함전분야)

　　0 1.31(금) 15:00 : 호주 (금융포함 전분야,통신제외)

2. 상기 협상관련 뉴질랜드는 내주초 아국에 REQUEST-LIST 를 전달할 예정이라고
하며 자국의 수정 OFFER 를 1.16(목) 제출하였다고 함.

　　한편 미국의 수정 OFFER 는 아직 제출되지 않았음.

(대사 박수길-국장)

수신처:(통기, 경기원, 재무부,농림수산부,문화부, 상공부, 건설부,보사부,노동부, 교통부
,체신부,과기처,공보처,항만청)

통상국	보사부	문화부	교통부	체정부	경기원	재무부	농수부	상공부
건설부	노동부	과기처	해항정	공보처				

PAGE 1   92.01.18   08:14 WH

外信 1과   통제관

0012

외 무 부

종 별 :

번 호 : GVW-0120   일 시 : 92 0117 1820

수 신 : 장 관(통기,경기원,교통부,항만청)

발 신 : 주 제네바 대사

제 목 : UR/GNS 협상

　　표제 협상관런 91.12.20자 DRAFT FINAL ACT에 반영되지 못하였던 해운 서비스와
운송 서비스분야 협상 현황에 관한 GNS 의장 서한을 별첨 송부함.

　　첨부: GNS 의장 서한 1부 끝

　　(GVW(F)-26)

　　(대사 박수길-국장)

통상국   교통부   경기원   해항청

PAGE 1   92.01.18   08:09 WH
                                          외신 1과 통제관
                                                      0013

주 제 네 바 대 표 부

번 호 : GVR(F) - 0026   년월일 : 2011   시간 : 1820
수 신 : 장   관 (통기. 경기천. 노동부. 항만청)
발 신 : 주 제네바대사
제 목 : GVW-0026 첨부

종 3 매(프지프함)

보 안 동 제	

| 외신과 동 제 | |

26-3-1

0014

MULTILATERAL TRADE
NEGOTIATIONS
THE URUGUAY ROUND

RESTRICTED

MTN.GNS/W/146
14 January 1992

Special Distribution

Group of Negotiations on Services

TRANSPORT SERVICES

At the request of the Chairman of the Group of Negotiations on Services, the following letter is being distributed to all participating countries.

———————

Dear Participant,

1.   In the latter part of the negotiations directed towards the completion of the draft of the Final Act (MTN.TNC/W/FA), participants in the GNS had intensive discussions pertaining to transport services. An annex on air transport services was developed and is contained in the draft General Agreement on Trade in Services. On maritime and road transport services, there was no agreement on whether an annex was necessary.

Maritime Transport Services

2.   With respect to maritime transport services, discussions focused largely on a proposal by the Nordic countries for a common approach to liberalization (MTN.GNS/W/135, Add.1 and 2). A proposal by Cameroon on behalf of twenty-four African countries members of the Ministerial Conference of West and Central African States on Maritime Transport (MINCOMAR) (MTN.GNS/W/128) was also examined.

3.   The Nordic countries proposed:

   (a)   the elimination of cargo sharing agreements;

   (b)   the progressive elimination of cargo reservation practices and the opening of access to non-military cargos;

   (c)   the progressive elimination of discriminatory measures affecting foreign shipping companies in the supply of shipping services;

   (d)   a standstill and a commitment to negotiate a liberalization of port and auxiliary services; and

   (e)   a commitment to ensure that access to, and use of, port and auxiliary services be accorded on reasonable and non-discriminatory terms and conditions.

4.   The proposal by Cameroon noted the importance of maritime transport services to the developing economies of countries in the West and Central African Sub-region and drew attention to the UN Convention on a Code of Conduct for Liner Conferences in this respect.

./.

GATT SECRETARIAT
UR-92-0007

0015

26-3-2

MTN.GNS/W/146
Page 2

5. The proposal by the Nordic countries had the support of a number of participants with important maritime transport industries, who considered the approach to be a means to ensure an acceptable level of liberalization commitments. Addenda 1 and 2 were produced in close cooperation with several other participants.

6. It was suggested that in addressing the issue of the progressive elimination of discriminatory measures affecting foreign shipping companies, consideration should be given to the restrictive practices of closed liner conferences.

7. While there was wide support for liberalization in maritime transport services, there was no consensus on whether an annex calling for liberalization commitments based on a common approach was needed. It was noted that the Articles of the Agreement provided an adequate basis for the negotiation of commitments to liberalize trade in services, including maritime transport services.

8. There was general agreement that the negotiating process leading to the liberalization of trade in maritime transport services would have to address the particular situation of developing countries, inter alia, through transitional arrangements.

9. Many participants were of the view that as the Agreement would not necessarily provide for improved access to, and use of, port and auxiliary services, further work would be necessary in order to ensure that this means of liberalization was properly addressed.

10. In the light of the importance of the maritime transport services sector and the general interest expressed in pursuing its liberalization, further work should be undertaken on maritime transport services in the near future.

Road Transport Services

11. With respect to road transport services, discussions focused on different aspects of the sector, including the regional character of transport services, the importance of the protection and rehabilitation of the environment to protect human, animal, plant life and health, and the need to provide for smooth traffic flows.

12. Though many participants recognized the importance and the special character of road transport services, there was no agreement on whether any of the peculiarities of the sector needed to be addressed specifically under the Agreement.

Yours sincerely,

Felipe Jaramillo
Chairman of the
Group of Negotiations
on Services

0016

26-3-7

주 제 네 바 대 표 부

제네(경) 20644-70

수신 : 외무부장관

참조 : 통상국장, 경제기획원장관

제목 : UR/GNS 협상 자료 송부

1992. 1. 18

92. 1. 17

　　　당관에서 작성한 UR/서비스 협정 초안 요약 해설자료를 별첨 송부하니
업무에 참고 바랍니다.

첨부 : 서비스 협정 초안 해설 자료 1부.　　끝.

주 제 네 바 대 사

선결				결재(공람)		
접수일시 1992. 1. 21	번호					

03956

0017

외 무 부

종 별 :

번 호 : GVW-0147

일 시 : 92 0121 1900

수 신 : 장 관(통기,봉일, 경기원, 체신부)

발 신 : 주 제네바 대사

제 목 : UR/GNS 협상

    표제협상 관련 1.21(화) 당관에 전달된 미국의 기본통신 서비스에 대한 대아국 추가 REQUEST LIST를 별첨 송부함.

    첨부: 미국의 추가 REQUEST LIST 1부

    (GVW(F)-0035).끝

    (대사 박수길-국장)

통상국   통상국   신일   체정부   경기원

PAGE 1

92.01.22   06:38 FN

외신 1과 통제관

0018

주 제 네 바 대 표 부

번 호 : GVR(F) - 0035   년월일 : 2/2/   시간 : 1700

수 신 : 장   관 (통기. 통곡, 경까원. 체신부)

발 신 : 주 제네바대사

제 목 : UR/GNS 협상

종   3 미(표지포함)

보 안	
통 제	

외신과	
통 제	

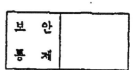

배부처	장차	차관	一차보	二차보	기획관리실	의전장	기신	보안	석순	아주국	미주국	구주국	중아국	국기국	경제국	통상국	문협국	영교국	총무과	감사관	공연원	외연대	청와대	총리실	안기부	공보처	경기인	상공부
	/	/	/	/	/	/									②										/		/	

35-3-1

UNITED STATES TRADE REPRESENTATIVE

1-3 AVENUE DE LA PAIX

12. GENEVA, SWITZERLAND

TELEPHONE: 732 08 70

January 21, 1992

The United States presents an addition to the request list presented to your country in October 1991. This request is in accordance with the U.S. proposal on basic telecommunications services outlined in GNS/w/145 and in accordance with the revised U.S. offer tabled with the Secretariat on January 17, 1992.

Nothing in the attached request list should be understood to diminish any rights acquired in bilateral or multilateral agreements.

The United States reserves the right in the course of negotiations on specific commitments on services to further modify the request list for your country, including adding requests in additional sectors.

The United States would appreciate the opportunity to discuss the basic telecommunications request and hold further discussions on any other U.S. request with your government at our next bilateral consultation. The United States would be pleased to provide clarification with regard to this request.

0020

35-3-2

Korea
Date 01/21/92

0021

Page 1

SERVICES BARRIERS TABLED BY THE UNITED STATES
GROUP ON NEGOTIATIONS ON SERVICES

ID # Barrier Category / Sector Code	Detail
1.808 Other Services Barriers, BES Telecommunications, Data Processing and Info Services	BASIC TELECOM: REQUEST COMMITMENT TO PROVIDE UNRESTRICTED MARKET ACCESS AND NATIONAL TREATMENT IN BASIC DOMESTIC (INTER-EXCHANGE) LONG-DISTANCE SERVICES AND BASIC INTERNATIONAL LONG-DISTANCE SERVICES, INCLUDING COMMITMENTS TO: 1) ALLOW AN UNLIMITED NUMBER OF COMPETITORS TO PARTICIPATE IN THE BASIC LONG DISTANCE SERVICES MARKET; 2) PERMIT FOREIGN ENTITIES TO PROVIDE BASIC LONG DISTANCE SERVICES BOTH THROUGH FACILITIES-BASED COMPETITION, INCLUDING THE RIGHT TO BUILD, OWN AND/OR OPERATE DOMESTIC AND INTERNATIONAL NETWORK FACILITIES, AND THROUGH RESALE OF SERVICES OF EXISTING SERVICES NETWORKS; 3) ALLOW UNRESTRICTED FOREIGN INVESTMENT FOR BASIC LONG-DISTANCE SERVICES; 4) AFFORD TRANSPARENT, NON-DISCRIMINATORY AND COST-BASED ACCESS AND INTERCONNECTION ARRANGEMENTS TO SERVICES AND NETWORKS OF INCUMBENT BASIC TELECOMMUNICATIONS PROVIDERS; 5) ESTABLISH A SYSTEM OF FAIR AND TRANSPARENT REGULATORY PROCEDURES ADMINISTERED BY AN INSTITUTION WITH INDEPENDENT REGULATORY OVERSIGHT.

35-3-3

외 무 부

종   별 :

번   호 : GVW-0154 　　　　　　　　　　일   시 : 92 0122 1800

수   신 : 장관(수신처 참조)

발   신 : 주 제네바 대사

제   목 : UR/GNS 비공식 협의

　　1.22.(수) 오전 JARAMILLO GNS 의장 주재하에 36개국비공식 협의가 개최되어 향후 협상 절차에 대하여 토의하였는바, 주요 내용 하기 보고함.

　　1. INITIAL COMMITMENTS 에 대한 협상 절차

　　- 의장이 제시한 다음 일정에 대하여 참가국간 이의없이 합의함.

　　0 2.10 : 새로운 OFFER 또는 수정 OFFER 사무국에제출

　　0 3.9 : 양자 협상 결과를 반영한 NATIONAL SCHEDULE초안(협상 참가국들의 확인조건) 사무국에제출

　　0 3.31 : 서비스 협정에 부속될 최종 NATIONALSCHEDULE 사무국에 제출

　　- 의장은 기 제시한바 있는 3.9-3.20 협상기간은 각국이 서비스 분야와 상품 분야 시장접근 협상결과를 종합하여 평가하고 최종 조정작업을하게될 것이라고함.

　　2. MFN 일탈에 관한 협상 절차

　　- 의장이 제시한 절차에 대하여 합의하지 못하고 다음주에 재협의키로 함.

　　0 의장은 MFN 일탈은 최소화 되어야 하며, 일탈이허용되는 경우에도 그 기간 및 범위가 엄격하게제한 되어야 한다는 것이 모든 국가의 의견이라고 전제하고, MFN 일탈을 원하는 국가는 그내용을 INITIAL COMMITMENT 에 대한 양자 협상과정에서 상대국에 알리고 국가간 협상을 통하여 합의된 최종 MFN 일탈 목록을 3.31 까지 사무국에제출 하는 방안을 제의

　　0 이에 대하여 양자 협상과정에서 MFN 일탈에대한 협상도 병행하는 점에 대하여는 이견이없었으나 미국, EC 는 협상을 진전시키기 위한현실적 방안이라고 지지한 반면, 그외 모든 국가는 각국의 MFN 일탈에 관한 정보 없이는 전체협상 결과에 대한 평가 를 할수 없기 때문에INITIAL COMMITMENT 에 대한 협상의 진행이어려우므로 MFN 일탈 신청 내용이 2.10 또는 3.9등 조속한 시일내에 다자간에 공개되어야 한다고주장함.

통상국	장관	2차보	외정실	정와대	안기부	법무부	보사부	문화부
교통부	체신부	경기원	재무부	농수부	상공부	건설부	노동부	과기처
해항정	공보처							

PAGE 1 　　　　　　　　　　　　　　　　　　　　　　92.01.23　08:27 BX

　　　　　　　　　　　　　　　　　　　　　　　외신 1과　통제관

3. 기타- 사무국은 다음주중에 다음 자료들을 배부하겠다고함.

0 각국의 OFFER 제출 목록

0 SCHEDULE 작성 안내서 수정판(동 안내서수정작업 과정에서 문제점들이 발견되고 있다고하는 한편 각국의 의견 개진 요청)

0 각국 REQUEST 의 요약(REQUEST 의 비밀성 유지한도내)

- 이집트는 2.17 경 개도국에 대한 SCHEDULING관련 세미나 개최를 요청하였는바, 의장은 가급적 동일자에 개최토록 하겠다고 함. 끝

(대사 박수길-국장)

수신처:(봉기, 경기원, 재무부, 법무부, 농림수산부, 문화부, 상공부, 건설부, 보사부, 노동부, 교통부, 체신부, 과기처, 공보처, 항만청)

o 자   문 : 은행감독원 감독기획과 조사역   이의성

　　　　　KIEP   연구위원   성극제

　　　　　KDI   연구위원   김지홍

　　　(단, 금융.보험분야에 국한된 별도의 양자협상이 개최될

　　　　경우 재무부 대표중 선임자를 교체 수석대표로 함)

4. 출장기간 : 92.1.26-2.2

5. 소요예산 : 해당부처 소관예산

6. 훈   령 :

o 앞으로 세차례의 양허협상이 있음을 고려, 협상을 진행하여 나가면서
  우리의 최종 입장을 정립하도록 하되 현재 작성된 수정 offer list를
  기초로 업종별로 상황 변화에 따라 신축성있게 대처토록 함.

o 기본적으로 Initial Offer 수준에서 대응토록 하고, 분야별로 상대방의
  요구가 불명확한 사항에 대해서는 상대측의 요구를 보다 정확하게
  파악하도록 함.

o '90.11월이후 개방화가 이루어진 통신, 유통, 금융, 운송, 관광
  분야등은 기본적으로 MFN 원칙이 적용될 것이며 동 추가 자유화
  내용도 향후 수정 Offer에 반영될 것임을 밝히도록 함.

o 우리나라의 주요국에 대한 Request List를 제출 함으로써 우리의
  협상력 강화를 도모토록 함.

o 상대측의 요구 수준이 낮거나 단순한 확인 요청사항에 대해서는
  관련되는 자료 및 정보를 성의있게 제공토록 함.   끝.

외 무 부 장 관

0024

재 무 부

우 427-760 경기도 과천시 중앙동 1 / 전화 (02)503-9266 / 전송 503-9324

문서번호 국금 22251-12

시행일자 '92. 1. 22 (   )

수신 외무부장관

참조

선결			지시	
접수	일자시간	'92.1.24	결재·공람	
	번호	2868		
처리과				
담당자				

제목 UR 서비스 양자협상 참여

1. GVW-0108('92. 1. 16)와 관련입니다.

2. UR 서비스 협상과 관련 스위스 제네바에서 '92. 1. 28~31간 개최되는 양자협상에 참여할 당부대표를 아래와 같이 파견코자 하오니 필요한 조치를 취하여 주시기 바랍니다.

아   래

자 격	성 명	소 속
교체수석대표 (금융, 보험분야)	김 창 록	재무부 국제금융과장
대 표	최 희 남	재무부 국제금융과 사무관
대 표	이 의 성	은행감독원 조사역

- 출장기간 : '92. 1. 26~2. 2

첨부 : 회의 참석대책. 끝.

재 무 부 장

0025

UR 금융서비스 양자협상 대책

'92. 1

국 제 금 융 국

1. 양자협상 개요

    가. 일시 및 장소 : '92, 1.28~ 1.31. 제네바 GATT

    나. 협상대상국 및 일정

        - 1.28(화) 09:00 : EC (은행, 증권, 보험, 회계)
                     15:00 : 스웨덴 (은행, 증권, 보험, 회계)
        - 1.29 (수) 14:00 : 미국 (보험, 회계)
        - 1.30 (목) 16:00 : 뉴질랜드 (은행, 증권, 보험, 회계)
        - 1.31 (금) 15:00 : 호주 (은행, 증권, 보험, 회계)

    다. 의 제

        - Request를 바탕으로 각국 서비스시장 개방에 대한 구체적인 협상

        ┌────────── 〈 국별 Request 현황 〉──────────┐
        │   │
        │ - 아국 Request : 6개국 49개 항목 (미국, EC, 일본 등) │
        │   │
        │ - 상대국 Request : 10개국 94개 항목 (미국, EC, 일본등) │
        │   │
        └──┘

    라. 대표단 구성

        - EPB 제2협력관외 관계부처 실무자 및 KIEP, KDI 전문가 참석

        - 금융분야는 국제금융과장을 교체수석대표로 하여 별도 협상토록 함.
           o 국제금융과 사무관, 은행감독원 실무자 참석

0027

2. 협상 대책

가. 협상 동향

- 금번 양자협의는 UR 협상 추진일정상 서비스 양허협상은 3월말까지 세차례의 양허협상을 통하여 마무리 지을 계획

  o '91.12. 9~13일간 미국, EC, 스웨덴, 카나다, 스위스, 핀란드등 6개국과 각국의 Request에 대한 양자협의 기실시

  o 향후 1.20~1.31, 2.17~2.28, 3.9~3.20등 3차례 양허협상이 예정되어 있음.

- 미국등 주요협상국은 서비스 일반협정 제정등 Rule making 작업이 일단락 지워짐에 따라 각국 서비스 시장의 개방확대를 위한 양허협상을 본격적으로 진행시키겠다는 계획이나

  o UR 협상의 시간제약 및 각국의 미온적인 태도를 고려시 추가적인 시장개방보다는 향후 금융서비스 시장개방의 기본틀로서 활용될 것임.

나. 기본협상 대책

- 아국은 미국, EC, 스위스등 주요국으로부터 Request를 받았으나 대부분 한미금융정책 회의시 제기되었던 사안들로서

  o 그동안 금융개방정책의 추진으로 상당부분을 수용하였으며, 개별 현안에 대하여 한미 양국간에는 상호이해가 존재

0028

o EC등 여타국에 대해서도 아국의 금융여건 및 금융시장 개방정책
  설명을 통하여 상대국의 이해를 촉구

o 특히 최근 우리가 Call시장 개선조치로서 blind brokerage system
  을 도입하는 등 금융시장 개방노력이 지속적으로 추진되고 있음을
  강조

- 또한 아국이 Request한 사항을 제기함으로써 상대국의 금융장벽을 부각

다. UR 금융서비스 협상의 기본 Position

- 우리의 경제규모가 증대되고 대외거래가 확대됨에 따라 경제의
  개방화 · 국제화가 요구되고 있음.

o 특히 개도국에서 선진국으로의 이행과정에 있는 우리로서는
  금융시장의 개방화 · 자율화 필요성을 잘 인식하고 있음.

- 이러한 우리자체의 필요에 의해서 우리 금융여건에 맞는 단계적인
  금융시장 개방을 추진하고 있으나

o 금융시장 개방과 자율화는 우리한테 익숙하지 않은 상황으로
  급속한 개방 및 자율화 추진은 내부적인 부작용을 발생시키는 바

o 국제수지 적자의 확대, 과소비 현상, 근로의욕 저하 등 '90,
  '91년에 나타난 우리경제의 어려움이 그러한 예라 할 수 있음.

0029

- 따라서, 어려운 경제여건하에서 자율화 · 개방화를 빠른 속도로 추진하는 경우 우리경제의 기반이 약화될 수 있으며

  o 이에 따라 우리가 목표로 하는 개방화 · 자율화 추진도 달성이 불가능할 것임.

- 이러한 전환기적 어려움에 처해 있는 우리경제의 어려운 상황에 대한 귀측의 이해를 구하며,

- 금융서비스의 자유화는 각국 금융제도의 특수성과 발전단계에 따라서 점진적이고 단계적으로 이루어져야 할 것이며

  o 또한 성공적인 금융자유화를 위하여는 금리자유화, 국제수지등 경제적 선행조건 안정이 필요하며

  o 금융분야의 의무부담이 다른 서비스 분야보다 과중하지 말아야 하며 기타 서비스 분야와 균형을 유지해야 할 것임.

0030

3. 국별 협상대책

가. EC

　(1) 아국에 대한 Request 검토

Request List	아국 설명 내용 *
① 공 통 　- 모든 금융분야를 양허 　- 선진국의 Negative 방식 수용 　- 현존 조치의 동결	- Positive 방식 채택으로 현단계 　에서는 수용 불가
② 은 행 　- 현지법인 설립 허용	- 신규은행 설립은 제한, 지점 　형태로 허용
- 외은지점 설치 조건 철폐	- 예금자 보호를 위해 일정기준 　필요
- 본점자본금 인정	- 본점은 아국 금융당국 감독 　범위 밖으로 수용 불가
- Call 시장 차별 시정	- Call 시장에서의 공정거래를 　위하여 blind brokerage system 　도입
- 추가지점 설치 조건 철폐	- 국내은행과 동일하게 적용
- 신탁업 인가조건 철폐	- 차별적인 인가조건 폐지
- 전산망 가입	- 국내은행과 협의후 가입방안 　마련
- 부동산 취득 허용	- 일정기준하에서 주거용 업무용 　부동산 취득 가능
③ 증 권 　- 지점 및 현지법인 설립조건 완화	- 설립조건은 자본시장의 건전한 　육성을 위한 요건으로 적절한 　것임.
- 영업기금 제한 완화	- 안정적인 증권업무 수행에 　필요한 수준임

* GATT Binding과는 무관

0031

Request List	아국 설명 내용 *

- 거래소 회원 가입조건 자유화	- 국내증권사와 동일하게 허용
	  ㅇ 특별회원권 제도 및 정회원
	    가입금의 분할 납부 인정

- 단위신탁업 허용	- 현재로서는 허용 검토계획 없음
- 주식시장 개방 확대	- 개방진전시 단계적 확대
④ 보 험	
- 현지법인 및 지점 설치조건 완화	- 요건 완화 불가
- 외국 국영보험사 설립 허용	- 기허용
- 재보험에 대한 우선 출재제도 완화	- 점진적 완화 검토
⑤ 회 계	
- 회계법인에 대한 외국인 투자	- 외국인투자 제한업종으로 외국인 투자가 허용되지 아니함

- 회계사 업무의 상호주의 폐지	- 회계사 자격취득 부여 방안으로
	  외국에서 공인회계사 자격 취득
	  한 사람에 대한 득혜 제공임

- 외국회계법인과의 제휴 허용	- 회계법인 설립은 한국공인회계사 자격을 지닌자에 한함

- 자격인정을 받은 회계사의
  업무범위 확대
	- 약식시험을 거쳐 공인회계사
	  자격을 인정받은 경우는 50%이상
	  합작기업이나 본국기업이 이해
	  관계에 있는 기업으로 회계업무
	  제한

* GATT Binding과는 무관

0032

(2) 아국의 대 EC Request

Request List	EC 입 장

① 은 행
 	
 A. 영국
 	
 - 영란은행의 창구지도 범위 축소
 	
 - 갑기금에 대한 지급이자의 손비
   인정 요구
 	
 B. 독 일
 	
 - 책임자본금 계산시 차별 철폐
 	
 - 본지점 대변잔에 대한 지준의무
   면제
 	
 - 외은지점의 독일국채 발행시
   연방채권 인수단 참여 허용
 	
 - 복수 점포장제 폐지
 	
 - 본국임원 채용시 연방은행
   감독청 승인기준 폐지
 	
 C. 프랑스
 	
 - 한국계 은행에 대한 여신규제
 	
 - 기업인수시 승인절차 차별 완화
 	
 - 외국은행의 프랑화 채권발행시
   주간사 역할 허용
	- 창구지도는 예금자 보호를 위한
	  것으로 무차별적임
	
	 o 구체적 내용은 추후 동보
	
	 - 구체적 내용 추후 동보
	
	  "
	
	 - 현지법인만 참여 가능
	
	 - 예금자 보호를 위한 것으로
	   불가피
	
	 - "
	
	 - 구체적 내용 추후통보
	
	  "
	
	  "

0033

Request List	EC 입 장

② 보 험
 	
A. 영국
 	
- 보험사 지급능력 요구의 차별
  철폐
 	
B. 프랑스
 	
- 보증기금액에 기준 불명화
 	
- 외국보험사 주식투자시 득별
  허가제 폐지
 	
- 외국보험사의 적하보험 제한
  철폐
 	
C. 네덜란드
 	
- 외국보험사의 보험광고 제한
  철폐
	- 구체적 내용 추후 통보
	
	"
	
	"
	
	"
	
	"

0034

나. 호 주

(1) 아국에 대한 Request 검토

Request List	아국 설명 내용 *
① 은 행	
- 본점자본금 인정	- 본점은 아국금융 당국 범위밖으로 수용 불가
- 은행자회사 설립	- 내국민에 대한 금융자회사 설립도 규제
- 은행 수용기준 폐지	- 예금자보호를 위해 일정기준 필요
- CD 발행한도 기준 차별 폐지	- 본점자본금 불인정으로 기준 차이 존재
- 은행설립시 전치요건 폐지	- 아국 금융여건 및 환경에의 적응기간 필요
- 비은행 금융기관의 설립 형태 확대	- 지점, 사무소, 합작투자, 현지법인 형태로 기진출(보험, 증권)
② 증 권	
- 증권사 지분참여 한도 확대	- 기한도 확대 (40%→50%)
- 주식시장 개방 조건 명시	- 주식시장 개방 방안 기발표
③ 보 험	
- MFN 원칙 적용	- MFN 원칙에 따라 기허용
- 손보사에 대한 지분율(20%) 제한 철폐	- 당분간 곤란
- 공적보험요율 결정 폐지 철폐	- 향후 보험요율 범위 확대

* GATT Binding과는 무관

0035

Request List	아국 설명 내용 *
④ 회 계 - 외국회계법인과의 financial link 허용 - 외국인의 공인회계사 시험응시 허용	- 회계업은 외국인투자 제한업종으로 외국인투자가 허용되지 않음 - 국적제한이 없으므로 외국인도 응시 가능

* GATT Binding과는 무관

(2) 아국의 대호주 Request

- 외국은행에 대하여 Trading banks의 설립을 금지하고 있으며, 현지법인 형태의 Finance Company만 허용되어 은행업에 대한 제약이 상존하므로 Trading banks 설립 허용 요구

  o bank 명칭 사용금지

  o Check 발행, 어음교환 참가 불가

  o 일반 고객으로부터 예금조달 불가

  o 중앙은행의 rediscount facilities 사용 불가

- 본지점 차입한도 확대

  o 자기자본의 6배 이내로 제한

0036

다. 미 국

(1) 아국에 대한 Request 검토

Request List	아국 설명 내용 *
① 보 험 - 독립대리점 또는 Broker 허용	- 국내보험시장 여건상 불가 　ㅇ 국내에 시행중인 전속대리점 　　만 허용
② 회 계 - 회계사 업무범위 제한철폐	- 국내회계사 자격취득시 업무 　제한이 없으나 약식절차에 　의하여 회계사 자격을 인정받은 　경우만 업무제한
- 회계사 자격취득시 국적요건 　철폐	- 국적제한 요건이 없음
- 외국회계법인과의 연계 허용	- 회계업은 외국인 투자제한 업종 　으로 외국인투자가 허용되지 　않음
- 외국회계법인 명칭 사용	- 외국회계법인 명칭사용을 금지 　하는 규정은 없으나, 회계사회 　의 자율규제로 유사명칭 사용을 　규제하고 있음

* GATT Binding과는 무관

0037

(2) 아국의 대미 Request

Request List	미 국 입 장
① 보 험 - 주별 면허취득을 전국 단일 면허로 전환 - Port of Entry 폐지 - 영업지역 확대시 타주에서의 성공적 영업실적 요건 폐지 - 인가시 Transparency 요구 - 외국보험사에 대한 차별적인 특소세 부과 폐지	- Multiple jurisdiction 적용 으로 국내보험사도 동일하게 적용 - 확인작업중 추후 통보 " "

라. 스웨덴, 뉴질랜드

- 구체적인 Request 사항이 없음.

0038

법   무   부

국심 20411-⟨8⟩   503-9505   1992. 1. 23.

수신 외무부장관

참조 통상국장

제목 UR서비스 양자협의 참석대표 추천

'92년 1월 스위스 제네바에서 개최되는 우루과이라운드 서비스
양자협의 본부 일원으로 아래 사람이 참석할 수 있도록 협조하여 주시기
바랍니다.

        0 소   속   : 국제법무심의관실
        0 출장자   : 김 영 철
        0 직   위   : 검 사
        0 생년월일   : 1959. 2. 27.
        0 출장지   : 스위스 제네바
        0 경   비   : 당부 부담
        0 출장기간   : 1992. 1. 26(일) - 2. 2(일)

첨부 국·영문 이력서 1부.   끝.

                법   무   부   장

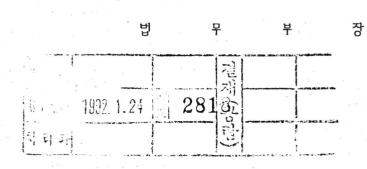

1992. 1. 24   281

0039

경 제 기 획 원

우 427-760 / 경기도 과천시 중앙동1 정부제2청사 / 전화 503-9149 / 전송 503-9141

문서번호 통조삼 10502-20

시행일자 1992. 1.23.

선결			지시		
접수	일자 시간	:	결재·공람		
	번호				
	처리과				
	담당자				

수신 외무부장관

참조 통상국장

제목 UR/서비스 양허협상 참석

　　　　1. 스위스 제네바에서 개최되는 UR/서비스 양허협상에 다음과 같이 참석코자
하니 협조하여 주기 바랍니다.

　　　　　　　　　　　- 다　　　음 -

가. 출장자

　　- 수석대표 : 경제기획원　제2협력관　　　　　　이윤재
　　- 대　　표 : 경제기획원　통상조정3과장　　　하동만
　　　　　　　　　　〃　　　　통상조정3과 사무관　김용준
　　　　　　　　재 무 부　국제금융과장　　　　김창록
　　　　　　　　　　　　　국제금융과 사무관　　최희남
　　　　　　　　법 무 부　국제법무심의관실 검사　김영철
　　- 자 문 관 : 은행감독원　감독기획과 조사역　이의성
　　　　　　　　KIEP　　연구위원　　　　　성극제
　　　　　　　　KDI　　　　〃　　　　　　김지홍

나. 출장기간 : '92. 1.26~2.2
다. 출 장 지 : 스위스 제네바
라. 경비부담 : 경제기획원, 각부처, KIEP, KDI등

첨부 : 출장일정 1부.　끝.

　　　　경 제 기 획 원　장

0040

出 張 日 程

'92. 1. 26(日)　12:40　　서울 발 (KE 901)
　　　　　　　　18:10　　파리 착
　　　　　　　　20:45　　파리 발 (SR 729)
　　　　　　　　21:45　　제네바 착

　1. 27(月)　┐
　　　　　　　│
　　~　　　　　│　　　UR/서비스 讓許協商
　　　　　　　│
　1. 31(金)　┘

'92. 2. 1 (土)　10:55　　제네바발(LH 1855)
　　　　　　　　12:15　　프랑크푸르트착
　　　　　　　　13:50　　　　　〃　　발(KE 916)

　2. 2 (日)　10:20　　서울착

0041

재 무 부

우 427-760 경기도 과천시 중앙동 1 / 전화 5388 / 전송 503-9324

문서번호 국금 22251-16

시행일자 '92. 1. 24 (   )

수신 외무부장관

참조 통상국장

선결			지시		
접수	일자시간		결재·공람		
	번호				
	처리과				
	담당자				

제목 UR 금융 협상

　　　　UR 서비스 협상중 우리 금융산업의 개방과 관련한 금융협상의 과정과 내용에 관하여
주요 선진국의 관심이 제고되고 있어 이를 효율적으로 대처하기 위하여 다음사항을
주제네바 대사에게 훈령하여 주시기 바랍니다.

다　　　　　　　음

　가. 엄 낙용 재무관을 1.28부터 3월까지 개최될 금융부문 쌍무간 협상에

　　　　계속 참여토록 하여 금융협상 내용 파악과 전략 등을 수립 보고토록 할 것.

　나. UR 쌍무간 금융협상이 주요선진국의 아국 금융산업 개방에 관한 잘못된

　　　　인식을 해소할 수 있는 계기가 될 수 있도록 양국 금융 당국자간의

　　　　협의 일정이 마련되도록 할 것.　　끝.

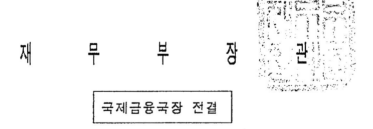

재　　무　　부　　장　　관

국제금융국장 전결

0042

외 무 부

110-760 서울 종로구 세종로 77번지 / (02)720-2188 / (02)725-1737 (FAX)

문서번호 통기 20644-28

시행일자 1992. 1. 27.(   )

취급		장 관
보존		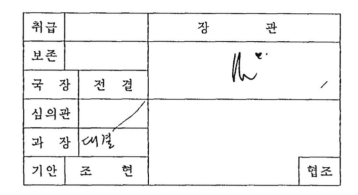
국 장	전 결	
심의관		
과 장	대결	
기안	조 현	협조

수신   수신처 참조

참조

제목   UR/서비스 협상 정부대표 임명 통보

　　　92.1.27-31간 제네바에서 개최되는 UR/서비스 양허협상에 참가할 정부대표단이 "정부대표 및 특별사절의 임명과 권한에 관한 법률"에 의거 아래와 같이 임명 되었음을 통보합니다.

　　　　　　　　　　　- 아　　　　　　　　　래 -

1. 회 의 명 : UR/서비스 양허협상

2. 회의 개최기간 및 장소 : 92.1.27-31, 스위스 제네바

3. 정부대표 :

　　O 수석대표 : 경제기획원 제2협력관　　　　　　　이윤재

　　O 대　　표 : 경제기획원 통상조정3과장　　　　　하동만

　　　　　　　　　　통상조정3과 사무관　　　　　　　김용준

　　　　　　재 무 부 국제금융과장　　　　　　　　　김창록

　　　　　　　　　　국제금융과 사무관　　　　　　　최희남

　　　　　　법 무 부 국제법무심의관실 검사　　　　김영철

　　　　　　주 제네바 대표부 관계관

0043

o 자　　문 : 은행감독원 감독기획과 조사역　　　　이의성

　　　　　　　KIEP　　　　연구위원　　　　　　　성극제

　　　　　　　KDI　　　　연구위원　　　　　　　김지홍

o 단, 금융.보험분야에 국한된 별도의 양자협상이 개최될 경우 재무부

　　대표중 선임자를 교체 수석대표로 함.

4. 출장기간 : 92.1.26-2.2

5. 소요예산 : 해당부처 소관예산

6. 출장 결과 보고서는 귀국후 2주일이내 외무부에 제출하여 주시기 바랍니다.

　　　　　　　　　　　　　　　　　　　　　　　　　　　　　　끝.

수신처 : 경제기획원장관, 재무부장관, 법무부장관

외　무　부　장　관

0044

노　　　동　　　부

우편번호 427-760, 경기 과천 중앙동1번지 /전화(02) 503-9750(5580) /전송(02)503-9771-2

___

문서번호　해고 32480-47

시행일자　'92. 1. 27. (　　　)

경유

수신　외무부장관

참조　주미대사

선결			지시		
접	일자 시간	92.1.28	결 재 · 공 람		
수	번호	326¡			
처리과					
담당자					

제목　자료수집 협조요청

___

　　　UR/서비스 양허협상과 관련 필수인력 (Managers,Executives,Specialists)의

정의에 참고하고자 하오니 다음 자료를 조사,통보하여 주시기 바랍니다.

- 자료 요청 사항 -

　　ㅇ　통신,유통,금융,운송,관광분야별로 대표적인 기업체 1개소씩을 선정한

　　　조직표 (영문기재)

　　ㅇ　필수인력의 구체적인 정의가 우리나라 기업의 어느직위에 속하는지의 비교표

　　ㅇ　미국 이민법 (연방규정 제214조의 2)에 의한 L 사증 (계열회사 전근자)발급에

있어서의 필수인력의 입국허용 범위 등 구체적인 사례

첨부 : 미국측이 제시한 UR/협상자료 1부.　끝.

노　동　부　장

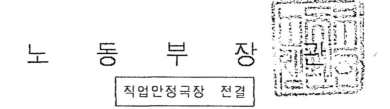

직업안정국장 전결

서비스 공급자의 일시적 입국

다음에 정의된 관리자, 임원, 전문가를 제외하고는 부담하지 아니함. 체약국의 시민권을 제한하면서 미국은 기본협정을 미국에 설립된 자사, 자회사, 제휴회사를 통하여 미국에서 서비스를 공급하는 기업의 고용인에게 적용하며, 미국외의 당해 기업에 입국신청일전 1년이상 고용되고 있는자 이어야함.

a. Managers 조직내에서 제1차적으로 조직전체, 조직일부 또는 하부조직을 지휘하며 타 감독직, 전문직, 관리직에 있는 고용인의 업무를 감독 또는 통제하고 해고권과 고용권을 갖거나 또는 해고, 고용, 인사문제 (승진, 휴가승인 등)에 관히 추천권을 갖으며 매일매일의 업무에 재량권을 행사하는 자.
전문가가 아닌한 제일선 감독자는 포함하지 않으며, 서비스 공급을 위해 필요한 업무를 1차적으로 수행하는 고용인도 포함하지 않음.

b. executives : 조직내에서 조직관리를 제1차적으로 지휘하며, 의사결정에 광범위한 범위를 행사하고 그 기업의 최고위 임원, 이사회, 주주로 부터 일반적인 지휘감독 만을 받는자. 임원은 서비스의 실질적인 공급 또는 조직의 서비스에 관련된 업무는 직접 수행할수 없슴

c. 전문가 : 조직내에서 상당한 수준의 경험에 의한 지식을 갖고 그 조직의 서비스, 설비조사 기술 또는 관리에 관한 독점적인 지식을 소유하는 자.
      (전문가 공인자력의 소지자를 포함할수 있슴)
미국은 미국내에서의 입국 및 임시체류에 관한 약속을 노사분쟁의 경우에는 적용하지 않슴

※ 일시적인 입국이라 함은 미국이민법에 의한 영구적인 거주의 목적 및 시민권에 관한 권리를 부여받지 않는 입국을 의미함.
일시적인 입국은 3년간으로 제한되며 5년을 초과하지 않는 범위내에서 연장할수 있슴. 기본협정의 약정 및 조건에 따라 입국 서비스 공급자 및 자연인의 입국은 즉, 이민, 노동, 근로조건에 관련된 모든법을 준수하여야 한다.
그러한자를 고용한 법인은 이 규칙을 집행하는 관계당국에 협조하여야 함. 0046

※ 참 고 사 료

미국의 비이민사증중 L사증 (계열회사 진근자) 발급대상
※ 비이민국적법 연방규정 제214조의 2

○ 중역직 (MANAGERIAL CAPACITY)

종업원으로서 단체 (ORGANIZATION) 및 관례상 인정된 동 단체의 부서 또는 지부를
지휘하고, 다른 종업원의 일을 감독하며, 다른 종업원을 고용 및 해교하는 권한과
기타 인사상 조치 (승진, 휴가허가 등)와 함께 당해 조치를 권고하는 권한을 가지
며, 일상업무에 대한 재량권을 행사하는 어느조직체내의 특정지위를 말하며,

- 중역직은 피감독대상 종업원이 중역이나 전문직이 아닌한 감독상 최고위층
  (THE FIRST LINE LEVEL)을 포함하지 않음

○ 지배인직 (EXECUTIVE CAPACITY)

종업원으로서 단체의 경영을 지휘하고, 조직의 목표 및 정책을 실정하며, 정책
결정에 있어 광범한 재량권을 행사함과 동시에 다만 보다 고위층인 수석간부,
중역회의 및 동 사업체의 주주로 부터의 일반적인 지휘,감독만을 받는 어느조직체
내의 특정지위

○ 전문지식 (SPECIALIZED KNOWLEDGE) 소유자

국내의 노동시장에서 쉽사리 입수할수 없는 어느 조직체의 산물 (PRODUCT),
용역,설비,기술,경영,기타 재산적 이익 등에 직접 관련된 개인이 갖추고 있는지식
당해 지식은 그 조직자체에 관련된 것으로서 사업의 확장과 직접 관련된 것이
거나 시장에 있어 자유경쟁적인 사업에 허용되는 것이어야 한다.

0047

주 미 대 사 관

USW(F) : 0431   년월일 :   시간 :

수 신 : 장 관 (통기, 통이, 통상) 상공부, 재무부,   보 안
                                청기원   면 제

발 신 : 주 미 대 사   INSIDE U.S. TRADE - January 24, 1992

제 목 : UR 금융서비스분야 관련 U/업계 입장   (출처 :   )
                        (3매)

FINANCIAL SERVICES INDUSTRY PRESSING FOR MORE U.S. LEVERAGE IN GATT TALKS

U.S. financial services companies are pressing the Administration for a commitment that the benefits of an Uruguay Round agreement in that sector would not be extended to other countries if they failed to make significant market access commitments based on negotiating guidelines outlined in the agreement, according to informed sources. If the Administration made it clear at the beginning of market access talks that failure to obtain such concessions would lead it to seek a derogation from the Most Favored Nation principle, countries may be more inclined to negotiate seriously, according to financial services industry sources.

They argue that the need for increasing U.S. leverage over the services market access negotiations scheduled to begin this week arose after the final draft services agreement failed to contain a provision

배부처	장관	차관	一	二	기획실	의전관	정석국장	아주국	미주국	구주국	중아국	경기국	통상국	문경국	영교국	총무과	감사관	공안원	외안리	청와대실	총리실	안기부	공보처	경기기	상공부	접수
			/									③										/	/		/	

(0431 - B - 1)   외신 1과
                        통 제

                                              0048

SERVICES INDUSTRY PRESSES ADMINISTRATION ON DRAFT AGREEMENT . . . begins page 1

that would have allowed trading partners not to apply the benefits of a sectoral agreement to a country that failed to ease its trade restrictions in that sector. Both U.S. government and industry sources concede it will be impossible to find support for this sectoral non-application provision, especially after the European Community agreed to drop it from the draft agreement tabled by the top official of the General Agreement on Tariffs & Trade on Dec. 20.

Financial services firms laid out their MFN derogation request to the Administration last week, seeking both a political commitment to apply it and a clarifications on how a derogation would work in practice, sources said. The firms put forward the position that full MFN status should only be extended if a critical mass of countries makes "significant" market access commitments consistent with the "understandings" listed on page 51 of the draft services text.

The draft services agreement allows countries to schedule commitments based on an alternative approach to that outlined in part III of the draft provided it is based on four "understandings." These stipulate that the alternative approach should not conflict with the provisions of the agreement and that it should not prejudice the right of any party to use Part III of the agreement to schedule market access commitments. The third and fourth understanding respectively state that commitments be applied on an MFN basis and that there is no presumption about the degree of liberalization to which a party is committing itself.

By linking the understandings to market access concessions, the U.S. industry wants to ensure that they become commitments, an industry source pointed out. The current draft text gives them the status of negotiating guidelines that countries may or may not follow, which is a weakening from an earlier draft, according to Administration officials and industry sources. The Administration also is concerned that the understandings now contained in the text are too weak to constitute an obligation for countries, according to one official.

The industry group did not specify what constituted the critical mass of countries, but one source said it would include members of the Organization for Economic Cooperation & Development, Korea and other newly industrialized countries as well as some Latin American countries. But that list varies for various sectors of the financial services industry, an industry source pointed out.

In last week's meeting with negotiators, company representatives wanted to clarify whether an MFN derogation applied to existing or future measures to liberalize the services market and how it would work against the national treatment and market access obligations, according to the source. They hoped to get an Administration reply as early as this week. Support of the financial services industry will be important to get an Uruguay Round agreement passed, industry sources pointed out. It is by far the largest sector within the services industry in terms of the revenues generated, so that its opposition would seriously undermine the chances of passing a services agreement, sources said.

Given the importance of the financial services industry and the danger that a push for an MFN derogation on financial services could unravel the entire services agreement, the Administration will have to weigh its response carefully, sources pointed out. The government may try to convey to the industry that it wants to wait until the market access negotiations are completed and it can assess the agreement in its entirety before it raises the threat of an MFN derogation, they said. An Administration official last week said that the option of not applying the whole services agreement if there are not sufficient concessions is "more viable" and "less farfetched" for the Administration than the industry may assume.

The U.S. could support a European Community idea that foresees a review of market access concessions three or four years after the agreement goes into effect, the official said. The European Community services industry represented in the so-called EC services group informally is floating this idea that foresees a general non-application of the agreement's benefits if a country did not follow through on market access commitments or failed to negotiate significant concessions in that interim period, an EC source said. In those two cases, the previous trade rules would snap back, he said. But the Administration source made it clear that such a provision, which is not included in the draft services agreement, will provoke opposition from developing countries. As these countries seek other changes, it could lead to the unraveling of the agreement, he pointed out.

Some industry sources pointed out that if the Administration raised the issue of an MFN derogation too early it could upset the political balance standing behind the current rules on MFN derogation. These are based on the political consensus that the exemptions should be limited to air transport, maritime services, basic telecommunications, and audiovisual services. The current rules stipulate that a country can take an exemption from MFN with the intent of not letting it stay in place for more than 10 years, and accepting a five-year interim review.

The EC idea of the second non-application is based on the understanding that a good framework and a series of initial liberalization commitments with the promise of future liberalization is acceptable to the EC industry, EC sources said. They speculated that the EC Commission would also find such an outcome of the negotiations acceptable. But one EC industry source raised concerns that U.S. industry would not be satisfied with such an outcome, partially because firms may feel they can achieve more market opening with section 301.

This week's services negotiation will not focus on the controversial provisions of the draft Uruguay Round services text, but deal instead on bilateral market access discussions as well as the unresolved provisions of the framework setting new rules to govern services trade. Trading partners left some parts of the framework aside and agreed to tackle them in 1992 because they ran out of time, according to an Administration official. The areas that need to be finished up in the framework are definitions, the air transport annex and the provisions on dispute settlement, he said.

On dispute settlement, trading partners will have to decide whether the services text should take over provisions of the Dunkel text, or if they should be adapted specifically for the services sector, the official said.

The Administration has not decided how and if to address the problems posed by the draft agreement, the official said. In the framework, the concerns include, but are not limited to, the issue of economic integration, which applies to customs unions and free trade areas. The article lays out the criteria of liberalization such trade areas should follow, including the rules for compensation that should be extended to trading partners that lose trade as a result of an a customs union and free-trade area being formed.

In its current provisions, the economic integration provision concerns the Administration because it "raises very ineffectually" the rights of third-country companies that are located in one of two countries entering into a free-trade agreement, one official pointed out. The benefits of a free-trade agreement could be denied to a company from a third country if it did not have substantive business operation in the territory of both countries. This provision was included at the insistence of Canada, which wants to protect its banking sector, he said. FTA signatories could also deny the benefits of the agreement to a third-country company if it was not established before the agreement was signed and if the signatories to the free-trade agreement do not provide common treatment to third countries with respect to the sector concerned.

It is hard to tell now exactly what the impact of that provision will be in the future, but it could have "major potential implication" for the treatment of U.S. companies under trade agreements, such as EC agreements with Eastern European countries, he said.

0431 - 3 - 3

0050

경 제 기 획 원

우 427-760 / 경기도 과천시 중앙동1 정부제2청사 / 전화 503-9149 / 전송 503-9141

문서번호 통조삼 10502-27

시행일자 1992. 1. 27

(경유)

수신 외무부장관

참조

선결			지시결재·공람	
접수	일자시간	92: 1.2		
	번호	3446		
처리과				
담당자				

제목 UR/서비스협상관련 상대국에 대한 추가 Request사항 제출

　　　UR대책 실무위원회(1.23) 결과에 따라 별첨 Request 사항이 1월 27일 주간의
양허협상기간중에 GATT 및 상대국에게 전달될 수 있도록 협조해 주시기 바랍니다.

첨부 : 상대국에 대한 추가 Request List사항(영문) 1부.　끝.

경 제 기 획 원 장

제 2 협 력 관 전결

0051

相對國에 대한 追加 Request 事項(英文)

< The United States >

Sector	Request
1. Engineering services	In some States, engineering-related documents must be prepared only by the U.S. licensed engineers and stamping on official documents such as drawing and specification must be done only by the U.S. professional engineers(e.g., Section 150 of Pennsylvania Legal Code).
	Allow foreign engineers to prepare official engineering-related documents such as drawing and specification and to stamp on them.
2. Banking	Eliminate the requirement whereby foreign banks wishing to operate in Chicago must locate within the Chicago Loop Zone.

< The European Community >

Sector	Request
1. Distribution	(All Countries) Liberalize the trading services of chemical products and precious metals. (France) Clarify the sectors of retail services in which authorization is required according to the economic needs or because of the given quotas. Clarify also the sectors of retail services in which nationality is required.

< Japan >

Sector	Request
1. Distribution	Increase the minimum floor space of stores subject to the coordination procedures from 500㎡ to 1,000㎡. Simplify the coordination procedures related to the opening of the large-scale store and shorten the time length of the procedures.

< Canada >

Sector	Request
1. Distribution	Make offer in distribution services.
2. Banking	Improve the transparency in the procedure of issuing visa to the home staff members and shorten the time length of the procedures.

< Australia >

Sector	Request
1. Telecommunication	Make a binding commitment on packet and circuit switched services. Remove any restrictions on market access such as licensing or approval system.
2. Distribution	Make offers in the sectors of wholesale trade, brokerage services, and counter trading services. Clarify whether the regulations and licensing related to retail and franchising services in relevant States or territories are discriminating foreigners.

0056

< Switzerland >

Sector	Request
1. Securities	Eliminate Gentlemen's agreement requiring that all orders to foreign securities firms be executed using Swiss banks as intermediaries.

< Norway >

Sector	Request
1. Telecommunication	Make a binding commitment on simple data transmission services including packet and circuit switching services. Remove restrictions on market access such as licensing or approval requirements.

< Newzealand >

Sector	Request
1. Telecommunication	Remove restrictions on market access such as licensing or approval requirement.

< Austria >

Sector	Request
1. Telecommunication	Make a binding commitment on packet and circuit switched services. Remove restrictions on market access such as licensing or approval requirement.

< Hong Kong >

Sector	Request
1. Telecommunication	Allow cross-border supply and international services. Make a binding commitment on packet and circuit switched services. Remove restrictions on market access such as licensing or approval requirement.

< Mexico >

Sector	Request
1. Telecommunication	Include packet and circuit switched services within the scope of other telecommunication services. Remove restrictions on market access such as foreign equity limitation, licensing or approval requirement.

< Indonesia >

Sector	Request
1. Engineering services	Simplify equipment-inspection procedures executed by the Societe Generale Surveilance to expedite the supply of equipment.
2. Telecommunication	Make a binding commitment on value-added telecommunication services. Allow a cross-border supply and remove joint-venture as well as approval requirements.
3. Distribution	Make a binding commitment on distribution services.

< Thailand >

Sector	Request
1. Engineering services	Reduce the conditions for foreign investment such as the foreign equity participation of 49% and the export obligation of foreign equity. Allow foreign engineering firms to participate in local construction supervision services. Eliminate the 20% tax on the foreign investors' remittance profit.
2. Distribution	In the wholesale business, remove the approval requirement or provide transparent criteria for approval. In the retail business, remove the equity restriction of 49%.

< China >

Sector	Request
1. Common Request	Make a binding commitment on movie & video distribution services, insurance and telecommunication services. Remove the foreign equity participation requirement of 25%. Eliminate the restriction on the duration period of joint venture in the area of hotel business and apartment construction business.

< India >

Sector	Request
1. Distribution	Make a binding commitment on distribution services.

3900

외 무 부

종 별 :

번 호 : GVW-0223   일 시 : 92 0130 1730

수 신 : 장관(통기)

발 신 : 주 제네바 대사

제 목 : 주재관 일시귀국

    대: WGV-0178

    대호 주재관 2 인 일시 귀국에 이견없음. 끝

    (대사 박수길-국장)

통상국

분류번호	보존기간

발 신 전 보

WGV-0178   920130 1831 FL   종별: 지급

번 호 :

수 신 : 주 제네바   대사. 총영사

발 신 : 장 관 (통 기)

제 목 : 주재관 일시귀국

　　　경제기획원 및 농수산부는 UR 서비스 분야 수정 Offer List 작성작업과 농산물 분야의
감축 약속 계획서 작성작업 등 UR협상 관련 업무협의를 위해 귀관 한철수 경협관보를
2.5-14간, 김종진 농무관보를 2.8-17간 각각 일시 귀국시켜 줄것을 희망하여 왔는바,
이에 대한 귀견 지급 보고바람.　　　　　끝.　　　　　　　　(통상국장 김 용 규)

		보 안 통 제	

안고재	92년 1월 30일	통기과	기안자 성명		과 장	심의관	국 장		차 관	장 관
			조현			전결				

외신과통제

0068

74　우루과이라운드 서비스 분야 양허 협상 1

경 제 기 획 원

수 427-760 / 경기도 과천시 중앙동1 정부제2청사 / 전화 50?-?149 / 전송 503-9141

<table>
<tr><td>문서번호 통상삼 10502-50</td><td colspan="2">접</td><td>지</td></tr>
<tr><td rowspan="2">시행일자 1992. 1. 30</td><td rowspan="2">접</td><td>일 자</td><td rowspan="2">시</td></tr>
<tr><td>시 간   : </td></tr>
<tr><td>(경유)</td><td></td><td>번 호</td><td>재·</td></tr>
<tr><td>수신 외무부장관</td><td></td><td>처 리 과</td><td>광</td></tr>
<tr><td>참조 통상국장</td><td></td><td>담 당 자</td><td>람</td></tr>
</table>

제목 주제네바 대표부 경협관보의 일시 귀국협조 요청

　　주제네바 대표부 한철수 경제관 ?????를 다음과 같이 일시 귀국시키고자 하니 협조하여 주기 바랍니다.

－ 다　　음 －

가. 기간 : '92.2.5~'92.2.14(9박 10일)

나. 목적

　－ UR/서비스 양허표 작성방법의 변경으로 아국은 '91.1월 GATT사무국에 제출한 Offer List의 수정작업을 하고 있는 바 동 수정작업에 현지 협상실무자로서 직접 참여

　－ 금년 2~3월중에 집중적으로 추진될 것으로 예상되는 UR/서비스 양허 협상에 대한 대응방안을 관계부처 관계관과 협의 추진

첨부 : 일정표 1부.

　　　　　　　경　제　기　획　원　장

出 張 日 程

'92. 2. 5 (水)   10:55   제네바발(LH 1855)
                  12:15   프랑크프르트착
                  13:50   프랑크프르트발(KE 904)

     2. 6 (木)   10:20   서울착

     2. 7 (金) ┐   UR/서비스협상 Offer List작성
        ~   │   참여
                │
     2.13 (木) ┘   UR/서비스협상대책 수립 참여

'92. 2.14 (金)   12:40   서울발(KE 901)
                  18:10   파리착
                  20:45   파리발(SR 729)
                  21:45   제네바착

농 림 수 산 부

우 427-760 / 주소 경기 과천시 중앙동 1번지 / 전화 (02) 503-7227 / 전송 503-7249

문서번호 국협20650-15

시행일자 1992. 1.31 (년)

(경유)

수신 외무부장관

참조 통상국장

선결			지시	
접수	일자시간	1992. 1.31	결재공람	
	번호	3776		
처리과				
담당자				

제목 주제네바 농무관보 일시귀국 요청

　　　　UR농산물협상과 관련한 Country Plan 작성 및 농업부문 통상현안등을 협의하기 위하여 주제네바 농무관보 김종진의 일시 귀국을 아래와 같이 요청하오니 조치하여 주시기 바랍니다.

- 아　　　래 -

가. 출장기간 : '92.2.8-2.17(10일간)
　　　　　　　단, 현지사정에 따라 불가피한 경우에는 본부와 협의후 조정가능

나. 귀국 소요경비 : 농림수산부 부담

다. 일시귀국 요청근기 : 재외공무원 복무규정 21조 4항

붙임 : UR국별이행계획 수립을 위한 실무작업단 운영계획 사본 1부.　끝.

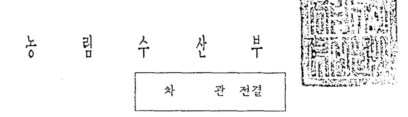

농 림 수 산 부

차　　관　전결

0071

발 신 전 보

분류번호	보존기간

번   호 : WGV-0186   920201 1127   F종별 : 암호송신

수   신 : 주   제네바   대사. 총영사

발   신 : 장   관 (통 기)<del>총이</del>

제   목 : 주재관 일시 귀국

연 : GVW-0178

귀관 한철수 경협관보와 김종진 농무관 보를 UR 협상 관련 업무협의차 2.5-14 및 2.8-17간 각각 일시 귀국 조치바람.   끝.   (통상국장   김 용 규)

총무과장 :

보 안 통 제	

양고재	92년 1월 31일	통기과	기안자성명		과 장	심의관	국 장		차 관	장 관	외신과통제
			조현				전결				

0072

MULTILATERAL TRADE

NEGOTIATIONS

THE URUGUAY ROUND

Group of Negotiations on Services

RESTRICTED

MTN.GNS/W/125/Rev.1*
28 January 1992

Special Distribution

Original: Spanish

COMMUNICATION FROM ARGENTINA

Conditional Offer of Argentina Concerning
Initial Commitments

Revision[1]

The following communication is circulated at the request of the delegation of Argentina.

The following is a preliminary offer of initial commitments which is conditional on the satisfactory conclusion of the current negotiations on the future General Agreement on Trade in Services. The offer will be revised in the light of the structure and final content of the aforementioned Agreement. Argentina reserves the right to withdraw its offer if it considers that any Agreement reached is not wholly satisfactory.

The offer is also conditional on the satisfactory conclusion of current negotiations in other Negotiating Groups of special interest to Argentina.

In addition, the offer is conditional on the inclusion in the Agreement of satisfactory disciplines on subsidies and safeguards.

The offer does not mention requirements related to prudential or professional practice considerations and they have not been listed as limitations or restrictions on access to the market or to national treatment (their inclusion in the national list will depend on the decision adopted in the GNS on the inclusion of non-discriminatory measures).

The offer includes references to a number of sectors and it is hoped that other parties will grant reciprocity in these sectors.

Finally, Argentina reserves the right to modify this offer in the light of the results of the consultations taking place, in particular with sub-national bodies.

---

[1]This document, initially circulated with the Annex in the original language, is now reissued with the Annex translated into English.

*English only

GATT SECRETARIAT
UR-92-0015

0073

SECTORS*	LIMITATIONS AND CONDITIONS ON MARKET ACCESS	CONDITIONS AND QUALIFICATIONS ON NATIONAL TREATMENT	COMMENTS
	1. Cross-border supply 2. Movement of consumers 3. Commercial presence 4. Movement of personnel	1. Cross-border supply 2. Movement of consumers 3. Commercial presence 4. Movement of personnel	

PROFESSIONAL AND BUSINESS SERVICES

SECTORS*	LIMITATIONS AND CONDITIONS ON MARKET ACCESS	CONDITIONS AND QUALIFICATIONS ON NATIONAL TREATMENT	COMMENTS
- Legal services (1.A.a.-861)	1. No limitations 2. No limitations 3. No limitations 4. Senior personnel and specialists	1. No limitations 2. No limitations 3. No limitations 4. No limitations	
- Accounting and auditing (1.A.b.-862)	1. No limitations 2. No limitations 3. No limitations 4. Senior personnel and specialists	1. No limitations 2. No limitations 3. No limitations 4. No limitations	
- Architecture (1.A.d.-8671)	1. No limitations 2. No limitations 3. No limitations 4. Senior personnel and specialists	1. No limitations 2. No limitations 3. No limitations 4. No limitations	
- Engineering services (1.A.e-8672)	1. No limitations 2. No limitations 3. No limitations 4. Senior personnel and specialists	1. Not bound 2. No limitations 3. Not bound 4. No limitations	
- Advertising (1.F.a.-871)	1. Not bound 2. No limitations 3. No limitations 4. Senior personnel and specialists	1. No limitations 2. No limitations 3. No limitations 4. No limitations	
- Market research and public opinion polling services (1.F.b.-864)	1. No limitations 2. No limitations 3. No limitations 4. Senior personnel and specialists	1. No limitations 2. No limitations 3. No limitations 4. No limitations	
- Management consulting services (1.F.c.-865)	1. No limitations 2. No limitations 3. No limitations 4. Senior personnel and specialists	1. No limitations 2. No limitations 3. No limitations 4. No limitations	
- Building-cleaning services (1.F.o.-874)	1. No limitations 2. No limitations 3. No limitations 4. Senior personnel and specialists	1. No limitations 2. No limitations 3. No limitations 4. No limitations	

---

*The sectoral classification is based on GATT secretariat document MTN.GNS/W/120 of 10 July 1991.

0074

- Translation services (1.F.t.-8790)	1. No limitations 2. No limitations 3. No limitations 4. Senior personnel and specialists	1. No limitations 2. No limitations 3. No limitations 4. No limitations
- Public relations services (1.F.t.-8790)	1. No limitations 2. No limitations 3. No limitations 4. Senior personnel and specialists	1. No limitations 2. No limitations 3. No limitations 4. No limitations

COMMUNICATION SERVICES

- Telecommunications (2.C.-752)	Monopoly suppliers exist. Argentina will ensure strict compliance with the provisions of Article VIII of the Framework Agreement (pages 343/4 of MTN.TNC/W/35/Rev.1)	
- Audiovisual services (2.D.-9611/3)	1. No limitations 2. No limitations 3. No limitations 4. Senior personnel and specialists	1. No limitations 2. No limitations 3. No limitations 4. No limitations

CONSTRUCTION

- General construction work for buildings (3.A.-512)	1. No limitations 2. No limitations 3. No limitations 4. Senior personnel and specialists	1. No limitations 2. No limitations 3. No limitations 4. No limitations
- Installation and assembly work (3.C.-514+516)	1. No limitations 2. No limitations 3. No limitations 4. Senior personnel and specialists	1. No limitations 2. No limitations 3. No limitations 4. No limitations
- Structural maintenance and repair (3.E.-511+515+518)	1. No limitations 2. No limitations 3. No limitations 4. Senior personnel and specialists	1. No limitations 2. No limitations 3. No limitations 4. No limitations
- Site preparations (3.A.-512)	1. No limitations 2. No limitations 3. No limitations 4. Senior personnel and specialists	1. No limitations 2. No limitations 3. No limitations 4. No limitations

FINANCIAL SERVICES

(A) Insurance

Direct insurance (7.A.a.-8121, 7.A.b.-8129)	1. Not bound 2. Not bound 3. No limitations 4. Senior personnel and specialists	1. Not applicable 2. Not applicable 3. No limitations 4. No limitations	Argentina undertakes to eliminate the taxes and penalties applying to insurance services not allowed in the country
Import and export insurance (7.A.b.-8129)	1. Not bound 2. Not bound 3. No limitations 4. Senior personnel and specialists	1. Not bound 2. No limitations 3. No limitations 4. No limitations	

Reinsurance (7.A.c.-81299)	1. Bound 2. No limitations 3. No limitations 4. Senior personnel and specialists	1. Bound 2. No limitations 3. No limitations 4. No limitations	All insurance companies must cede the 40 per cent of premiums to the State reinsurance company
(B) Banking (7.B)	This sector is covered by another communication		

TOURISM AND RECREATIONAL SERVICES

- Hotels (1.A.a.-641)	1. No limitations 2. No limitations 3. No limitations 4. Senior personnel and specialists	1. No limitations 2. No limitations 3. No limitations 4. No limitations
- Restaurants (9.A.-643)	1. No limitations 2. No limitations 3. No limitations 4. Senior personnel and specialists	1. No limitations 2. No limitations 3. No limitations 4. No limitations
- Tourist agencies (9.B.7471)	1. No limitations 2. No limitations 3. No limitations 4. Senior personnel and specialists	1. No limitations 2. No limitations 3. No limitations 4. No limitations
- Tour operators services (9.B.-7471)	1. No limitations 2. No limitations 3. No limitations 4. Senior personnel and specialists	1. No limitations 2. No limitations 3. No limitations 4. No limitations

0076

외　무　부

종　별 :

번　호 : GVW-0242　　　　　　　　　　일　시 : 92 0131 1700

수　신 : 장관(수신처참조)

발　신 : 주제네바대사

제　목 : UR/서비스 양자협상(2)

1.30(목) 개최된 일본 및 뉴질랜드와의 양자협상내용을 하기 보고함.

1. 일본과의 협상(14:30-16:00)

가. 협상 개요

- NATIONAL SCHEDULE 작성에 관한 기술적 사항, 인력이동, MFN 일탈등 수평적 문제에 대한 의견 교환에 그쳤으며 시간 부족으로 양국의 분야별 REQUEST 에 대한 협상은 하지 않았음.

0 일본은 비공식 수정 OFFER 초안을 제시하였음.

나. 인력이동

- 아측은 일본 수정 OFFER 초안에 인력 이동에대하여 UNBOUND 한 이유에 대하여 질의한바

0 일본은 자국의 출입국 관리 규제 체계가 매우 자세하기 때문에 새로운 협정에따라 국내법규를 조정하기가 어려워 계속 검토중이라고 하는 한편

0 인력이동에 COMMITMENT 한 나라의 경우 입국 허가및 취업허가등 이중 규제 체계로 되어있어 취업허가 절차 때문에 COMMITMENT 가 무의미하게 될 우려가 있는 반면자국의 경우 취업 허가 절차가 없다고 함.

- 아측은 일부 인력에 대하여 COMMITMENT 할 계획임을 밝히고 그 정확한 범위는검토중이라고 언급함.

다. MFN 일탈

- 일본은 다음사항에 대한 MFN 일탈 신청을 고려하고 있다고 함.

0 항공: 항공부속서의 MFN 일탈 대상에 포함되지 않은 SOFTRIGHTS

0 CABOTAGE: 상호 주의하에 외국인 토지 취득허가

0 외국인자문 서비스: 상호주의에 의하여 특정국가의 변호사 자격 소지자에 한하여

통상국	2차보	통상국	통상국	법무부	보사부	문화부	고통부	체신부
경기원	재무부	농수부	상공부	건설부	과기처	해항정	공보처	

PAGE 1　　　　　　　　　　　　　　　　　　　　　92.02.01　　06:23 DQ

외신 1과 통제관

0077

외국법 자문서비스 허용

　O RADIO LAW: 상호주의 하에 RADIO STATION 허가

　O 사업법: INTERNATIONAL TRADE FORWARDER

　O PUBLIC DAMAGES ACT

　- 또한 일본은 아국 해운분야 관련 WAIVER 발급 대상에서 일본 선박 배제, 한.일정기항로에 일본선사 배제 문제는 MFN 일탈을 신청하여야 할 것이라고 지적함.

　2. 뉴질랜드와의 협상

　가. 협상 개요

　- 별첨 뉴질랜드의 REQUEST 에 대한 아측입장을 밝혔으며 뉴질랜드의 수정 OFFER가 대상 분야에 있어서 포괄적이고 자유화 수준도 완전개방 상태에 가깝기 때문에 아측 REQUEST에 대하여는 토의하지 않았음.

　나. 뉴질랜드 REQUEST 에 대한 아측 답변

　- 인력이동: 아국 수정 OFFER 에 일정 범주인력에 대해 COMMITMENT 할 예정임.

　- 외국인 투자 제도: 아국 OFFER 은 STANDSTILL이상의 COMMITMENT 를 담고있으나동 COMMITMENT는 당연히 서비스 전 분야가 아니라 OFFER된 분야에 한하여 적용됨.

　- 컴퓨터 관련 서비스: 아국 OFFER 에 사무국 LIST상 서비스가 거의 모두 포함되어 있음.

　- 농업 및 임업 부수 서비스: 임업 관련 서비스는 외국인 투자 금지업종이며 농업 관련 서비스는 일부가 신고제임.(뉴질래드는 특히 목축 분야에 고도의 전문가들이있다고함)

　- 교육 서비스: 아국의 경우 교육서비스는 공공기능에 속하므로 아국내에 교육기관 설립은 불가능함.

　소비자 이동(뉴질랜드로 유학하는 경우)의 경우에는 COMMITMENT 하지 않더라도 실제 별다른 장애가 없을 것임.(뉴질랜드는 자국내에 외국유학생 유치에 1차적 관심이있다고 함)

　- 오락서비스: 추가 검토하겠음.

　- 관광: 해외여행 경비 사용에 실질적 제한이없음.

　- 항공서비스: 지상 조업서비는 OFFER 에서 삭제할것을 검토중임.(뉴질랜드는 공항에서의 농산물검역 수수료등의 원가 지향 의무에 관한 메카니즘 마련을

희망하였으나 구체적 방안은 없었으며 아국의 제한 조치 사례도 없었음)

다. MFN 일탈

- 뉴질랜드는 다음 사항에 대하여 MFN 일탈을 고려하고 있으나 그 경제적 효과는매우 작다고 함.

0 영화 공동 생산 협정: 조세감면 혜택 부여목적의 것임

0 인력이동에 관한 협정: 주변 저개발국과의 취업 허가에 관한 특별 협정, 영연방 학생의 일시 취업에 관한 협정

첨부: 뉴질랜드 REQUEST 1부. (GVW(F)-0066)

(대사 　　　　　　　　　　　　　　　　　　　　　　　　　박수길-국장)

수신처:통기,통일,통삼,경기원,재무부,법무부,농수산부,상공부,건설부,보사부,교통부,체신부,문화부,공보처,과기처,항만청.

주 제 네 바 대 표 부

번 호 : GVW(F) - 0066   년월일 : 20/31   시간 : 1700

수 신 : 장   관 (통재. 동업. 동이. 동산. 경기원. 재정박. 법무박. 상공박. 건설박. 내자박

발 신 : 주 제네바대사   노동부. 교통부. 체신부. 문화부. 농수산부. 공보처. 과기처. 항만청)

제 목 :

증 4 매 (프지프합)

보 안 동 제	

외신구 동 제	

36/78/1

NEW ZEALAND PERMANENT MISSION TO THE
OFFICE OF THE UNITED NATIONS AT GENEVA

28 A, CHEMIN DU PETIT-SACONNEX
P.O. BOX 334
1211 GENEVA 19   —   TEL. 734 95 30

23 January 1992

H.E. Mr Soo Gil Park
Ambassador
Permanent Mission of the Republic of Korea
Route de Pre-Bois 20
1216 Cointrin
Geneva

Dear Ambassador,

In accordance with the procedures agreed to by the GNS and
in view of the forthcoming negotiations on initial
commitments in services, I am pleased to enclose for your
consideration a copy of the list of requests submitted by
New Zealand in respect of the Republic of Korea. New
Zealand reserves the right to modify or make additions to
the enclosed list of requests in the light of developments
in the negotiations.

Yours sincerely

A M Bisley
Permanent Representative

Enc

66-4-2

0081

GENERAL AGREEMENT ON TRADE IN SERVICES
SPECIFIC COMMITMENTS
REQUESTS FROM NEW ZEALAND TO THE REPUBLIC OF KOREA

Movement of Natural Persons Providing Services

Request that Korea undertake a commitment on the movement of natural persons providing services for all sectors and sub-sectors included in its offer and for those additional sectors and sub-sectors requested below.

Foreign Investment

Request that Korea undertake a commitment to standstill on its foreign investment regime with horizontal effect across all sectors.

Computer and Related Services

Request that offer be expanded to include market access and national treatment with no limitations or conditions on services in this sub-sector as listed in document MTN.GNS/W/120.

Services Incidental to Agriculture and Forestry

Request that offer be expanded to include market access and national treatment with no limitations or conditions in this sub-sector as listed in document MTN.GNS/W/120.

Educational Services

Request that offer be expanded to include market access and national treatment with no limitations or conditions for educational services as listed in document MTN.GNS/W/120.

Entertainment Services

Request that offer be expanded to include market access and national treatment with no limitations or conditions for entertainment services as listed in document MTN.GNS/W/120.

0082

66-4-3

2

Tourism and Travel Related Services

Request that offer be expanded to include market access and national treatment with no limitations or conditions for tourism and travel related services as listed in document MTN.GNS/W/120.

Air Transport Services

Request that offer be expanded to include market access and national treatment <u>with no limitations or conditions</u> for;

- aircraft ground handling services

√ - computer reservation services

√ - the selling and marketing of air transport services

- aircraft repair and maintenance services

Request that Korea undertake as an additional commitment that air <u>transport (eg airport) user charges</u> be limited to the <u>approximate cost</u> of services rendered.

0083

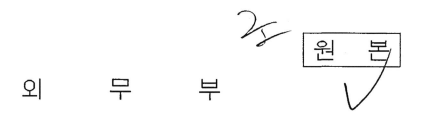

외 무 부

종 별 :

번 호 : GVW-0259   일 시 : 92 0203 1200

수 신 : 장관(수신처참조)

발 신 : 주제네바대사

제 목 : UR/서비스 양자협상(3)

　　1.31.(금) 개최된 EC 및 호주와의 양자협상 내용을 하기 보고함.

　　1. EC와의 협상(1.31.오전)

　　가. 아측 REQUEST 에 대한 EC측 답변

　　- 금융보험 분야

　　0 영란은행의 창구지도는 무차별적인 은행감독의 일환으로서 PRUDENTIAL MEASURE 임. 만약 사실상 차별이 있다면 분쟁의 제기도 가능함.

　　0 독일의 경우 은행 임원의 언어 요건은 감독기관과의 의사 소통을 위한 것으로서 공식적인 시험이 아니라 신축성 있게 운영되고있으며 EC 회원국에도 똑같이 적용됨. ADDITIONAL COMMITMENT 대상은 될수 있을 것임.

　　0 이태리의 보험 사업자 요건은 이태리내에 설립된모든 회사에 적용되는 것이며 EC 회원국에도 똑같이 적용됨.

　　- 유통분야

　　0 한국측 지적대로 OFFER 에서 제외되는 화학제품의 범위가 너무 포괄적이므로보다 구체적으로 기재하는 방안에 대하여 검토하겠으나 한국측도 유통업종 음식물, 화장품, 비료등에 대하여 개방약속을 해주기 바람.

　　0 프랑스의 NEEDS TEST 는 소형상점을 보호하기위해 큰 슈퍼 설립을 제한하는 것으로서 지방정부가 인가권을 행사하고 있음.

　　나. 해운분야 협상문서(12.15자 사무국 문서)에 대한의견 교환

　　- EC측은 동 문서를 다양한 각국입장을 현실적으로 타협시킬수 있는 대안이라고평가한다고하는 한편

　　0 국제해운에 대한 MFN 일탈과 관련, 아프리카국가들이 UN LINER CODE 하에서 동맹선 화물중 40퍼센트 자국 적취보장에 대하여 강한 집착을 보이고 있으므로

통상국	차관	2차보	통상국	통상국	안기부	법무부	보사부	문화부
교통부	체신부	경기원	재무부	농수부	상공부	건설부	노동부	과기처
해항정	공보처							

PAGE 1   92.02.04   06:18 ED

외신 1과 통제관

0084

이를철폐하는 것이 정치적으로 어려운 현실을 직시하여야 하며 또한 그 경제적 효과가극히 작다는 것도 고려하여야 한다고 지적함.

- 아측은 기존 정부입장에 따라 10년간 MFN일탈은 너무 장기이며 해운보존 서비스 사업자유화를 PACKAGE 로 추진하는 것은 문제가 있으며 FRAMEWORK 에 따라야 할것이라고 언급함.

2. 호주와의 협상(1.31. 오후)

가. 협상개요

- 양측 REQUEST OFFER 의 명료화 작업 위주로 진행되었는바, 아측은 호주에 대해 주로 금융보험 및 유통분야에 대하여, 호주측은 아측에 대해 금융, 보험 및 회계, 법률, 엔지니어링, 광고등에 대하여 질의하였으며 양측 모두 상대국 REQUEST에 대하여 1차적으로 수용불가 입장을 견지하였음.

0 한편 호주는 아국 수정 OFFER 제출과 관련특히 서비스 분야 포괄범위 확대에 대하여 관심을 표명하였으며 아측의 해운분야 WAIVER제도와 관련 미국, 덴마크,싱가폴에 대하여는 WAIVER 제도 적용을 면제해주고 있다고 지적함.

나. MFN 일탈

- 호주는 자국의 경우 아래와 같이 MFN 일탈을 고려중이라고 함.

0 영화 공동생산 협정:카나다, 영국,뉴질랜드,프랑스등 4개국과 협정을맺고있으며이태리, 독일, CIS중 일부국가와도 현재 추진중인바 2개 협정상에 금융 지원과 관련 MFN 문제가 있음.

0 항공분야 SOFT RIGHTS: 항공기 수선유지,CRS.항공권 판매 서비스등 보조서비스에 대하여 이미 OFFER 하였으나 타국가들이 이를 OFFER 하지않고 또한 MFN 일탈 할경우 자국도 일탈할것임.

(조건부 일탈)

0 증권거래소 회원가입: 현재 상호주의하에 운영되고 있으나 타국가들이 MFN 적용하면 자국도 상호주의를 포기하겠음(조건부 일탈)

- 아측은 미국,EC,일본등 주요 국가들이 너무 많은 MFN 일탈을 시도하고 있는 것과 관련 우려를 표명하였는바 호주 역시 MFN 일탈이 국가간에 연쇄효과를 일으키고 있는 점에 우려를 표명하고 이를 최소화 하도록 공동으로 압력을 가할 필요가 있다고 언급함.

3. 관찰 및 평가

PAGE 2

0085

- 금번 양자 협상을 통하여 지금까지 GATT 사무국에만 비밀리에 제출되었던 각국의 MFN일탈 신청 내용의 윤곽이 드러나게 됨.

0 '91년말까지 제출된 MFN 일탈 신청은 MODEST하다는 사무국의 평가가 있었음에비추어 금번양자 협상과정에서 각국이 밝힌 MFN 일탈신청 대상은 당초 보다 크게 늘어난 것으로서 향후협상 전망을 어둡게 하고 있음.(각국의 MFN일탈이 제한되지 않을경우 협상 타결이 난관에 봉착하게됨)

- 금번 양자 협상을 통하여 파악된 각국이 고려하고있는 MFN 일탈 신청 내용은 다음과 같이 3개유형으로 분류됨.

1) 역사적 이유, 지리적 조건등에 따라 양국간에 맺어진 협정에 관한 사항:

영화 공동생산 협정, 해운협정(UN LINER CODE),인접 국가간의 국경간 육상 운송협정 및CABOTAGE 협정, 인력이동 협정등

2) 상대국의 양허수준 확보를 목적으로 하는 조건부MFN 적용: 기본통신, 금융서비스

3) 기타 상호주의에 근거한 조치 및 일방조치:국내법상 상호주의 규정등을 이유로 일본이 제시하고 있는 외국법 자문, 토지취득, RADIOSTATION 등, CRS 등 항공분야SOFTRIGHTS(미국.일본), 해운분야의 일방조치(미국)

0 상기 유형중 1)은 대부분 기존 양자 협정이 있고 그 경제적 영향이 크지 않기때문에 정당화 하기용이할 뿐만 아니라 많은 나라에 보편적으로 존재하는 것임.

0 상기 항 2)은 특히 미국,EC가 상대국의 시장접근 약속을 끌어내기 위한 수단으로 사용코자하는 것으로서 그 경제적 영향이 클뿐만 아니라 협정 제 2조의 무조건적 MFN 에 상치되는 개념이기 때문에 많은 나라가 반발하고 있음.

0 상기 3)항 역시 그 경제적 영향이 큰 사항으로서 주로 일본이 제시하고 있는이들 문제는 많은 논란이 예상됨.

- 이번 협상과정에서 아국은 MFN 원칙에 충실한다는 기본입장에 따라 별도의 MFN 일탈신청 사항을 제기하지 않았는바 향후 협상에 대비하는 과정에서는 아국에 상기 첫번째 유형에 해당하는 사항이 있는가를 재점검할 필요도있다고 보임.

- 또한 OFFER 수정작업에 있어서는 상기 MFN 일탈문제 뿐만 아니라 대상분야 포괄 범위확대, 자유화 수준 제고등 질적인 개선 노력도 필요한 것으로 판단됨.

- 향후 협상 일정 별첨 송부함.

첨부: 향후 협상 일정에 관환 GNS 의장 NOTE1부

PAGE 3

0086

(GVW(F)-0259).끝

(차석대사 김삼훈-국장)

8수신처: 통기,통일,통삼,경기원,재무부,법무부,상공부,
농수산부, 건설부,보사부,노동부,교통부,체신부,문화부,공보처,과기처,항만청

PAGE 4

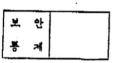

주 제 네 바 대 표 부

번 호 : GVR(F) - 0071   년월일 : 20203   시간 : 1200
수 신 : 장   판 (통과.통일.동이.통상. 경가원.재정부. 법무부. 상공부. 건설부.내자부
발 신 : 주 제네바대사 노동부. 교통부. 해선부 문체부, 농수산부, 공보처, 내기처, 당만처)
제 목 : GVW-0259

총 4 매(표지포함)

	보 안	
	통 제	

	외신과	
	통 제	

4

기 - 4 - 1

0088

30.1.92

<u>Group of Negotiations on Services</u>

<u>INFORMAL NOTE BY THE CHAIRMAN</u>

<u>M.f.n. Exemptions and Negotiations of Initial Commitments</u>

1.   As agreed in the meeting held on 13 January 1992, the Chairman of the
TNC indicated that participants should engage in "Intensive non-stop
negotiations ... with continuous multilateral monitoring on initial
commitments in services under the GNS ... . Substantial and meaningful
results for all parties in this area are also necessary for final agreement
by parties to the total package."

2.   In my letter to all participants of 14 January 1992, I initially
suggested the following dates during which the secretariat would provide
logistical support for delegations engaging in initial commitments
negotiations.

  -   20-31 January;
  -   17-28 February;   and
  -   9-20 March.

3.   The <u>Substantive Guidelines for the Negotiations of Initial Commitments
during the Uruguay Round</u> are those attached to the text of the Draft
General Agreement on Trade in Services (MTN.TNC/W/FA, page 56).

4.   Regarding m.f.n. exemptions, the Annex on Article II Exemptions and
its attachment, (MTN.TNC/W/FA, pages 32-3) establish the conditions under
which m.f.n. exemptions will be granted.

5.   Discussions in the GNS have revealed that all participants have a
clear preference to limit the number and scope of the exemptions so as not

7/-4-2   42-MISC4

- 2 -

to undermine the principle of unconditional m.f.n. Therefore, I suggest participants restrict the number, scope and duration of any exemption to the absolute minimum.

7. The procedure described below applies to the period prior to the acceptance of the GATS by all participants in the Uruguay Round. The adoption of the GATS means the adoption of the Articles of the Agreement, its annexes, decisions and understandings and the national schedules of commitments.

8. Parties are expected to make known to other Parties their intentions with respect to m.f.n. exemptions in the course of their bilateral negotiations.

9. After consultations with delegations, I am proposing procedures for the presentation of new or revised offers and draft lists of intentions for m.f.n. exemptions as well as for the final stages of the negotiating process. The proposed timetable is:

- New or revised offers should be submitted to the secretariat for distribution to participants by 10 February 1992;

- Draft lists of intentions with respect to m.f.n. exemptions shall be presented to the secretariat by 5 March 1992 to be circulated to participants who have made offers on a confidential basis.

- A stocktaking of the situation with respect to m.f.n. exemptions and the negotiations on initial commitments shall be conducted on 10 and 11 March 1992;

- Intensive negotiations should continue with a view to arriving at a balanced package of specific commitments and m.f.n. exemptions; draft schedules and revised lists of m.f.n. exemptions, subject to verification by participants, should be submitted to the secretariat by 16 March 1992 and circulated to all participants;

기-4-3

42-MISC4

- 3 -

- The final content of the schedules and the lists of m.f.n.
  exemptions agreed among participants to be annexed to the General
  Agreement on Trade in Services should be submitted to the
  secretariat by <u>31 March 1992</u>.

10. The secretariat will provide technical assistance to those developing
countries that require assistance relating to all aspects of the process
described above.

71-4-4

42-MISC4

TOTAL P.04

0091

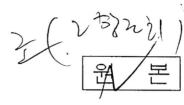

외　무　부

종　별 :

번　호 : GVW-0286　　　　　　　　　　일　시 : 92 0205 1730

수　신 : 장 관(봉기, 경기원, 재무부, 한국은행)

발　신 : 주 제네바대사대리

제　목 : UR 서비스 양자 협의 관련 자료송부

　　1. 91.12.12.카나다와의 서비스 분야 OFFER 에 대한 양자 협의시 아측이 제기한 · 금융 분야 REQUEST 에 대한 답변을 서면으로 송부하여 온바, 이를 별첨FAX 송부함.

　　2. 아울러 카나다측도 '카'측 금융분야 REQUEST 에 대한 아측의 서면 답변을 요구하고 있으니 조속 회신바람.

　　첨부: 아측 금융분야 REQUEST 에 대한 카측 답변1부

　　(GVW(F)-0082).끝

　　(차석대사 김삼훈-국장)

통상국　　2차보　　경기원　　재무부

PAGE 1　　　　　　　　　　　　　　　　　92.02.06　　07:49 WH

　　　　　　　　　　　　　　　　　　　　외신 1과　통제관
　　　　　　　　　　　　　　　　　　　　　　　0092

주 제 네 바 대 표 부

번 호 : GVR(F) - 0082   년월일 : 2.02.05   시간 : 1750

수 신 : 장   관 (통기, 경기)친, 재무부, 한국은행)

발 신 : 주 제네바대사

제 목 : GVW - 0286 첨부

총   5 매(표지포함)

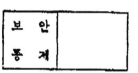

보 안 통 제	

외신과 통 제	

82 - 5 - 1   0093

The Permanent Mission of Canada
to the United Nations

La Mission Permanente du Canada
auprès des Nations Unies

1, rue du Pré-de-la-Bichette
1202 Geneva

February 4, 1992

Mr. Chol Soo Han
Assistant Attaché (Economic Affairs)
Permanent Mission of the Republic
of Korea
20, route de Pré-Bois
1216 Cointrin

Dear Mr. Han,

     Following our bilateral discussions of December 12,
1991 on access in services, please find herewith Canadian answers
to questions put by your Delegation in respect of financial
services.

     My colleagues and I look forward to the written answers
of the Korean Delegation to Canadian questions related to
Canadian requests in financial services.

Yours sincerely,

François Nadeau
Counsellor

82-5-2

0094

· COMMENTS REGARDING KOREA'S REQUESTS
ON INITIAL COMMITMENTS WITH RESPECT TO CANADA

2.   **Banking**

a.   **Foreign banks cannot set up branches in Canada**

o   Foreign banks are required to establish a subsidiary to operate in Canada, i.e.,
     they cannot open branches directly.

o   This prudential requirement exists for all foreign banks and Canadian regulators
     view this as an essential part of Canada's approach to the regulation and
     supervision of financial institutions.

o   Among other things, it helps to ensure that the Canadian entity and depositors
     are protected from problems which may arise for the parent bank and because of
     the uncertainties surrounding the application of Canadian and foreign bankruptcy
     and liquidation laws to branches.

b.   **The procedures for obtaining a banking license are complicated, non-transparent
     and long**

o   Regarding transparency and complexity, we would note that there is a published
     guide on the application process and procedures. We are not aware of any
     particular difficulties in this regard. As for the length of time to complete the
     process, this will vary from case to case and will in part depend on the time
     taken by the applicant in fully providing information requested by Canadian
     authorities.

c.   **12% ceiling on foreign bank assets**

o   The restriction, introduced when the entry of foreign banks into Canada was first
     allowed in 1980, is a reflection of our uncertainty regarding the effect of
     liberalization on Canadian markets and institutions. As a practical matter, we
     note that there remains room for further growth of non-U.S. foreign bank assets.
     Moreover, it should be recalled that the ceiling was doubled in 1984 to 16%
     from 8% in part to accommodate the interests of foreign banks (it was
     subsequently adjusted in 1989 to 12% to take account of the exemption
     provided to the U.S. under the Free Trade Agreement).

o   Any movement in this area would depend on the overall balance of concessions
     within the financial services sector, including a corresponding degree of
     liberalization undertaken by Korea.

2 82-5-3   0095

d. **Restrictions on the establishment of Schedule II banks:**

Yearly license renewal for first five years

o The yearly licensing provision has not ben carried forward under the new Bank Act (expected to come into force in the Spring of 1992). Under the new Act, the Superintendent for Financial Institutions will issue orders of indeterminate duration approving the commencement and carrying on of business by any <u>domestic or foreign bank</u>. Any license that was issued to a foreign bank will be deemed to be an order of indeterminate duration. Foreign banks will be treated the same as domestic banks in this regard.

Ratio of assets to authorized capital

o This provision, which provides the mechanism by which the 12% foreign asset ceiling is administered, has not been carried forward under the new Bank Act. It has been replaced by a new provision which limits the average domestic assets of non-U.S. foreign banks to an amount fixed by Order by the Minister of Finance.

Not more than 50% of funds can be obtained from abroad

o The requirement is in part prudential, I.e., it is prudent to diversify funding from a number of sources and to match the funding and asset-generating activities within a country. Moreover, deposit-taking by foreign banks fulfils an important policy objective of enhancing domestic competition.

e. **Restrictions on upstream lending**

o Such loans are generally prohibited for prudential reasons. On the other hand, any foreign or domestic bank may transfer assets to a related financial institution bank in the normal course of business according to arrangements approved by the Superintendent.

f. **"Thin capitalization"**

o This is a tax matter which applies to any foreign company -- financial institution or other -- operating in Canada. The objective is to help ensure that Canada can retain an appropriate tax base.

g. **Board of Directors**

o One-half of the Directors of any company incorporated in Canada must be resident Canadian, reflecting our view that, for prudential reasons, there should be resident Canadians held accountable for a company's activities. We are not aware that this is a particularly onerous requirement for foreign bank subsidiaries.

h. **Designation of accounting firms**

82-5-4

0096

o   Under the new Bank Act, domestic and foreign banks will only be required to
    designate <u>one</u> accounting firm (unless shareholders decide otherwise).

8 2 — 5 — 5

0097

외 무 부

종 별 :

번 호 : USW-0663   일 시 : 92 0207 1804

수 신 : 장 관 (봉이,재무부)

발 신 : 주 미 대사

제 목 : U.R. 금융서비스 협상

    - 미재무성 LUNDSAGER 한국담당 과장이 당관 허재무관에게 문의한 내용과
관련사항으로서

    - U.R. 금융서비스 협상시 제출된 INITIAL OFFERLIST 에 대한 REVISED OFFER LIST
제출을 위한 한국측 진행사항을 회보바람. 동 제출시한은 2.10(월)임.끝.

    (대사 현홍주-국장)

통상국   2차보   재무부

PAGE 1   92.02.08   10:15 WG

DRAFT

The United States offer of trade in services makes the following commitment pursuant to Article XVI of the agreement.

ENTRY AND TEMPORARY
STAY OF SERVICES PROVIDERS

Unbound, except for managers, executives and specialists, as defined below. Limited to citizens of parties to which the United States applies the Agreement who are employees of firms that provide services within the United States through a branch, subsidiary, or affiliate established in the United States and......

Affiliate means:

1) one of two subsidiaries both of which are owned and controlled by the same parent or individual, or

2) one of two legal entities owned and controlled by the same group of individuals, each individual owning and controlling approximately the same share or proportion of each entity, or

3) in the case of a partnership that is organized in the United States to provide accounting services along with managerial and/or consulting services and that markets its accounting services under an internationally recognized name under an agreement with a worldwide coordinating organization that is owned and controlled by the member accounting firms a partnership (or similar organization) that is organized outside the United States to provide accounting services shall be considered to be an affiliate of the United States partnership if it markets its accounting services under the same internationally recognized name under the agreement with the worldwide coordinating organization of which the United States partnership is also a member.

MPAFFIL.LAN
2/5/92

owned and controlled

110-2-2

0099

발 신 전 보

분류번호	보존기간

번   호 : WUS-0604   920210 1834 BU   종별 : _____

WGV -0231

수   신 : 주   미   대사. 총영事   (사본 : 주 제네바 대사)

발   신 : 장 관 (통 기)

제   목 : UR/서비스 협상

~~과 반선, 필수인력 정의에~~   가지정지정

UR/서비스 양허협상에 참고코자 하니 아래 사항을 조사, 보고바람.

o 통신, 유통, 금융, 운송, 관광 분야별로 각 한개씩 대표적인 기업체의 영문
   조직표

o 미국의 필수인력(Managers, Executives, Specialists)이 우리나라 기업의 어느
   직위에 속하는지 비교할 수 있는 자료

o 미국 이민법 (연방규정 제214조의 2)에 의한 L사증 (계열회사 전근자) 발급에
   있어서 필수인력의 입국 허용범위등 구체적인 사례.   끝.

(통상국장   김 용 규)

보 안 통 제	〣

앙 고 재	92 년 2 월 7 일	통 기 과	기안자 성 명 조 현		과 장	심의관	국 장 전결		차 관	장 관

외신과통제

0100

발 신 전 보

WUS-0617   920211 1347   FJ

분류번호	보존기간

번   호 :   종별 :

수   신 : 주   미   대사. 총영사

발   신 : 장 관 (통 기)

제   목 : UR/금융 서비스 협상

대 : USW-0663

대호 UR 금융서비스 협상 관련 미측 문의에 대해 아국은 2.12(수) 관련부처 회의를

거쳐 2.17(월)경 갓트에 수정 offer list를 제출 예정임을 ~~짜아~~ 설명바람.   끝.

(통상국장 김 용 규)

	보 안 통 제	〰

앙고재	92년2월10일 통기과	기안자 성명 준현		과 장 〰	심의관 기	국 장 전결	차 관	장 관 버	외신과통제

0101

외 무 부

종   별 :

번   호 : GVW-0329 　　　　　　　　　　일   시 : 92 0211 1030

수   신 : 장관(수신처 참조)

발   신 : 주제네바대사대리

제   목 : UR/서비스협상 비공식 협의

　　1. 92.2.10. 16:00 칼라일 사무차장은 서비스협상 결과관련 남아있는 기술적문제(MTN.TNC/W/FAP103)에 대한 향후 작업계획에 관하여 4개국 대표(아국,싱가폴,홍콩,이집트)를 초청 의견교환을 가졌는바, 동 회의는 금일 오후 갑작스런 통보에 의한 것이었음.

　　(갓트측 참석자: 칼라일 차장, 하라미요의장, 호주호스대사, 샘슨서비스 국장외실무자)

　　2. 칼라일 차장은 먼저 수개 국가별로 유사한 모임을 갖고 있다고 설명한후 향후작업관련 내주(2.17주)에 호주 호스대사 주재로 21조(양허수정),34조(정의)(1조 포함) 봉신 및 항공 부속서에 관한 논의를 할 예정이라고 하고, 동 논의는 TRACK 3차원의기술적문제에 국한되고 그범위도 최소화되어야 할것이라고 강조하면서 동문제에대한참가국의 의견개진을 요청함.

　　3. 아국은 향후 동 논의가 기술적문제에 국한되어야 한다는 점에 동의하고 특히항공부속서관련 일부국가가 고려중인 CRS 의 동부속서 배제는 실질문제이기 때문에논의되어서는 안된다는 입장을 밝히고, 이집트가 기존의 입장인 통신부속서 5.2항(원가조항)의 수용에 어려움이 있음을 개진함. 홍콩이 양허수정조문관련 입장을 개진하고자 한 바, 사무국측은 별첨자료를 배포함.

　　4. 특히 금일회의는 서비스협정안에 대한 각국의 관심사항을 알아보기 위한 것으로 보였으나, 참가국들이 갑작스런 회의로 사전준비가 없었기때문에 의견개진이 적은것으로 보임

　　5. 내주부터 있을 상기 작업과 관련 본부입장 회시바람.

　　첨부: 21조 양허수정 관련 사무국 문서 1부

　　(GVW(F)-0091).끝

통상국	2차보	정와대	안기부	법무부	교통부	체신부	경기원	재무부
농수부	상공부	건설부	과기처	장관	차관	이검설	분석관	

PAGE 1 　　　　　　　　　　　　　　　　　　　92.02.11　　20:58 DW

주 제 네 바 대 표 부

번 호 : GVF(F) - 0091   년월일 : 20211   시간 : 1030

수 신 : 장   관(통여, 경기원, 재무, 법무부, 농수산부, -상공부, 건설부, 교통부, 체신부, 과기처).

발 신 : 주 제네바대사

제 목 : GVW-032j 전달

총 3 매(표지포함)

보 안 통 제	かり

외신과 통 제	

91 - 3 - 1

0103

Draft
7.2.92

Issues to be resolved regarding Article XXI:
Modification of Schedules

Paragraph 2(a):

The withdrawal of benefits under this Article raises questions concerning the protection, if any, of acquired rights.

The issue of whether the number of Parties that may request compensation should be limited, and if so on what basis, needs to be clarified.

Once the issue of whether cases of non-violation nullification or impairment may be brought under this Agreement has been resolved, consideration may need to be given to whether the procedures of this Article should apply to cases proven under that standard.

Paragraph 3(a):

The time to be allotted for such negotiations needs to be established.

Issues to be addressed in clarifying the arbitration procedures include: (a) panel selection procedures; (b) timetable for completion of arbitration proceedings; (c) which Parties may participate in the arbitration; (d) nature and scope of the arbitration panel's mandate; (e) criteria, if any, for determining the trade value of the modified or withdrawn commitments. (In the event that the Uruguay Round dispute settlement text contains an arbitration provision applicable to the GATS, the arbitration provisions of this Article may need to be co-ordinated with and modified in light of a general arbitration provision applicable to the GATS.)

0104

91 - 3 - 2

14A-HAW

- 2 -

Paragraph 4(b):

Consideration will be given to the issue of whether compensatory withdrawal of benefits should be on an m.f.n. or non-m.f.n. basis. If withdrawal is permitted on a non-m.f.n. basis, the question of when and how such withdrawals should terminate would need to be decided. If benefits may be withdrawn on an m.f.n. basis the question of what rights would accrue to Parties affected by such withdrawals would need to be decided.

91 - 3 - 3

14A-HAW   0105

외 무 부

원 본

종 별 : 지 급

번 호 : GVW-0332   일 시 : 92 0211 1700

수 신 : 장 관(통기,경기원)

발 신 : 주 제네바 대사

제 목 : UR/서비스분야 일본측 수정 OFFER 송부

서비스분야 일본측 수정 OFFER LIST 를 별첨 FAX송부함.

첨부: 서비스분야 일본측 수정 OFFER LIST 1부

(GVW(F)-0093).끝

(차석대사 김삼훈-국장)

통상국   경기원

PAGE 1   92.02.12   02:20 FN

경 제 기 획 원

우 427-760 / 경기도 과천시 중앙동1 정부제2청사 / 전화 503-9149 / 전송 503-9141

문서번호 봉조삼 10502-33

시행일자 1992. 2. 10

(경유)

수신 수신처참조

참조

선결			지시	
접수	일자시간	92. 2. 11	결재·공람	
	번호	4658		
	처리과			
	담당자			

제목 UR대책 서비스분야 실무소위원회 개최

　　　1. UR서비스협상 관련 주요국회의(1.21)에서 협상참가국들은 2월 10일까지 각국의 수정양허표를 제출토록 하고 3월말까지 양허협상을 종료시킬 것을 합의한 바 있습니다.

　　　2. 이에 따라 정부는 그간 주요국과의 2~5차에 걸친 양자협상결과 및 서비스 최종협정(안)의 새로운 양허표 작성방식에 의거한 수정양허표를 조속한 시일내에 GATT에 제출할 계획입니다.

　　　3. 그간 관계부처와의 협의를 거쳐 작성된 수정양허표를 대외협력위원회의 의결을 거쳐 확정시키고자 다음과 같이 최종 실무협의를 위한 표제회의를 개최코자 하니 반드시 소관사항에 대한 책임있는 결정을 할 수 있는 소위원회 위원이 직접 참석하여 주시기 바랍니다.

　　　　　　　　　- 다　　　　음 -

- 일　　시 : '92. 2.12(수), 15:00
- 장　　소 : 경제기획원 대회의실(과천청사 1동 727호)
- 안　　건 : 우리의 수정양허표(안)(별도송부)
- 참석범위 : (별첨참조). 끝.

경　제　기　획　원　장

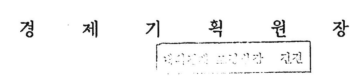

수신처 : <u>외무부장관</u>, 내무부장관, 재무부장관, 법무부장관, 농림수산부장관,
　　　　상공부장관, 건설부장관, 보사부장관, 노동부장관, 동력자원부장관,
　　　　교통부장관, 체신부장관, 문화부장관, 환경처장, 공보처장, 항만청장,
　　　　특허청장, 대외경제정책연구원장, 한국개발연구원장

0107

(別添)

參 席 範 圍

所　屬	參 席 對 象 者	備　　考
經濟企劃院	第2協力官	會議主宰
	通商調整3課長	
外　務　部	通商機構課長	
內　務　部	地籍課長	
財　務　部	國際金融課長	
法　務　部	國際法務審議官室	
	擔當檢事,	
	出入國企劃課長	
農林水産部	國際協力課長	
商　工　部	流通産業課長	
建　設　部	海外協力課長	
保　社　部	國際協力課長	
勞　動　部	海外雇傭課長	
動力資源部	國際協力課長	
交　通　部	國際協力課長	
遞　信　部	通信協力課長	
文　化　部	映畵振興課長	
環　境　處	政策調整課長	
公　報　處	廣告政策課長	
港　灣　廳	振興課長	
特　許　廳	指導課長	
KIEP	박태호, 성극제,	
	김태준 研究委員	
KDI	김지홍 研究委員	

0108

UR/서비스 讓許協商對策

1. 修正 讓許計劃表 作成·提出

   - UR對策 서비스分野 實務小委員會 開催 : 2.12

   - 第14次 對外協力委員會 書面決意   : 2.14

   - GATT에 提出 및 各國配布   : 2.17

2. 2月中 讓許協商對策

   - 修正 讓許計劃表를 중심으로 協商에 對應

   - 代表團 構成

        ○ 首席代表 : 經濟企劃院 第2協力官
        ○ 代   表 : 經濟企劃院 通商調整3課長外 2
                     財 務 部 國際金融課長, 銀行課長外 3
                     法 務 部 擔當檢事
                     海運港灣廳 擔當官
        ○ 諮 問 官 : KIEP, KDI, 外換銀行의 專門家

   - 協商 期間 : 2.24(月) ~ 2.28(金)

   - 協商相對國 : 美國, EC, 日本, 캐나다, 濠洲, 뉴질랜드,
                  스위스, 핀란드, 노르웨이등 9개국

0109

UR/서비스協商關聯

韓國의 修正讓許計劃表 提出對策

1992. 2. 12

UR/對策 서비스實務小委員會

0110

目　　　次

Ⅰ. 修正 讓許計劃表 提出經緯 및 向後協商日程 1

Ⅱ. 讓許計劃表 主要修正內容 2

Ⅲ. 向後 讓許協商 關聯對策 5

　　1. 讓許協商對策 5

　　2. 最惠國待遇(MFN) 逸脫對策 8

　　3. 協商關聯 國內對策의 차질없는 推進 9

〈 添附 〉 韓國의 修正讓許計劃表(案) : 國 · 英文

Ⅰ. 修正讓許計劃表 提出經緯 및 向後協商日程

- UR/서비스 협상과 관련하여 우리정부는 1991.1.9 對外協力
委員會의 議決을 거쳐 최초의 讓許計劃表(Initial Offer
List)를 GATT에 제출

- 그간 UR협상의 진전에 따라 1991.12.20 全體協商議題에 대한
最終協定文案(Draft Final Act)이 제출되었으며 서비스분야
일반협정초안도 거의 합의된 상태로 제시

   ○ 서비스 讓許表 作成方式에 대한 합의형성

   ○ 향후협상일정

      · '92.1~3월중 2~3차에 걸친 國家別 讓許協商 진행
      · '92.2.10까지 각국의 修正讓許計劃表 제출
        (현재 美國, EC, 日本, 濠洲, 뉴질랜드등 제출)
      · '92.3.9까지 讓許協商結果를 반영한 양허표 및 MFN
        逸脫事項(3.6) 제출
      · '92.3.31까지 서비스 一般協定에 포함될 國家別 最終
        讓許計劃表 확정

- 政府는 그동안 關係部處 實務協議를 거쳐 새로운 讓許計劃表
作成方式과 그간의 國家別 兩者協議(1~4회) 및 讓許協商
(1.28~1.30, 美國, EC등 7개국)結果를 반영한 修正讓許
計劃表案을 마련

- 同 讓許修正計劃表를 대외협력위원회의 의결을 거쳐 第2次
讓許協商이 진행되는 2월중순까지 GATT에 제출할 방침

0112

Ⅱ. 讓許計劃表 主要修正內容

1. 修正讓許計劃表上 등재업종의 調整

가. 業種分類의 變更

- 우리의 1次 讓許計劃表는 8개분야 42개 細部業種을 등재

- 修正讓許計劃表 業種分類는 GATT사무국 서비스 분류표에
  따라 11개분야중 8개 분야(敎育서비스, 保健社會서비스,
  文化娛樂서비스 제외)를 등재하고 韓國標準産業分類 및
  國內法規에 의거 57개(15개 추가) 세부업종을 등재

< 業種分類 比較 >

最初의 讓許計劃表		修正 讓許計劃表	
分 野	細部業種	分 野	細部業種
1. 視聽覺서비스	2	1. 事業서비스	22(12)
2. 事業서비스	10	2. 커뮤니케이션	5 (-)
		가. 通信	3 (-)
		나. 視聽覺서비스	2 (-)
3. 通信	3	3. 建設	2(-1)
4. 建設	3	4. 流通	2 (-)
5. 流通	2	5. 環境關聯서비스	2 (2)
6. 金融	7	6. 金融	9 (2)
7. 運送	11	7. 觀光	3(-1)
8. 觀光	4	8. 運送	12 (1)

* (   )내는 業種의 細分化 및 追加讓許에 따른 증가업종수

나. 追加 讓許業種

① 業種의 細分化에 따른 追加

- 엔지니어링서비스 → 엔지니어링서비스, 종합엔지니어링
  서비스
- 컴퓨터관련서비스 → 컴퓨터설비자문업, 소프트웨어시행
  서비스, DP서비스, DB서비스
- 銀行 → 預金 및 관련업무, 貸出 및 관련업무, 外換업무
- 여행알선서비스 → 여행알선서비스, 통역안내서비스

② 各國의 讓許協商結果에 따른 業種追加

- 이미 外國人投資가 자유화된 업종으로서 협상과정에서
  상대국의 요구가 비교적 강하고 讓許하여도 우리로서는
  부담이 적은 것으로 검토된 업종을 추가
  ㅇ 도시계획 및 조경설계서비스, 自然科學 R&D서비스,
    시장조사및 여론조사, 축산관련서비스, 지질조사 및
    탐사서비스, 속기사, 특정폐기물 처리, 폐수수탁
    처리

③ 最初 讓許計劃表('90.11월기준) 작성이후의 追加自由化
  事項 반영

- 廣告(외자지분 제한폐지), 通信(국제서비스 허용), 流通
  (매장면적 및 점포수 확대), 陸運分野(개방시기 단축)의
  자유화수준 반영
- 鐵道小運送業은 업종추가

④ 除外業種 : 外國人專用 觀光紀念品 販賣業

2. 讓許表 作成方式의 變更에 따른 修正

- UR/서비스 일반협정초안에서 제시된 讓許表 作成方式에 따라 前文 및 分野別 記載事項을 수정

〈 讓許表 前文 〉

O 최초의 양허표에서는 商業的駐在(외국인투자 및 외국환 관리법상의 공통제한사항), 토지취득및 이용, 外換管理에 대하여 共通制限事項을 명기

O 修正讓許表에서는 기본적으로 외국인투자, 토지취득 및 이용에 대하여는 國內制度를 보다 명료하게 기재하고 外換管理에 관한 실질적인 제한사항은 各 業種別로 記載

O 人力移動에 있어서는 상업적주재에 따른 必須人力의 범위를 정의하고 同 人力의 일시적 입국을 양허

〈 分野別 自由化約束 關聯事項 〉

O 최초의 양허표에서는 國境間 供給, 海外消費, 商業的駐在 등 3가지 서비스 거래형태에 대한 규제사항을 기재하였 으나 修正讓許表에서는 去來形態에 대한 구분없이 각종 규제사항만을 기재

O 최초의 양허표에서는 일부 登錄·許可要件을 기재하였 으나 修正讓許表에서는 시장접근에 따른 수량제한등 制限措置(일반협정 16조관련)와 內國民待遇上의 차별 사항(17조관련)만을 기재하고 內·外國人이 동등하게 적용되는 등록요건등은 不記載(필요시 주석으로 명기)

O 최초의 양허표에서는 現存規制水準 讓許를 Standstill로 표기하였으나 修正讓許計劃表에서는 규제내용을 구체적 으로 기재하여 양허

Ⅲ. 向後 讓許協商 關聯對策

1. 讓許協商對策

가. 主要國의 開放要請(Request)에 대한 對應

- 현재 우리에게 서비스시장 개방을 요청하고 있는 나라는
  美國, EC, 日本, 濠洲, 뉴질랜드, 카나다, 스위스, 스웨덴,
  노르웨이, 핀랜드, 印度, 폴란드등 모두 12개국이며, 이번
  修正讓許計劃表에서는 이들 국가의 요청사항중 극히 일부만
  반영

< 主要國의 開放要求事項 >

	開放要求業種	備 考
美國	회계, 광고, 시청각, 보건시설관리, 봉신, 엔지니어링, 건설, 프랜차이징, 보험, 법무, 소매업, 관광	엔지니어링 반영
EC	법무, 회계, 세무, 컴퓨터관련서비스, 광고, 봉신, 건설, 유통, 금융, 호텔, 관광, 해운, 항공, 육운, 금융, 사업서비스(종합엔지니어링, 도시계획, R&D, 광업관련서비스, 속기서비스, 패션디자인, 시장조사 및 여론조사, 환경관련서비스)	事業서비스, 環境 關聯서비스 반영
日本	사업서비스(장비임대, 전문직서비스, 엔지니어링), 시청각, 금융, 해운	-
캐나다	금융, 보험, 봉신, 해운, 항공, 관광, 건설, 컴퓨터 및 소프트웨어 서비스, 사업서비스, R&D, 시장조사 및 여론 조사, 광업관련서비스, 지질관련서비스, 환경관련서비스, 화물주선서비스	事業서비스, 環境 關聯서비스 반영
濠洲	회계, 광고, 항공, 건설, 엔지니어링, 금융, 법무, 해운, 봉신	-
스위스	유통, 금융	-
北歐(스웨덴, 노르웨이, 핀랜드)	봉신, 건설, 유통, 금융, 해운, 육운, 법무, 회계, 설계, 엔지니어링, 광고, 컨설팅, 관광, 환경, 컴퓨터관련서비스	-
뉴질랜드	농업(축산)관련서비스, 교육서비스등	축산관련서비스 반영

0116

- 앞으로 讓許協商에서 각국이 공식적으로 개방을 요청한
  사항에 대해서는 보다 강도높은 압력 예상

  ○ 1차적으로 현재의 修正讓許計劃表上에 제시된 수준을
    가지고 讓許協商에 대응

  ○ 각국이 계속 追加的인 自由化約束을 요구할 경우에는
    다음 代案을 가지고 신축성있게 대응

    ① 法務서비스(外國法에 대한 法律諮問 허용)

      · 변호사 자격요건중 國籍要件을 폐지한 수준에서
        양허표에 등재용의 표명(방침 기확정)

    ② 醫療施設管理서비스

      · 의료시설의 소유권과는 별개 용역업으로서의 開放
        檢討意思 표명(방침 기확정)

    ③ 公認會計서비스(상호사용 및 업무제휴등)

      · 國內規制制度의 본질을 침해하지 않는 범위내에서
        수용여부 검토

    ④ 현재 국내제도상 자유화된 업종중 讓許表에 등재되지
      않고 있는 업종

      · 同 業種에 대해서는 이미 개방키로 결정한 사항
        으로서 일부국가에는 이미 약속된 상황이므로 開放
        計劃을 철회할 의사가 없는 한 등재 불가피

      · 同 業種에 대한 개방요구에 대해서는 個別法 및
        外換管理上의 規制등을 검토한 후 신축성있게 대응

    ⑤ 기타 새로운 要求事項은 별도검토

  ○ 金融서비스에 있어서는 美國, EC등 선진국들의 MFN原則
    適用 제한움직임을 정확히 파악하여 대응

나. 우리가 開放要請한 事項에 대한 對策

- 그동안 우리나라는 美國, EC, 日本등 15개국에 대하여 금융,
  유통, 통신, 건설등 업종에서 상대국의 서비스市場 開放을
  요청

  ○ 美國등은 유통등 일부분야에서 追加讓許

- 우리가 중점적으로 개방을 요청한 나라들은 대부분 先進國
  으로서 우리와의 개방격차가 큰 실정이기 때문에 동등한
  협상력을 발휘하는데는 한계가 있으나 우리의 입장을 방어
  하는 차원에서 開放要請事項을 계속 주장

< 우리의 開放要請事項 >

主 要 國	開放要請事項	備 考
美國	통신, 건설, 유통, 은행, 보험, 육운, 창고, 관광, 엔지니어링	流通반영
EC	통신, 건설, 유통, 은행, 보험, 육운, 관광	-
日本	통신, 건설, 유통, 은행, 육운, 관광	-
캐나다	통신, 은행, 유통	-
濠洲	통신, 은행, 유통	-
스위스	통신, 은행, 증권	-
스웨덴, 핀랜드 노르웨이,뉴질랜드, 홍콩, 멕시코	통신	-
인도네시아	엔지니어링, 통신, 유통	-
泰國	엔지니어링, 유통	-
中國	영화 및 비디오, 보험, 통신, 건설	-

2. 最惠國待遇(MFN) 逸脫對策

- 그간 最惠國待遇原則은 다자간 서비스협상의 기본원칙으로써 반드시 준수되어야 함을 강조

  ○ 이에 따라 우리는 最惠國待遇 逸脫要請은 가급적 최소한에 그치겠다는 입장표명

- 금년 1월 들어 美國, EC, 日本등 상당수의 국가들이 MFN 逸脫意思를 표명하고 있기 때문에 우리도 이에 伸縮性있게 대응필요

- 2월중 讓許協商 過程에서 우리의 MFN 일탈사항을 조건부로 제시함으로써 우리의 協商力 強化(공식제출시한 : 3.6)

  ① 콤퓨터 豫約서비스(CRS)

    ○ 韓·美 航空協定('91.6)에 따라 美國에 개방키로 한 SITA를 통한 CRS공급('92.4) 서비스는 美國을 제외한 여타국에 대하여 개방을 유보

    ○ 상기 MFN 逸脫內容은 UR/서비스협상에서 각국의 CRS 개방에 대한 開放約束程度에 따라 변경 가능

  ② 海運

    ○ 定期外航貨物船의 국적선 우선이용제도에 대한 適用 免除 對象國은 우리나라와 해운협정을 맺고 있는 美國, 獨逸, 덴마크, 싱가폴, 台灣, 파키스탄, 노르웨이, 말레이지아, 나이지리아에 한정(海運産業育成法에 근거)

    ○ 1995.1월부터 同 制度 폐지가능

3. 協商關聯 國內對策의 차질없는 推進

- 우리의 修正讓許計劃表는 대부분 현재 개방된 업종 및
  자유화수준을 반영하고 있으나 일부 분야에서 開放日程
  計劃 및 國內規制의 緩和를 양허하고 있기 때문에 이를
  차질없이 추진해 나가는 것이 필요

  ① 開放日程 提示業種

    ○ 建築設計 : 한국건축사와 공동계약 허용('96.1)

    ○ 附加通信 : 외국인 지분제한 폐지('94.1)

    ○ 一般建設 : 외국인 지분제한 폐지('94.1) 및 지사설치
                 허용('96.1)

    ○ 專門建設 : 외국인 지분제한 폐지('94.1) 및 지사설치
                 허용('96.1)

    ○ 海   運 : 정기선 화물국적선 이용제도 폐지('95.1)

    ○ 航   空 : 항공기 수선 및 항공서비스 판매 합작투자
                 허용('97.1)
                 컴퓨터예약업 외국인 지분제한 폐지('94.1)

    ○ 貨物트럭킹 및 鐵道小運送 : 연차적으로 영업지역 확대
                 ('97.1부터 전국 허용)

  ② 技術用役育成法의 改正

    ○ 外國用役發注承認制 및 主契約者制度의 폐지

    ○ 登錄制를 申告制로 전환

- 9-9 -

대외협력위원회 서면 결의 안건 검토 의견

1992. 2.14.
통상기구과

1. 안 건

o UR/서비스 협상 관련 아국의 수정 양허 계획표

o 향후 협상 대책

2. 수정 양허 계획표 제출 경위

o 아국은 91.1.9 대외협력위원회 의결을 거쳐 갓트에 최초의 양허 계획표
(Initial Offer List) 제출

o UR/서비스 협상의 진전에 따라 92.2.10까지 협상 참가국은 수정 양허 계획표
(Revised Offer List) 제출 필요

3. 수정 양허 계획표 제출

o 11개 서비스 분야 55개 업종 양허

o 최초 양허 계획표(8개분야 42개 업종)를 기초로 작성

- 91년도중 서비스 양자협상 결과에 따라 상대국의 요구가 비교적 강하고
양허해도 부담이 적은 7개 업종 추가 (도시계획 및 조경설비 서비스, 시장조사 및 여론조사 등)

- 업종을 세분화 함으로써 4개 업종 추가 (여행알선을 여행알선서비스 및 관광안내서비스로
세분 등)

- 최초 양허 계획표 이후 아국이 자발적으로 자유화 조치를 취한 1개 업종
추가 (철도 소운송업)

0121

4. 향후 협상 대책

o 앞으로 수정 양허표에 대해 각국의 추가 양허 요구가 있는 경우,
법무 서비스, 의료시설 관리 서비스, 공인회계 서비스등 분야에서 대안 제시
o 협상 상대국에 대한 우리의 개방 요구(request)도 병행 실시

5. 평 가

o 수정 양허 계획표는 그간 관련부처간 실무회의를 거쳐 확정된 것으로서,
최종적인 것은 아니며 향후 협상 과정에서 상대국의 추가적인 요청이 있을
경우 협상 대책에 따라 신축적으로 대응이 가능함.

o 따라서 수정 양허 계획표 제출 및 향후 협상 대책에 관한 대외협력위원회
결의에 찬성이 가함.   끝.

0122

발 신 전 보

<table>
<tr><td>분류번호</td><td>보존기간</td></tr>
<tr><td></td><td></td></tr>
</table>

번   호 : WGV-0265   920214 1838 DW   종별 : _____

수   신 : 주 제네바 대사. 총영사.

발   신 : 장 관 (통 기)

제   목 : UR/GNS 협상

1. 주한 미 대사관은 미측이 UR/GNS 한미 양자간 양허 협상을 2.26(수) 제네바에서
    개최하기를 희망하며 아측이 가급적 금융, 통신, 노동력 이동분야의 본부대표를
    파견 할것을 요청한다고 통보하여 왔으며 본부는 이를 검토 중임.

2. 상기 미측의 요청사항을 귀지 주재 미 대표부에 확인 바라며, 여타국과의 GNS/양자
    협상계획도 있으면 아울러 보고바람.

                                          끝.   통상국장 김 용 규)

<table>
<tr><td>보 안
통 제</td><td></td></tr>
</table>

<table>
<tr><td rowspan="2">앙
고
재</td><td>42
년
2
월
14
일</td><td>통
기
과</td><td>기안자
성명</td><td>과 장</td><td>심의관</td><td>국 장</td><td colspan="2">차 관   장 관</td></tr>
<tr><td></td><td></td><td>조현</td><td></td><td></td><td>전결</td><td></td><td></td></tr>
</table>

<table>
<tr><td>외신과통제</td></tr>
</table>

0123

외 무 부

원 본

종 별 : 지 급

번 호 : GVW-0355

일 시 : 92 0214 1000

수 신 : 장관(통기, 경기원)

발 신 : 주제네바대사대리

제 목 : UR/서비스 분야 OFFER LIST 작성지침(수정분)송부

서비스분야 OFFER LIST 작성관련 91.12.31자 지침의 수정분을 별첨 FAX 송부함.

첨부: UR/서비스 OFFER LIST 작성지침 1부

(GVW(F)-0103).끝

(차석대사 김삼훈-국장)

통상국   2차보   경기원

PAGE 1

92.02.15   05:51 DQ

외신 1과 통제관

0124

주 제 네 바 대 표 부

번 호 : GVR(F) - 0/03　　　년월일 : 202/4　　시간 : /000

수 신 : 징　　　관 (동거.경기원)

발 신 : 주 제네바대사

제 목 : GVW - 0355 첨부

종　　　매(표지포함)

보 안	
봉 제	

외신관	
봉 제	

103 — /2 — /

0125

12.2.92

SCHEDULING OF INITIAL COMMITMENTS IN TRADE IN SERVICES:

EXPLANATORY NOTE[1]

Introduction

1.   This Note is intended for persons who are preparing offers, requests and national schedules of initial commitments. Its objective is to explain, in a concise manner, how commitments should be set out in schedules in order to achieve precision and clarity. It is based on the view that some standardization of format is necessary to ensure comparable and unambiguous commitments. The Note cannot answer every question that might occur to persons responsible for scheduling commitments; it does attempt to answer those questions which are most likely to arise. The answers should not be considered as an authoritative legal interpretation of the GATS.

2.   The GATS contains two sorts of provisions: general obligations, applying uniformly to all signatories in all sectors, and specific commitments, which are negotiated sectoral undertakings particular to each GATS signatory. Specific commitments, upon the conclusion of negotiations, are recorded in national schedules which are attached to, and form an integral part of, the GATS. By virtue of Article XXVIII:1, every signatory must attach to the GATS its national schedule.

3.   In taking stock of the negotiating process thus far, it is apparent that the offers that have been submitted in the form of schedules differ in their presentation. These differences include the types of measure scheduled, their description, the method of referring to measures, the use of modes of supply, the classification of service sectors, and terminology.

---

[1] This note is circulated by the Secretariat in response to requests by participants. It is a revised version of a 13 December 1991 draft entitled Scheduling of Commitments in Trade in Services: Explanatory Note. References to the General Agreement on Trade in Services (GATS) and related Annexes and other Documents are all based on the text contained in document MTN.TNC/W/FA of 20 December 1991, which is part of the Draft Final Act Embodying the Results of the Uruguay Round.

0126

/63-/2-2

- 2 -

This Note answers two main questions: what items should be entered on a schedule, and how should they be entered?

PART I

WHAT ITEMS SHOULD BE SCHEDULED?

4. A schedule contains three main types of information: limitations[2] to market access, limitations to national treatment, and additional commitments other than market access and national treatment. If a participant undertakes a commitment in a sector then it must indicate, for each mode of supply in that sector:

- what limitations, if any, it maintains on market access;

- what limitations, if any, it maintains on national treatment; and

- what further commitments, other than market access and national treatment, it may decide to undertake.

A. Limitations on Market Access (Article XVI)

5.   A Party under the GATS grants full market access in a given sector and mode of supply when it does not maintain in that sector or mode any of the types of measures listed in Article XVI. The measures listed comprise four types of quantitative restrictions (subparagraphs a-d), as well as limitations on forms of legal entity (subparagraph e) and on foreign equity participation (subparagraph f). The list is exhaustive, and includes measures which may also be discriminatory according to the national

---

[2] The term "limitations" will be used throughout this Note to refer to the "terms", "conditions", "limitations", and "qualifications" used in the GATS, in particular in Articles XVI and XVII.

0127

103-12-7

- 3 -

treatment standard (Article XVII). The quantitative restrictions can be
expressed numerically, or through an economic needs test.

> Example: A law specifies that a restaurant will be granted a
> license to operate only if the applicant
> demonstrates that market conditions justify an
> additional restaurant. This is a measure contrary
> to paragraph 2(a) of Article XVI.

A participant which maintains a measure listed in Article XVI in a sector
and mode of supply in which it is making a commitment has a choice: in the
light of the results of negotiations it may either remove the measure, or
it may record the measure on its schedule as a limitation to market access.

B. Limitations on National Treatment (Article XVII)

6.   A Party grants full national treatment in a given sector and mode of
supply when it accords in that sector and mode conditions of competition no
less favourable to services or service suppliers of other Parties than
those accorded to its own services and service suppliers. This requirement
may result from treatment which is either formally identical, or formally
different; the standard thus covers both _de jure_ and _de facto_
discrimination. Unlike Article XVI, the national treatment commitment is
not defined through an exhaustive listing of the types of measure which
would constitute limitations.

> Example: A law requires that all accountants practicing in a
> country be its nationals. Such a measure discriminates
> explicitly on the basis of the origin of the service
> supplier and thus constitutes formal, or _de jure_, denial
> of national treatment.

> Example: A law requires that all accountants be graduates of local
> universities. Although the measure does not formally
> distinguish service suppliers on the basis of national
> origin, it _de facto_ offers less favourable treatment to
> foreign service suppliers by modifying in an unfavourable
> way the conditions of competition in relation to the like
> service supplier of national origin.

0128

103-12-6

- 4 -

7.   As mentioned in paragraph 5, a measure of a Party may be contrary to both market access (Article XVI) and national treatment (Article XVII) commitments assumed by a Party. Such a measure, if it is to be maintained, should be entered in the market access column. In this case, the entry will be considered to provide a limitation as well to a national treatment commitment in that sector.

C. Additional Commitments (Article XVIII)

8.   A Party may, in a given sector, make commitments other than market access and national treatment. Such commitments can include, but are not limited to, undertakings with respect to professional qualifications, technical standards, licensing procedures, and other domestic regulations referred to in Article VI, even though these measures may be consistent with full market access (Article XVI) and national treatment (Article XVII). Unlike market access and national treatment, additional commitments are expressed in the form of undertakings, not limitations.

PART II

HOW SHOULD ITEMS BE SCHEDULED?

9.   Schedules record, for each sector, the legally enforceable commitments of each Party. It is therefore vital that schedules be clear, precise and based on a common approach and terminology. This section describes how commitments should be entered on schedules. It is based on the model schedule in the Annex.

The main elements are:

    A.   horizontal measures;
    B.   sector-specific measures;
    C.   sectoral classification;
    D.   modes of supply; and
    E.   use of common terms.

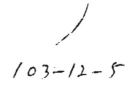

0129

103-12-5

- 5 -

A. Scheduling of horizontal measures

10.   A horizontal measure is a measure which affects trade in services in more than one service sector. In order to avoid repetition, it is advisable to enter these measures in a separate section at the beginning of the schedule. The entry should describe the measure concisely, indicating the elements which make it inconsistent with Articles XVI or XVII, and include a legal reference to any relevant law or regulation.

Some horizontal measures may be specific to only one mode of supply:

> Example: Legislation may refer to foreign investment, formation of corporate structures or land acquisition regulations. Such measures affect above all the presence of juridical persons.

> Example: Legislation may stipulate requirements regarding entry, temporary stay and work as well as define the scope of personnel movement covered by a particular offer. Such measures affect above all the presence of natural persons.

Other horizontal measures may affect more than one mode of supply:

> Example: Legislation may provide for tax measures which are contrary to national treatment, or for competition laws which affect market access. Such measures would normally affect more than one mode of supply.

B. Scheduling of sector-specific measures

11.   A sector-specific measure is a measure which affects trade in services in only one sector. Such a measure, if maintained, must be entered as a limitation in the appropriate column (either market access or national treatment), of the appropriate sector. The entry should describe the measure concisely, indicating the elements which make it inconsistent with Articles XVI or XVII, and include a legal reference to any relevant law or regulation.

0130

103-12-6

- 6 -

C. Sectoral Classification

12.   The classification of sectors and sub-sectors should be based on the secretariat's revised Services Sectoral Classification List.[3] Each sector contained in the secretariat list is identified by the corresponding CPC (Central Product Classification) number. Where it is necessary to refine further a sectoral classification, this should be done on the basis of the CPC. The most recent breakdown of the CPC, including explanatory notes for each sub-sector, is contained in the UN Provisional Central Product Classification.[4]

> Example: A Party wishes to indicate an offer or commitment in the sub-sector of map-making services. In the secretariat list, this service would fall under the general heading "Other Business Services" under "Related scientific and technical consulting services" (see item 1.F.m). By consulting the CPC, map-making can be found under the corresponding CPC classification number 86754. In its revised offer/schedule, the Party would then enter the sub-sector under the "Other Business Services" section of its schedule as follows:
>
> Map-making services (86754)

If a Party wishes to use its own sub-sectoral classification or definitions it should, for the purpose of ensuring legal certainty, provide concordance with the CPC in the manner indicated in the example noted above.

D. Modes of supply

13.   The four modes of supply listed in the schedules correspond to the scope of the GATS as set out in Article I:2. The modes are essentially defined on the basis of the origin of the service supplier and consumer, and the degree and type of territorial presence which they have at the

---

[3] Document MTN.GNS/W/120, dated 10 July 1991.

[4] Statistical Papers Series M no. 77, Provisional Central Product Classification, Department of International Economic and Social Affairs, Statistical Office of the United Nations, New York, 1991.

0131

103-12-7

- 7 -

moment the service is delivered. This classification is intended to correspond to the categories of regulatory measures which commonly affect trade in services. The modes of supply may be illustrated as follows:

MODES OF SUPPLY

Supplier Presence	Other Criteria	Mode
Service supplier not present within the territory of the Party	Service delivered within the territory of the Party, from the territory of another Party	CROSS-BORDER SUPPLY
	Service delivered outside the territory of the Party, in the territory of another Party, to a service consumer of the Party	CONSUMPTION ABROAD
Service supplier present within the territory of the Party	Service delivered within the territory of the Party, with supplier present as a juridical person	PRESENCE OF JURIDICAL PERSON
	Service delivered within the territory of the Party, with supplier present as a natural person	PRESENCE OF NATURAL PERSON

14.   It is important to have a common interpretation of what each mode covers along the lines of what is suggested above. Further examples and explanations are given below.

a)   Cross-border supply

15.   The supply of a service through telecommunications, mail, and services embodied in goods (eg. a computer diskette, or drawings) are all examples of cross-border supply, since the service supplier is not present within the territory of the Party where the service is delivered.

0132

103 - 12 - 8

- 8 -

b)   Consumption abroad

16.   Tourism and ship repair abroad are examples of this mode. In the case of tourism, the service consumer is abroad when the service is delivered, whereas in the ship repair example the consumer typically is not abroad when the service is delivered.

c)   Presence of juridical persons

17.   This mode covers not only the presence of juridical persons in the strict legal sense, such as corporations, but also other legal entities such as partnerships and joint ventures, which share some of the same characteristics (see definitions in Article XXXIV).

d)   Presence of natural persons

18.   This mode covers natural persons who are themselves service suppliers, as well as natural persons who are employees of service suppliers.

e)   Relation between modes of supply

19.   Where a service transaction requires in practical terms the use of more than one mode of supply, coverage of the transaction is only ensured when there are commitments in each relevant mode of supply.

> Example: A signatory has made a commitment in the cross-border supply of architectural services (eg. by telecommunications or the mails). This commitment alone does not extend to the presence of natural persons (eg. visits by architects). A separate commitment would have to be taken under 'Presence of natural persons' to cover this case.

E.   How should commitments be recorded?

20.   Since the terms of a participant's schedule create legally binding commitments, it is important that the terms used, notably in expressing presence or absence of limitations to market access and national treatment, be uniform and precise. Depending on the extent to which a participant has limited market access and national treatment, for each commitment four cases can be foreseen:

0133

103-12-P

- 9 -

a)   Full commitment

21.   In this case the participant does not seek in any way to limit market access or national treatment in a given sector and mode of supply through measures inconsistent with Article XVI and XVII. The participant in this situation should mark in the appropriate column: NONE. However, any relevant horizontal limitations will still apply.

b)   Commitment with limitations

22.   Two main possibilities can be envisaged in this case. The first is the binding of an existing regulatory situation ("standstill"). The second is the binding of a more liberal situation where some, but not all, of the measures inconsistent with Articles XVI or XVII will be removed ("rollback"). Here, the participant must describe in the appropriate column the measures maintained which are inconsistent with Articles XVI or XVII. The entry should describe each measure concisely, indicating the elements which make it inconsistent with Articles XVI or XVII, and include a legal reference to any relevant law or regulation. It would not be sufficient to merely enter in a column words such as "bound" or "standstill".

c)   No commitment

23.   In this case, the participant remains free in a given sector and mode of supply to introduce or maintain measures inconsistent with market access or national treatment. In this situation, the participant must record in the appropriate column the word: UNBOUND. This case is only relevant where a commitment has been made in a sector with respect to at least one mode of supply. Where all modes of supply are "unbound", and no additional commitments have been undertaken in the sector, the sector should not appear on the schedule.

0134

103-12-10

- 10 -

e)   **No commitment technically feasible**

24.   In some situations, a particular mode of supply may not be
technically feasible. An example might be the cross-border supply of hair-
dressing services. In these cases the term NOT APPLICABLE should be used.
Where the mode of supply thought to be inapplicable does in the future
become possible, the term "not applicable" should be understood to mean
"unbound".

0135

/03-12-11

DRAFT

ANNEX: SCHEDULE OF COMMITMENTS OF COUNTRY X

Sector or Sub-sector	Limitations on Market Access	Limitations on National Treatment	Additional commitments
	(1)	(1)	(1)
	(2)	(2)	(2)
	(3)	(3)	(3)
	(4)	(4)	(4)
	(1)	(1)	(1)
	(2)	(2)	(2)
	(3)	(3)	(3)
	(4)	(4)	(4)

Key: (1) Cross-border supply   (3) Presence of juridical persons
     (2) Consumption abroad   (4) Presence of Natural Persons

NOTE: The schedule shall also specify where appropriate the time-frame for implementation of commitments and their date of entry into force.

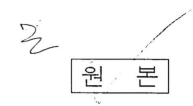

외 무 부

종 별 :

번 호 : GVW-0365

일 시 : 92 0214 1700

수 신 : 장 관(봉기, 경기원, 법무부, 재무부, 상공부, 건설부, 보사부, 교통부, 체신부,

발 신 : 주 제네바 대사대리   과기처, 항만청)

제 목 : UR/서비스 양자협상 일정

　　92.12.14. 현재 확정된 아국의 제2차 서비스분야 양자협상 일정 (대부분 국가 금융분야 포함)을 아래 봉보함.

　　- 아래 -

　　- 92.2.24(월) 14:30 스위스

　　- 92.2.25(화) 10:00 놀웨이

　15:00 뉴질랜드

　17:30 핀랜드

　　- 92.2.26(수) 09:30 미국

　15:00 일본

　　- 92.2.27(목) 09:00 EC

　15:00 카나다. 끝

　　(차석대사 김삼훈-국장)

통상국	2차보	법무부	보사부	교통부	체신부	경기원	재무부	상공부
건설부	과기처	해항청						

PAGE 1

92.02.15　09:15 WG

외신 1과 통제관

0137

발 신 전 보

	분류번호	보존기간

번 호 : WGV-0271　920215 1507　FE　종별 : _____

수 신 : 주 제네바　　　대사. 총영사

발 신 : 장 관 (통 기)

제 목 : UR/GNS 수정 양허계획표 제출

　　92.2.15. 대외협력위원회 결의를 거친 아국의 UR/서비스분야 수정 양허
계획표를 2.16. 귀임하는 귀관 한철수 경협관보편에 송부하니 1.17중 갓트에
제출바람.　　　끝.

　　　　　　　　　　　　　　　　　　(통상국장　김 용 규)

0138

경 제 기 획 원

우 427-760 / 경기도 과천시 중앙동1 정부제2청사 / 전화 503-9149 / 전송 503-9141

문서번호 봉조삼 10502-37

시행일자 1992. 2. 15.

(경유)

수신 외무부장관

참조 통상국장

선결			지시	
접수	일자시간	∴	결재·공람	
	번호			
	처리과			
	담당자			

제목 UR/서비스협상관련 한국의 수정양허계획표 GATT제출에 관한 협조

1991.1.14 GATT에 제출한 UR/서비스협상관련 최초의 양허계획표를 대외협력위원회의 의결을 거쳐 별첨과 같이 수정하여 GATT에 제출코자 하니 조치하여 주시기 바랍니다.

첨부 : 한국의 수정양허계획표.   끝.

경 제 기 획 원 장

0139

외 무 부

종 별 :

번 호 : GVW-0372 일 시 : 92 0217 1730

수 신 : 장 관(통기,경기원)

발 신 : 주 제네바 대사

제 목 : UR/서비스 협상 카나다의 수정 OFFER 송부

2.17. GATT 에 제출된 카나다와의 수정 OFFER 를 별첨 송부함

첨부: 카나다의 수정 OFFER 1부(GVW(F)-0109). 끝 개판정.

(대사 박수길-국장)

통상국 2차보 경기원

PAGE 1

92.02.18 08:21 WG

외신 1과 통제관

0140

외 무 부

종 별 :

번 호 : GVW-0373

일 시 : 92 0217 1730

수 신 : 장 관(통기,경기원,법무부,노동부)

발 신 : 주 제네바 대사

제 목 : UR/서비스 협상

연: GVW-226

연호 1.29 개최된 UR/서비스 한.미 양자 협상시 아측이 요청한 제휴기업 (AFFILIATE)의 정의에 대한 미측 서면 답변을 별첨 송부함.

첨부: 제휴기업의 정의에 대한 미측 서면답변 1부

(GVW(F)-0110).끝 버뜨림.

(대사 박수길-국장)

통상국   2차보   법무부   경기원   노동부

PAGE 1

외 무 부

원 본

종 별 :

번 호 : GVW-0384

일 시 : 92 0218 1800

수 신 : 장관(수신처참조)

발 신 : 주 제네바 대사

제 목 : UR/GNS 협상

    2.18(화) 당관에 전달된 오지리의 대아국서비스분야 REQUEST-LIST 를 별첨 송부함.

      첨부: 오지리의 REQUEST LIST 1부.(GVW(F)-114)

      (대사 박수길-국장)

    수신처: 통기, 경기원, 재무부, 법무부, 농림수산부, 문화부, 상공부, 건설부, 보사부, 노동부, 교통부, 체신부, 과기처, 공보처, 항만청)

| 통상국 | 차관 | 2차보 | 안기부 | 법무부 | 보사부 | 문화부 | 교통부 | 체신부 |
| 경기원 | 재무부 | 농수부 | 상공부 | 건설부 | 노동부 | 과기처 | 해항청 | 공보처 |

PAGE 1

92.02.19   04:57 ED

외신 1과 통제관

0142

148 우루과이라운드 서비스 분야 양허 협상 1

주 제 네 바 대 표 부

번 호 : GVR(F) - 0114   년월일 : 20 2/8   시간 1800

수 신 : 장   관 (통제. 통일. 동아. 통상. 경기원. 재정부. 법무부. 상공부. 건설부. 내무부

발 신 : 주 제네바대사   노동부. 교통부. 체신부. 문화부. 농수산부. 공보처. 과기처. 보건사회부)

제 ,목 : UR/GNS협상 (브라질의 Request List)

총 6 매(표지포함)

보 안	
통 재	

외신과	
통 재	

배부처	장관실	차관실	일차보	이차보	기획실	의장실	분석관	의전장	아주국	미주국	구주국	중아국	국기국	경제국	통상국	문협국	영교국	총무과	감사관	공보관	외연권	청와대	총리실	안기부	공보처	경기원	상공부	재무부	법무부	건설부	내무부	노동부	교통부	체신부	문화부	농수부	과기처	항만청
	1	1	1	1		1	1							1/4										1	1	1	1	1	1	1	1	1	1	1	1	1	1	1

114 - 6 -1

0143

ÖSTERREICHISCHE STÄNDIGE VERTRETUNG
Mission Permanente de l'Autriche
Austrian Permanent Mission

CH-1211 Genf 20, 9-11, rue de Varembé, Tel. 733-77-50, Fax 734-45-91

TELEFAX-DEPESCHE
Begleitblatt

AN: TO/POUR ___all participants in the GATS negotiations___

TELEFAX-Nummer: _____ **Telefon-Nummer:** _____

VON: FROM/DE Verfasser ___R. Hochörtler___ **DATUM:** DATE ___17.2.1992___

SEITEN: PAGES ___5___
(inkl. Begleitblatt total)

Bemerkungen: Note

In accordance with the procedures agreed to by the GNS, Austria hereby presents its general requests concerning movement of personnel and establishment to all participants of the negotiations on trade in services.

Austria reserves her right to submit additional country specific requests at a later stage.

Austria would appreciate the opportunity to discuss the attached requests at an appropriate time and would be pleased to provide clarification or background details.

Richard Hochörtler
Deputy Permanent
Representative

0144

AUSTRIAN REQUEST LIST ON SERVICES
TO ALL PARTICIPANTS

1. Liberalization commitments on the movement of natural persons providing services under the Agreement.

Austria requests from all parties, without requiring compliance with economic needs test :

(i) the temporary access , as intra-corporate transferees, of natural persons in the following categories, provided that such persons have been employed by the company concerned for at least the year immediately preceding such movement:

  (a) senior employees of an organization who primarily direct the management of the organisation, receiving general supervision or direction principally from the board of directors of stockholders of the business, including :
  - directing the organization or a department or subdivision of the organisation;
  - supervising and controlling the work of other supervisory, professional or managerial employees;
  - having the authority personally to hire and fire or recommend hiring, firing of other personnel actions.

  (b) Persons employed by an organization who are indispensable for the provision of a specific service by reasons of high or uncommon :
  - qualifications referring to a type of work or trade requiring specific technical knowledge;
  - knowledge essential to the organizations service, research equipment, techniques or management.

0145

114 - 6 - 3

- 2 -

(ii)   the temporary access of natural persons in the
       following categories:

   (a)   Persons based in the territory of Austria
         who are representatives of a service provider
         and who are seeking temporary entry for the
         purpose of negotiating for the sale of services
         and of entering into agreements to sell services
         for that service provider, where those
         representatives will not be engaged in making
         direct sales to the general public or in
         supplying services themselves.

   (b)   Persons meeting the criteria of category (i) (a)
         who are responsible for the setting up of a
         commercial presence of the service provider in the
         territory of another party when:

         - the representatives are not engaged in making
           direct sales or supplying services and
         - the service provider has no representatative,
           branch or subsidiary in the territory of the party
           concerned.

0146

- 3 -

2. Liberalization commitment on establishment

According to the Austrian legislation the right of
establishment and consequently the granting of national
treatment with regard to most service sectors including
financial services is contingent upon a reciprocity and/or
economic and local interest test.

Austria requests all parties to undertake in their national
schedules effective commitments on establishment, including
the acquisition of majority participation in domestic
companies, on the basis of national treatment.

Consistent with the application of unconditional MFN under
the GATS Austria is prepared to renounce recourse to such
measures as described above in relation to GATS parties,
provided that a satisfactory balance of commitments can be
achieved.

If this condition is met the right of establishment and
national treatment would be extended on m.f.n. basis to all
parties. This means that in such case Austria would renounce
application for a m.f.n. derogation.

The Austrian offer/request pertains to most services
contained in the Austrian conditional offer
(MTN.TNC/W/66/Add. 1 of 23 May 1991).

0147

114 - 6 - 5

- 4 -

Taking as a basis the classification list MTN.GNS/W/120 the following services are affected:

1. A. Business services excluding "Professions Liberales"
1. B; 1.D; 1.E; 1. F; 3.; 4.; 5. partly; 6.; 7.; 8. partly; 9.;
10. partly;
11. auxiliary transport services and maintenance and repair;
12. - hair-dresser
    - auctioning of movable goods and chattels
    - debt collection agencies
    - equalization procedures out of court.

0148

114-6-6

경 제 기 획 원

우 427-760 / 경기도 과천시 중앙동1 정부제2청사 / 전화 503-9149 / 전송 503-9141

문서번호 통조삼 10502-3♪

시행일자 1992. 2. 18

(경유)

수신 수신처참조

참조

선결			지시	
접	일자시간	9~.2.20	사결	
수	번호	5892	재·공	
	처리과			
	담당자		람	

제목 UR/서비스협상 관련자료 배포

　　　　1. GATT사무국이 작성한 UR/서비스업종 분류표와 현재 UN에서 작업중에 있는 CPC 분류표, 미국, 일본 및 뉴질랜드의 수정 Offer List를 별첨과 같이 통보하니 업무에 참고하시기 바랍니다.

　　　　2. 특히 각부처는 양허표(National Schedule)에 등재할 업종의 명칭 및 포괄범위 를 명확히 하기 위하여 동 업종이 GATT사무국의 분류표, 한국표준산업분류표 국내법규상 어떤 업종에 해당되는지를 검토하여 다음양식에 따라 당원(통상조정3과)에 2.26(수)까지 통보해 주시기 바랍니다.

- 다　　　　음 -

최종 양허표에 등재할 업종명	신한국표준산업분류 표상의 포괄범위 (분류번호 포함)	국내법규상의 포괄 범위	GATT사무국 분류표 상의 포괄범위 (분류번호 포함)

첨부 : 1. UR/서비스업종 분류표 1부.
　　　 2. 각국의 수정 Offer List(Ⅲ) 1부.
　　　 3. 각국의 수정 Offer List(Ⅳ) 1부.　끝.

경 제 기 획 원 장

제 2협력관 전결

수신처 : <u>외무부장관</u>, 내무부장관, 재무부장관, 법무부장관, 교육부장관, 문화부장관
　　　　　농림수산부장관, 상공부장관, 보건사회부장관, 건설부장관, 교통부장관,
　　　　　노동부장관, 동자부장관, 체신부장관, 체육청소년부장관, 과학기술처장관,
　　　　　환경처장관, 공보처장관, 경찰청장, 특허청장, 해운항만청장

0149

발 신 전 보

분류번호 | 보존기간

번 호 : WUK-0305   920219 1910 CJ 종별 : _____

수 신 : 주   영   대사. 총영사/

발 신 : 장 관   (통 기)

제 목 : UR/서비스 협상

1. 2.24-28간 제네바에서 개최되는 UR/서비스 양허 협상에 참가할 아국 대표단에
    귀관 최낙정 해무관을 포함시키고자 하는바, 귀관 업무 형편상 동인의 제네바
    파견이 곤란한 경우, 지급 보고바람.

2. 동인 ~~출장자~~ 출장기간은 2.23-29 간이며 예산은 해운항만청에 지원 예정임.

                                      끝.   (통상국장 김 용 규)

보 안 통 제

외신과통제

0150

외 무 부

종 별 :

번 호 : GVW-0392

일 시 : 92 0219 1500

수 신 : 장 관(수신처참조)

발 신 : 주 제네바 대사

제 목 : UR/서비스 협상(노르웨이의 수정 OFFER)

2.19(수) 당관에 전달된 노르웨이의 수정 OFFER를 별첨 송부함.

첨부: 노르웨이의 수정 OFFER 1부

(GVW(F)-0117).끝

(대사 박수길-국장)

통상국	통상국	통상국	통상국	안기부	법무부	보사부	문화부	고통부
체신부	경기원	재무부	농수부	상공부	건설부	노동부	과기처	해항청
공보처								

PAGE 1

92.02.21   07:50 FN

외신 1과 통제관

0151

주 제 네 바 대 표 부

번 호 : GVN(F) - 0117   년월일 : 2021P   시간 : 1500

수 신 : 장   관 (도해·통상, 동미, 통상, 국기관, 제2정책, 경제국, 상공부, 전자북, 내자국

발 신 : 주 제 네바대사   노동부. 고용국. 해건북 민사국, 농수산국, 공보처, 과기처, 상공부)

제 목 : GVN-03P호 첨부

총 20 매(표지포함)

보 안 통 제	

| 외신과
동 재 | |

117-20-1

THE PERMANENT MISSION OF NORWAY
IN GENEVA   17 February 1992

COMMUNICATION BY NORWAY

Conditional Offer by Norway
concerning Initial Commitments

Revision 1 to MTN\W\63\Add.1.

1. Norway presented its Conditional Offer concerning Initial
Commitments on 22 May 1991 in the document MTN\W\63\Add.1. The
attached revision is based on the draft final text of the
General Agreement on Trade in Services and its attached texts
of 20 December 1991 (document MTN.TNC\W\FA). The offer is
subject to revision to take account of any amendments to these
texts. It reflects the bilateral negotiations on initial
commitments which Norway has conducted after the issuance of
the previous offer. It also incorporates some technical changes reflecting the content of the relevant articles in the
framework agreement and the sectoral annexes and attachments.

2. Progressive liberalization of trade in services is an
essential goal for Norway in the Uruguay Round negotiations.
Comprehensive initial commitments on market access and national treatment by all participating countries in the Uruguay
Round as part of the General Agreement on Trade in Services
are thus of relevance for the assessment for the overall results of the Uruguay Round negotiations. To this end Norway is
prepared to continue actively bilateral negotiations with
other trading partners on the basis of the offers for additional commitments in market access and national treatment as
outlined in the work programme by the Chairman of the Group of
Negotiations in Services.

3. This revised offer is presented in the expectation of
corresponding offers with widest possible sectoral coverage by
other participants in the Uruguay Round negotiations. A balanced outcome of the negotiations would require that other
parties are ready to bind their regulatory measures in the
areas of interest to Norway.

4. This offer is conditional and Norway reserves its right to
modify, reduce or withdraw this offer based on the following
criteria:

-   The quality and number of offers by other participants in
    order to foster the progressive liberalization of all
    services sectors;

-   The scope and economic value of the MFN-derogations
    sought for by the other participants;

-   The final contents of the framework agreement and the
    sectoral annexes.

0153

2

5. The initial commitments in this offer and any additional
commitments resulting from the initial commitment negotiations would be bound in the Norwegian national schedule as a
part of the balanced expectation that other parties would make
corresponding initial commitments and further additional
commitments of special interest to Norway.

0154

Sector/subsector	Article XVI (market access)	Article XVII (national treatment)
All sectors:		
General authori-zation procedures:		
Act of 14th, December 1917., Acquisitions of waterfalls, mines and other real properties	According to the Act of 14th December 1917 relating to acquisitions of waterfalls, mines and other properties, foreigners/foreign-controlled *) Norwegian companies need a concession for purchases of real property, whether building and/or land, without regard to the purpose for which the property will be used. Leases of real property for a period of more than 10 years are subject to concession requirement. If the property is to be used for manufacturing purposes, a concession is required without regard to the lease period.	Requirements::Chairman/majority of the board of directors are Norwegian citizens. BOUND.
	Foreign citizens residing in Norway who purchase or lease real property for housing, secondary residences and business activities without a concession, are subject to the condition that the real property is acquired for their own personal use.	
	According to the Act of 1917 a concession can only be granted when it is not contrary to the public interest. The concession terms are stipulated by the Ministry of Industry or the Ministry of Petroleum and Energy (in the case of waterfalls). Transactions/agreements between Norwegian parent/foreign company must be based on realistic pricing.	
	*)A foreign controlled company: *The company is owned by foreigners/foreign-controlled companies or the chairman and the majority of the board of directors are not Norwegian citizens.*	

0155

Sector/subsector	Article XVI (market access)	Article XVII (national treatment)
Joint Stock Companies Act 4th of June 1976		According to the Act of 1976 the manager in a joint stock company, at least half the members of the board of directors, the corporate assembly and the committee of representatives must be permanent residents of Norway and have resided there for the last two years. The Ministry of Industry may grant exemptions from these rules.

Corporations registered in Norway, where more than 1/3 of the voting rights are controlled by non-nationals or foreign controlled companies, or where the chairman and the majority of the board members are non-nationals, are subject to concession when acquiring real estate or entering into certain lease contracts with regard to such objects. BOUND. |
| **Labour movement**

- Entry into and residence in the national territory | Entry into and residence in the national territory are regulated by the Norwegian immigration law, according to which work permit is required for foreign nationals if the purpose of entry into Norwegian territory is to undertake work. Permit will be issued according to Norwegian labour market tests and practices, of which natural persons as intra-corporate transferees with managerial positions and temporary assignments, are exempt. Norway does not contemplate any changes in these regulations as a result of this offer. UNBOUND. | |
| - Temporary entry of service providers | Norway shall permit, without requiring compliance with the labour market tests, the temporary entry of the following service providers as intra-corporate transferees:

1) Executives - persons who primarily direct the management of the organisation, establish its goals and generally have a wide decision making authority. Executives would not necessarily perform tasks related to the actual provision of the service.

2) Managers - persons who direct the organization or its department and are in a senior level position responsible for the service | Full compliance with Norwegian labour laws and labour market practices required. Observance of wage levels, terms and conditions for work etc. practised on the local market, whether based on law or through collective agreements. BOUND. |

Sector/subsector	Article XVI (market access)	Article XVII (national treatment)
	providing functions of the organization by supervising and controlling and having also authority to hire and fire personnel or recommend such and other personnel actions.	
	Work permit will be issued in compliance with the labour market tests to those intracorporate specialists, who possess knowledge at an advanced level of expertise or otherwise essential or proprietal to the organizations's service, research equipment, techniques or management.	
	Service sellers - persons who as representatives of a service provider are seeking temporary entry (up to 90 days) in purpose of negotiations for the sale of services or entering into agreements to sell services for that service provider, where this selling activity is not directed to the general public. BOUND.	
1. BUSINESS SERVICES		
A. Professional services		
a) Legal services		
- Legal advice on foreign law	Legal advice activities on foreign law and international law: Tribunal Act of 13 August 1915 no. 5 § 218 subsection 2 no. 5. Foreign advocates may apply for permission to give advice on foreign law and international law. BOUND.	No limitations. BOUND.
- Legal representation in courts	As a main rule licence to operate as an advocate is required. Main criteria: Norwegian law exam; two years professional experience (including some experience from legal representation in courts); course covering different subjects of importance to operate; as an advocate. (Tribunal Act of 13 August 1915 no. 5 §§44 final subsection, Criminal Procedure Act of 22 May 1981 no 25 § 95 subsection 3.) BOUND.	No limitations. BOUND.

Sector/subsector	Article XVI (market access)	Article XVII (national treatment)
b) Accounting auditing and bookkeeping services (862)		
- registered auditors	Public certification required. Requirements are stipulated concerning i.a. education/ examination, relevant practice and proper conduct. Audit reports must be drafted in Norwegian. The Ministry of Finance may give further regulations. Such regulations must remain strictly within the scope of the acts governing audits and auditors, and may not establish requirements for obtaining registration or license as an auditor not provided for in the acts themselves. BOUND.	Permanent residence in Norway required. BOUND.
- licensed auditors	Public certification required. General requirements as for registered accountants. In addition, special examination as licensed auditor and higher, relevant academic education or longer practice required. The Ministry of Finance may give further regulations.; Such regulations must remain strictly within the scope of the acts governing audits and auditors, and may not establish requirements for obtaining registration or license as an auditor not provided for in the acts themselves. BOUND.	
d) Architectural services (8671)	No limitations. BOUND	No limitations. BOUND.
e) Engineering services (8672)		
- Advisory and consultative engineering (86721)	No limitations. BOUND.	No limitations. BOUND.
- Engineering design services (86722)	No limitations. BOUND.	No limitations. BOUND.
- Engineering design services for industrial processes and production (86725)	No limitations. BOUND.	No limitations. BOUND.
f) Integrated engineering	No limitations. BOUND.	No limitations.

Sector/subsector	Article XVI (market access)	Article XVII (national treatment)
services (8673)		BOUND.
g) Urban planning and landscape architectural services (8674)	No limitations. BOUND.	No limitations. BOUND.
Related scientific and technical consulting services (8675)	No limitations. BOUND.	No limitations. BOUND.
h) Medical and dental services	Formal certification required to practice on their own responsibility. Main criteria: formal medical or dental education and professional experience, must speak Norwegian and have passed certain national exams in different areas. Further details by the Ministry of Health and Social Affairs. Foreign exams giving equivalent competence may be recognized on a case-by-case basis. BOUND.	No limitations. BOUND.
i) Veterinary services (932)	Formal certification required to practise on their own responsibility. Main criteria: formal education and professional experience. Foreign exams giving equivalent competence may be recognized on a case-to-case basis. BOUND.	No limitations BOUND.
j) Nursing and other personal care services (including daycare) (parts of 93191)	Formal certification required to practice on their own responsibility. Main criteria: formal medical education and professional experience, must speak Norwegian and have passed certain national exams in different areas. BOUND.	No limitations. BOUND.
B. Computer and related services		
a) Consultancy services related to the installation of computer hardware. (841)	No limitations. (Technical certification requirement for supervisor in charge of installation work. Foreign exams giving equivalent competence may be recognized.) BOUND	No limitations Bound.
b) Software implementation (842)	No limitations. BOUND	No limitations. Bound.

Sector/subsector	Article XVI (market access)	Article XVII (national treatment)
c) Data processing services (843)	No limitations. Bound	No limitations Bound.
C. Research and development services		
- Economic and behavioural research	No limitations. BOUND.	No limitations. BOUND.
D. Real Estate services (822)	Permission from the Ministry of Finance is required in order to establish a real estate agency in Norway. Criteria for permission include a minimum guarantee capital and a requirement that an authorized real estate agent must be in charge of the agency. The Ministry of Finance may give further regulations. BOUND.	
Real estate agents	in order to operate as an "authorized real estate agent", a licence from the Ministry of Finance is required. Authorization is based on the following requirements: Education/examination, at least 2 years of relevant practice, financially solvent and proper conduct. Upon request, education/examination from abroad may be accepted. An attorney at law practising in Norway may operate as a real estate broker without special authorization. BOUND.	
E. Rental/leasing services without operators		
a,b,c) ships, aircraft, other transport equipment (83103, 83104, 83102, 83105)	No limitations. BOUND.	No limitations. BOUND.
c) Car hiring (83101)	Motor vehicles belonging to a foreign car hire firm can not be hired out to persons permanently domiciled in Norway. When returning from a foreign country a person permanently domiciled in Norway may however be given permission to import and temporarily use a hired car, registered abroad, provided: - entry takes place at an operative customs house, - the customs authorities give permission by endorsement on the hire contract,	

8

0161

Sector/subsector	Article XVI (market access)	Article XVII (national treatment)
	- the motor vehicle must immediately be reexported or handed over to the local representative of the hire firm. UNBOUND.	
d) Relating to other machinery and equipment		
- Non-transport: Computers, construction/demolition (83107, 83108)	No limitations. BOUND.	No limitations. BOUND.
F. Other Business Services		
a) Advertising services (871)	No limitations. Rules regarding personal integrity must be followed. BOUND.	No limitations. BOUND.
b) Market research and opinion polling (864)	No limitations. BOUND.	No limitations. BOUND.
c,d) Management and administrative services (including management, consultancy) (865, 866)	No limitations. BOUND.	No limitations. BOUND.
f,g) Services incidental to Agriculture, forestry and fishing (881, 882)	No limitations. BOUND.	
h) Services incidental to mining (883 i.e. oil and gas)	No limitations. BOUND.	No limitations. BOUND.
k) Labour recruitment and provision of personnel (nationals and residents with work permit) (872)	Government monopoly. Exceptions to this rule granted within areas such as accountancy, office and secretary work. Companies which wish to open up a practice within one of the above-mentioned areas must register as joint-stock companies or have a guarantee from a bank or an insurance company of NOK 50.000,-. Further details by the Ministry of Labour and Government	

//9-20-10

Sector/subsector	Article XVI (market access)	Article XVII (national treatment)
l) Investigation and security activities (873)	Administration. BOUND.	Licence can be granted only for Norwegian citizens. BOUND.
m) Related scientific and technical consulting services (8675)	Formal authorization by government agency required. Min. age requirement: 21. BOUND.	No limitations. BOUND.
o) Building cleaning services (874)	No limitations. BOUND	No limitations. BOUND.
p) Photograpic services (875)	No limitations. BOUND.	No limitations. BOUND.
r) Printing and publishing	No limitations. Rules regarding personal integrity must be followed. BOUND.	No limitations. BOUND.
s) Exhibition Management services (87909)	No limitations. BOUND	No limitations. BOUND.
2. COMMUNICATION SERVICES		No limitations. BOUND.
A. Postal services (7511)	Public service function. Publicly owned monopoly under direct governmental and parliamentary control. When specific activities are sub-contracted public procurement regulations apply. BOUND	No limitations on sub-contracted activities. BOUND.
B. Courier services (7512)	No limitations except as specified for transportation services. BOUND.	No limitations. BOUND.
C. Telecommunications		
- Value added services *)	The provision of these services may be subject to registration and/or licencing procedures. BOUND.	No limitation. BOUND.
- Packet and circuit switched data transmission services **)	The provision of these services may be subject to licensing requirement. UNBOUND.	No limitation. UNBOUND.

Sector/subsector	Article XVI (market access)	Article XVII (national treatment)
Other types of satellite mobiles services	Subject to further consideration	Subject to further consideration
*) **)	*This does not include voice telephony, telegraph and telex. Pending parliamentary approval. (i.e. UNBOUND)*	
o) Other communication services		
- News and press	No limitations. BOUND.	No limitations. BOUND.
D. Audiovisual services (cultural and non-cultural)		
a) Motion picture and video tape production and distribution services (9611)	No limitation. BOUND.	Film support schemes only allocated to Norwegian nationals.
b) Motion picture projection service (9612)	No limitation. BOUND.	No limitation. BOUND.
c) Radio and television services (9613)	No limitation on cross-border transmission into or reception within national territory. Licence required for frequency allocation and transmission from national territory. Public service function may be imposed. BOUND.	Domestic preference may be applicable to frequency allocation for transmission from national territory. BOUND.
	Subsidies and preferential allocation of facilities may be granted to maintain and promote (i.a.) freedom of expression and information, the availability, quality, diversity and pluralism of cultural services, as well as national and regional languages, cultural identity, the dissemination of news and information, educational and minority needs. BOUND.	Domestic preference may be applied to frequency allocation for transmission from national territory. BOUND.
d) Radio and television	To obtain a local broadcasting licence the holder of the licence and	No limitations.

0163

11 - 20 - 12

Sector/subsector	Article XVI (market access)	Article XVII (national treatment)
transmission services (7524)	at least two thirds of the broadcasting companies' shareholders must be resident in the area for which the licence is granted. BOUND.	BOUND.
3. CONSTRUCTION AND RELATED SER-VICES.	The Act regulating services conducted by building contractors is ad-ministered by the Ministry of Industry. It sets conditions for being approved as a contractor. The following requirements must be followed:	
Act of construction and engineering services		The contractor must have lived in Norway for at least one year and still be a resident in the country. Exceptions are granted under special cir-cumstances. The applicant must certify know-ledge of Norwegian rules and regulations in this area. If the contractor moves from the country, the applicant will not be approved before residen-cy is resumed. BOUND.
	Contractor required to have certified supervisor in charge of construction or installation work. Same requirements for supervisor as mentioned above as for the contractor concerning residence. Local authorities must be notified about the chosen supervisor to be in charge of the project. Compliance with technical norms and standards applicable to equipment and materials used. BOUND.	No limitations. BOUND.
	Land owner is required to have authorization for proposed purpose of land use. National, regional and local laws and zoning regu-lations apply. Builder required to have authorization for all technical plans and drawings. Technical norms and standards apply. BOUND.	No limitations. BOUND.
C. Installation and ass-embly work		
- Installation and assem-bly work (other than construction)	Technical certification requirement for supervisor in charge. BOUND.	No limitations. BOUND.
- Electrical work (5164)	Competence certification required. Main criteria: formal education and professional experience. Foreign exams giving equivalent competence may be recognized on a case-by-case basis. BOUND.	No limitations. BOUND.

0164

117-20-13

Sector/subsector	Article XVI (market access)	Article XVII (national treatment)
- Plumbing (5162)	Competence certification required. Main criteria: formal education and professional experience. Foreign exams giving equivalent competence may be recognized on a case-by-case basis. BOUND.	No limitations. BOUND.
- Water and sanitation	Competence certification required. Main criteria: formal education and professional experience. Foreign exams giving equivalent competence may be recognized on a case-by-case basis. BOUND.	No limitations. BOUND.
- Interior design.	No limitations. BOUND	No limitations. BOUND.
4. DISTRIBUTION SER-VICES		
B. Wholesale trade ser-vices	- Law on trade in alcoholic beverages of 2. june 1989 regulates all sale and import of alcohol. Government monopoly on import and trade in alcohol. Licence necessary to sell alcohol. - Trade in arms not included. - First hand sale of fish not included in this offer. - Law of 27. june 1928 § 17 regulates first hand sale from farmers and import of grain. UNBOUND	
C. Retailing services	Trade act of 6. june 1980 nr. 21. The main criteria for performing retailing services are: - Age over 18 years. - Not under investigation for bankrupcy BOUND.	- Is a resident and has been so for the last two years. BOUND.
5. EDUCATION SERVI-CES	Primary and secondary education are public service functions. Local government authorities are responsible for primary and secondary education, supervised by national government agency. Authori-zation may be given to foundations and other legal entities to offer additional parallel or specialized education on a commercial or non-commercial basis. BOUND.	
A. Primary education services. (921)		
B. Secondary education services. (922)	Financial assistance to educational institutions or to students only available for studies at certified establishments. Specialized courses	No limitations. BOUND.

Sector/subsector	Article XVI (market access)	Article XVII (national treatment)
	and other educational services may be offered without authorization. For such education no public financial assistance is available. When specific activities are subcontracted public procurement regulations apply. BOUND.	
7. FINANCIAL SERVICES		
A. Insurance	Foreign insurance companies are entitled to offer insurance services in Norway, subject to the possible application of a reciprocity requirement. Such services may be offered through the establishment of either a subsidiary or a branch. In both cases an authorization is required in accordance with terms and conditions stipulated in the 1988 Insurance Activities Act. Other than foreign insurance companies may not hold a Norwegian insurance company as a subsidiary. The operations of any insurance company in Norway and any branch in Norway of a foreign insurance company is restricted to one of the following three areas: Life insurance, non-life insurance or credit risk insurance BOUND.	
B. Banks	Permission by the Ministry of Finance is required for establishment of banks. Permission may be given to establish a bank owned by one or more foreign banks, or by one or more foreign banks together with one or more Norwegian banks, provided that one single foreign bank owns more than 50 % of the share capital in the new bank. Establishment in Norway of branches of foreign banks is not permitted. In a domestically owned bank 66 2/3 % or more of the share capital must be owned by Norwegian citizens. The following legal persons are considered as Norwegian citizens: The national government; institutions and foundations governed by the national government; Norwegian municipalities; Norwegian banks; Norwegian corporations and foundations which are of public utility and where all members of the board of directors are Norwegian citizens domiciled in Norway; joint-stock companies and other limited liability companies established in Norway and in which all members of the board are Norwegian citizens and at least 2/3 of the share capital belongs to the national government, Norwegian municipalities or Norwegian citizens. BOUND.	Members of the board of directors and committee of representatives must be Norwegian citizens residing in Norway. Subsidiaries of foreign banks: Up to 1/3 of the members of the board of directors and the committee of representatives may be foreign citizens residing outside Norway. In both bodies the chairman must be a Norwegian citizen permanently residing in Norway. BOUND.
C. Other		
Financing companies	Permission is required for the establishment of financing companies.	Practice is less liberal for non-residents who wish

119 - 20 - 15

1992-02-19   17:24   KOREAN MISSION GENEVA   2 022 791 0525   P.02

Sector/subsector	Article XVI (market access)	Article XVII (national treatment)
	Only Norwegian citizens residing in Norway may establish a financing company in Norway. If a financing company is organized as a limited liability joint-stock company, others than Norwegian citizens may jointly own up to 33 1/3 % of the share capital. The same provisions as those cited for banks above govern the definition of "Norwegian citizens". A foreign financing company may be authorized to establish or acquire a Norwegian financing company as a subsidiary. BOUND.	to operate financing companies in Norway. BOUND.
Securities brokers	In order to trade securities on a commercial basis in Norway a joint stock company must be established and registered. In general, total foreign ownership in a Norwegian securities firm is subject to an upper limit of 10 pct. of the share capital. Upon request the King (Ministry of Finance) may in individual cases raise the upper limit to 25 pct. In this respect Norwegian banks, whether owned by Norwegians or foreigners, are considered as "Norwegian". BOUND.	Foreign securities brokers may not conduct activities in Norway and may not hold a Norwegian securities broker company as a subsidiary. BOUND.
Management of collective institutions	Management of collective investment institutions must be organized as a limited joint-stock company. Up to 10 % of the shares in such companies may be owned by non-nationals. BOUND.	
Foreign exchange regulations	Most foreign exchange restrictions were abolished as from 1 July 1990. The following restrictions remain: Only foreign exchange banks are permitted to engage in cross-border payment transfers as a business activity. In general, borrowing in foreign currency is not allowed for local governments (municipalities). Export and import of domestic or foreign banknotes in excess of the equivalent of NOK 25.000 per person per journey must be reported to the customs authorities. In general, for all payments and transfers between a resident and a non-resident the resident is obliged to report the payment or transfer to Norges Bank (Bank of Norway). BOUND. (If the payment is made through a Norwegian bank, the bank undertakes the reporting.)	Residents are obliged to use a Norwegian security broker as intermediary when trading securities with non-residents. Residents are not allowed to take out insurance other than non-life insurance from a foreign insurance company. BOUND.

Sector/subsector	Article XVI (market access)	Article XVII (national treatment)
9.TOURISM AND TRA- VEL RELATED SERVI- CES.		
A. Hotels, camping sites and other commercial accommodations Restau- rants, cafes, pubs, bars etc.		Managers of enterprises in accommodations, restaurants and cafes must have been residents for the last two years and have good command of the language. Local authorities may grant exemptions to this requirement. BOUND.
B. Travel agencies and tour operators	Commercial presence and movement of personnel: in order to operate travel agencies associations or companies with limited liabilities must obtain a licence; the applicant must have stayed in Norway permanently for at least two years. In order to obtain a licence for tour operations the applicant must raise a guarantee and pay a cash fee. Once these requirements have been complied with, a licence is automatically issued. BOUND.	No limitations. BOUND
C. Tourist guides ser- vices	No limitations. BOUND.	No limitations. BOUND.
D. Other		
- Hotels and restaurants (including catering)	Health and sanitary inspection of facilities required. BOUND.	No limitations. BOUND.
11. TRANSPORT SER- VICES		
A. Maritime transport	A ship is regarded as Norwegian and may be registered in the ordinary Norwegian Ship Register when owned by Norwegian citizens or by a Norwegian company where Norwegian citizens own at least 60% of the capital. When the company is a limited liability company, it must be headquartered in Norway. Exemptions from the 60% rule may be granted.

In the Norwegian International Ship Register (NIS) there are no such limitations. However, a ship with more than 40% foreign ownership | The majority of members of the board, including the Chairman, must be Norwegian nationals resident in Norway for at least the last two years. |

0168

Sector/subsector	Article XVI (market access)	Article XVII (national treatment)
	must be operated by a Norwegian shipowning company with the head office in Norway, or by a Norwegian management company. If the ship is registered directly in the NIS by a foreign company, a Norwegian representative is required.	
	Scheduled maritime transport of persons requires a licence. A permanent personal and/or business address in Norway is a prerequisite for such a licence.	No limitations. BOUND.
International shipping	No limitations. BOUND.	No limitations. BOUND.
Cabotage/inland waterways transport	No limitations. UNBOUND.	No limitations. UNBOUND.
	Passengers and shippers of cargo allowed access to and use of any available maritime transport service. BOUND.	No limitations. BOUND.
Services auxiliary to transport	No limitations. BOUND.	No limitations. BOUND.
C. Air transport (freight and passengers) including auxiliary services		
General requirement	Authorization required for all commercial air transport service operations, scheduled and non-scheduled. Compliance with national air safety regulations required. Compliance with conditions in bilateral agreements and domestic regulations required, all such conditions in conformity with the Chicago Convention. New bilateral agreements may be implemented. UNBOUND.	Home state jurisdiction over work and operational conditions on board foreign registered carriers is recognized inside Norwegian territory and air space. All SAS-operations treated as domestic. BOUND.
International traffic	Charter and taxi flights into and out of Norway may be carried out only upon permission granted by the Civil Aviation Administration. Concession to operate scheduled air services to and from Norway is granted where bilateral agreements with Norway exist or by special permission from the air transport authorities. BOUND.	
Cabotage	Cabotage reserved to national airlines.	

0169

Sector/subsector	Article XVI (market access)	Article XVII (national treatment)
	Passengers and shippers of cargo allowed access to and use of any available air transport service. BOUND.	No limitations. BOUND.
Ground handling	Foreign airlines normally not allowed to establish and maintain their own airport infrastructure facilities due to space and capacity constraints. Authorization may be granted by the Civil Aviation Administration and airport authorities on case-by-case basis. Taxes, fees and other charges in conformity with international obligations. BOUND.	No limitations, except in certain cases, operating conditions as authorized. BOUND.
Sales and marketing		
Reservation systems	National carrier system displays only national carriers, scheduled flights of its member carriers and selected other carriers. Requests for membership are considered on the basis of "reciprocity" acceptable to the national carrier. BOUND.	No limitations. BOUND.
E. Rail Transport Services. International rail transport including transportation of passengers and freight between Norway and third countries.	Limitations. Bilateral agreements regulate traffic volume and frequency.	Limitations.
Rail Cabotage	Authorization not extended to foreign trains and rolling stock.	Not applicable. UNBOUND.
F. Road Transport Services		
Land transport	Cabotage is reserved to national hauliers. Third country traffic is prohibited as a rule. Exceptions may be granted. Access to the market is regulated through bilateral agreements. Practice has been rather liberal in according access for those countries which offer access on a reciprocity basis. UNBOUND.	
Road Cabotage	Bilateral agreements regulate traffic volume and frequency. UNBOUND.	No limitations. BOUND.
International road transportation including transportation of freight and passengers between Nor-	Passengers and shippers of cargo allowed access to and use of any	No limitations.

Sector/subsector	Article XVI (market access)	Article XVII (national treatment)
way and third countries	available land transport service. BOUND.	BOUND.
Combined transport services	No limitations. BOUND.	No limitations. BOUND.
Buses	Coach operators whose vehicles are registered outside Norway may freely undertake round trips within Norway provided that passengers' starting and finishing locations are located abroad; shuttle services and other regular trips are subject to concession or authorization if the starting location is within Norway. Passenger road transport operations restricted in the case of: - Transport within the country (cabotage). - Picking up or setting down on an international journey. BOUND.	

UR(우루과이라운드)-서비스 분야 양허협상, 1992. 전6권(V.1 1-2월)   177

발 신 전 보

WUS-0796   920220 1608 DW

번 호 :   종별 :

수 신 : 주   미   대사. 총영사/

발 신 : 장 관 (통 기)

제 목 : UR/서비스 수정 양허 계획표

대 : USW-0781

2.17 갓트에 제출된 UR/서비스 분야 아국 수정 양허 계획표 2부를 금번 한.미
경제협의회 아국대표단이 지참, 귀관에 전달 예정이니 동부는 대호 미 재무부 Lundsager
한국담당과장에게 전달바람.   끝.   (통상국장 김 용 규)

	보 안	
	통 제	

앙고재	92년 2월 20일	통기과	기안자 성명		과장	심의관	국장		차관	장관	
							전결				

외신과통제

외 무 부

종 별 :

번 호 : GVW-0402

일 시 : 92 0220 1430

수 신 : 장관(봉기, 경기원, 재무부, 법무부, 농림수산부, 문화부, 상공부, 건설부, 항만청,

발 신 : 주 제네바 대사   보사부, 노동부, 교통부, 체신부, 과기처, 공보처)

제 목 : UR/서비스 양자협상 일정

연: GVW-365

연호 2.24(월)-2.27(목) 까지의 양자협상 (8개국)외에 다음 2개국과의 협상이 추가 되었음.

0 2.28(금) 10:00 : 호주

0 2.28(금) 14:30 : 스웨덴.끝

(대사 박수길-국장)

통상국	2차보	법무부	보사부	문화부	교통부	체신부	경기원	재무부
농수부	상공부	건설부	노동부	과기처	해항청	공보처		

PAGE 1

92.02.21   09:59 WG

외신 1과 통제관

0173

외 무 부

110-760 서울 종로구 세종로 77번지   / (02)720-2188   / (02)725-1737 (FAX)

문서번호 통기 20644-

시행일자 1992. 2.20.(   )

취급			차 관	장 관
보존			전 결	
국 장				
심의관		제2차관보		
과 장				
기안	조 현			협조

수신   내부결재

참조

제목   UR/서비스 협상 정부대표 임명

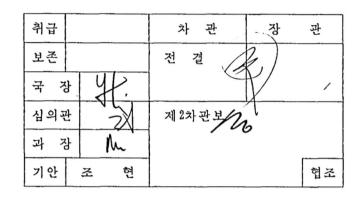

　　　92.2.24-28간 제네바에서 개최되는 UR/서비스 양허협상에 참가할 정부대표단을
"정부대표 및 특별사절의 임명과 권한에 관한 법률"에 의거 아래와 같이 임명코자
건의하오니 재가하여 주시기 바랍니다.

　　　　　　　　　　　- 아　　　　　　　　　래 -

1. 회 의 명 : UR/서비스 양허협상

2. 회의 개최기간 및 장소 : 92.2.24-28, 스위스 제네바

3. 정부대표 :

　　　ㅇ 수석대표 : 경제기획원 제2협력관　　　　　　이윤재

　　　ㅇ 대　　표 : 경제기획원 통상조정3과장　　　　하동만

　　　　　　　　　　통상조정3과 사무관　　　　　　김용준

　　　　　　　　　　통상조정1과　　〃　　　　　　　주형환

　　　　　　재 무 부 국제금융과장　　　　　　　　　김창록

　　　　　　　　　　은행과장　　　　　　　　　　　진영욱

　　　　　　　　　　증권정책과 사무관　　　　　　　우기종

　　　　　　　　　　보험정책과 사무관　　　　　　　임승태

　　　　　　　　　　국제금융과 사무관　　　　　　　최희남

0174

법 무 부 국제법무심의관실 검사   정기용

~~주 제네바 대표부 관계관~~

주 영국 대사관 해무관   최낙정

ㅇ 자   문 : 외환은행   한일석

　　　　 KIEP 연구위원   성극제

　　　　 KDI 연구위원   김지홍

　　　　(단, 금융·보험분야에 국한된 별도의 양자협상이 개최될

　　　　 경우 재무부 대표중 선임자를 교체 수석대표로 함)

4. 협상일정 (양자협상 대상국)

　　ㅇ 2.24(월) 15:00   스 위 스

　　ㅇ 2.25(화) 10:00   노르웨이

　　　　　　 15:00   뉴질랜드

　　　　　　 17:30   핀 랜 드

　　ㅇ 2.26(수) 09:00   미   국

　　　　　　 15:00   일   본

　　ㅇ 2.27(목) 09:00   E   C

　　　　　　 15:00   캐 나 다

　　ㅇ 2.28(금)   여타국가

5. 출장기간 : 2.23-3.2   (3.17~3.22)

6. 소요예산 : 해당부처 소관예산

7. 훈   령 :

　　ㅇ 2.17 제출한 아국의 수정 offer list를 기초로 협상에 임하도록 함.

　　　- 수정 offer 내용을 충분히 설명토록 함.

　　　- 상대국으로부터 추가 개방 요구가 있을 경우 동 요구의 우선 순위등

　　　　 그 내용을 명확히 파악, 차기 협상에 대비토록 함.

　　ㅇ MFN 일탈 신청과 관련 각국의 입장을 파악, 아국의 MFN 일탈 신청에

　　　 대비토록 함.   끝.

외 무 부 장 관

0175

법 무 부

우 : 427-760   경기 과천시 중앙동 1   / 전화 : 503-9505   / 전송 : 504-1378

문서번호 국심 23010-17

시행일자 1992. 2. 14.

(경 유)

수   신   외무부장관

참   조

선결			지시		
접수	일자시간	92.2.17	결재·공람		
	번호	5451			
처리과					
담당관					

제   목   UR서비스 협상회의 참석대표 추천

　　　'92.2.24 - 3.1 까지 스위스 제네바에서 개최되는 UR서비스 협상회의에 참석할 대표자로 당부소속 검사 정기용(Chung, Ki-Yong)을 추천합니다.

　　　※ 정기용검사는 제48차 유엔인권위원회에 추천되어 있음을 참고로 알려 드립니다. 끝.

법 무 부 장 관

0178

경 제 기 획 원

우 427-760 / 경기도 과천시 중앙동1 정부제2청사 / 전화 503-9149 / 전송 503-9141

문서번호 통조삼 10502-40

시행일자 1992. 2. 18

(경유)

수신 수신처참조

참조

선결			지시	
접수	일자시간	92.2.20	시결	
	번호	5891	재·공	
	처리과			
	담당자	宋용	람	

제목 UR/서비스 양허협상 대표단 구성

　　　1. UR/서비스 양허협상이 별첨과 같이 2.23일주간에 스위스 제네바에서 미국,EC, 일본,핀랜드,캐나다,노르웨이,뉴질랜드,스위스등과 열릴 예정입니다.

　　　2. 이에따라 본부협상대표단을 구성하여 대응코자 하니 귀부(기관)의 책임있는 과장급 대표(또는 연구책임자)를 선정, 지급 통보해 주시기 바랍니다.

별첨 : '92.2월 UR/서비스 양허협상일정 및 대표단구성 1부.　끝.

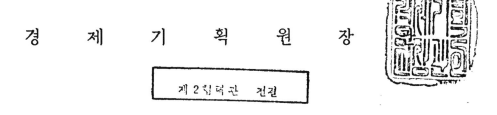

경 제 기 획 원 장

제2협력관　전결

수신처 : 외무부장관, 재무부장관, 법무부장관, 체신부장관, 교통부장관,
　　　　해운항만청장, 대외경제정책연구원장, 한국개발연구원장

0177

< 別添 >

'92年 2月 UR/서비스 讓許協商日程 및 代表團構成

Ⅰ. 協商日程 및 分野

日　時	對象國家	分　野
2.24(月) 15:00	스위스	-
2.25(火) 10:00	노르웨이	-
15:00	뉴질랜드	-
17:30	핀랜드	-
2.26(水) 09:00	美國	金融, 通信分野 포함
15:00	日本	-
2.27(木) 09:00	EC	-
15:00	캐나다	-
2.27(金)	여타국가	對象國 및 時間 아직 未定

Ⅱ. 協商代表團의 構成

가. 出張期間 : 2.23～3.2

나. 代表團構成

- 首席代表 : 經濟企劃院　第2協力官
- 代　　表 : 經濟企劃院, 外務部, 財務部, 遞信部,
　　　　　　交通部, 海運港灣廳 擔當課長 및
　　　　　　法務部 擔當檢事
- 諮問官 : KIEP 성극제 研究委員
　　　　　KDI　김지홍 研究委員

0178

재　무　부

우 427-760 경기도 과천시 중앙동 1　/ 전화 5388　　　/ 전송 503-9324

문서번호 국금 22251-42

시행일자 '92. 2. 18　　( )

수신 외무부장관

참조

선결			지시		
접수	일자시간	92-2-20	결재·공람		
	번호	5986			
처리과					
담당자	조영근				

제목 UR 금융서비스 양자협상 참석

　　　UR 금융서비스협상과 관련 스위스 제네바에서 '92.2.22~28간 개최되는 양자협상에 참여할 당부대표를 아래와 같이 파견코자 하오니 필요한 조치를 취하여 주시기 바랍니다.

아　　　래

자　　　격	성　　　명	소　　　속
교체 수석 대표 (금융, 보험 분야)	김 창 록	국제금융과장
"	진 영 욱	은 행 과 장
대　　　표	우 기 종	증권정책과 사무관
"	임 승 태	보험정책과 사무관
"	최 희 남	국제금융과 사무관
자 문 관	한 일 석	외환은행

　　- 출장기간 : '92. 2. 22~3. 1.　　끝.

첨부 : UR 금융협상에 대한 훈령

재　무　부　장

0179

UR 금융협상에 대한 훈령

1. 아국이 최근 제출한 UR 금융서비스 수정 offer list를 충분히 설명함으로서 최소한의 양허가 이루어질 수 있도록 노력하고, 아국의 Request에 대한 상대국의 수정 offer에 대하여도 논의를 함으로써 규제 완화에 최선을 다할 것.

2. 각국의 MFN 일탈 신청 내용과 이에 대한 각국의 입장을 예의 주시하여 신축적으로 대응하고 필요한 경우 다음과 같이 대처할 것.

   o 아국의 금융자율화 일정작성 계획 등을 설명하여 개방의지를 표명함으로써 상대국을 최대한 설득할 수 있도록 하며,

   o 필요한 경우 상대국의 우선 요구순위를 파악하고, 3월 협상시 구체적인 협상안을 제시할 수 있음을 표명할 것.

0180

경 제 기 획 원

우 427-760 / 경기도 과천시 중앙동1 정부제2청사 / 전화 503-9149 / 전송 503-9141

문서번호 통조삼 10502-442

시행일자 1992. 2. 18

(경유)

수신 외무부장관

참조 통상국장

선결			지시	
접수	일자시간	· . ·	결재·공람	
	번호			
	처리과			
	담당자			

제목 UR/서비스 양허협상 참석

　　　1. 스위스 제네바에서 개최되는 UR/서비스 양허협상에 다음과 같이 참석코자
하니 협조하여 주기 바랍니다.

- 다　　　음 -

　가. 출장자

　　　- 수석대표 : 경제기획원　제2협력관　　　　　이윤재
　　　- 대　　표 : 경제기획원　통상조정3과장　　　하동만
　　　　　　　〃　　　　통상조정3과 사무관　　　김용준
　　　　　　　〃　　　　통상조정1과 사무관　　　주형환
　　　- 자문관 : KIEP　　연구위원　　　　　　성극제
　　　　　　　KDI　　　　〃　　　　　　　김지홍

　나. 출장기간 : '92. 2.23～3.2
　다. 출 장 지 : 스위스 제네바
　라. 경비부담 : 경제기획원, KIEP, KDI등

첨부 : 출장일정 1부.　끝.

　　　　경　제　기　획　원　장

0181

出 張 日 程

'92. 2. 23(日)   12:40   서울 발 (KE 901)

18:10   파리 착

20:45   파리 발 (SR 729)

21:45   제네바 착

2. 24(月)

~   UR/서비스 讓許協商

2. 29(土)

'92. 3. 1 (日)   18:05   제네바발 (AF 969)

19:10   파 리 착

20:30   〃 발 (KE 902)

3. 2 (月)   17:30   서울착

0182

해 운 항 만 청

우 110-410 서울 종로구 인의동 112-2 / 전화 (02)744-4730, FAX 745-9595

문서번호   진흥 33700-154

시행일자   1992.02.19

수신   외무부장관

선결			지시결재·공람		
접수	일자시간	92. 2. 20 :			
	번호	5983			
처리과					
담당자					

제목   UR 서비스 양허 협상개최에 따른 협조 요청

1. 경제기획원 통조삼 10502-40('92. 2. 18)의 관련입니다.

2. '92. 2. 24부터 제네바에서 개최예정인 UR서비스 양허 협상에 주영한국대사관 소속 해무관을 아래와 같이 참석토록 하고자 하오니 조치하여 주시기 바랍니다.

- 아   래 -

가. 회의기간 : '92. 2. 24 - 2. 28 (출장기간 : '92. 2. 23 - 2. 29)

나. 장 소 : 제네바

다. 회의참석자

　　ㅇ 소속 및 직위 : 주영한국대사관 해무관

　　ㅇ 성 명 : 최 낙 정

라. 예 산 : 해운항만청 예산. 끝.

해 운 항 만 청

0183

외 무 부

110-760 서울 종로구 세종로 77번지   /   (02)720-2188   /   (02)725-1737 (FAX)

문서번호 통기 20644-2L

시행일자 1992. 2.21.(   )

취급		장 관	
보존		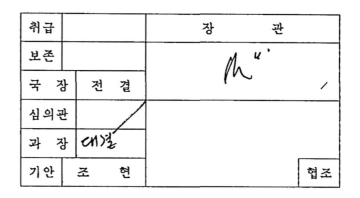	
국장	전결		
심의관			
과장	대결		
기안	조 현		협조

수신 수신처 참조

참조

제목 UR/서비스 협상 정부대표 임명 통보

1. 92.2.24-28간 제네바에서 개최되는 UR/서비스 양허협상에 참가할 정부대표단이 "정부대표 및 특별사절의 임명과 권한에 관한 법률"에 의거 아래와 같이 임명 되었음을 통보합니다.

- 아   래 -

가. 회 의 명 : UR/서비스 양허협상

나. 회의 개최기간 및 장소 : 92.2.24-28, 스위스 제네바

다. 정부대표 :

　　　ㅇ 수석대표 : 경제기획원 제2협력관   이윤재

　　　ㅇ 대   표 : 경제기획원 통상조정3과장   하동만

　　　　　　　　　　　　통상조정3과 사무관   김용준

　　　　　　　　　　　　통상조정1과 사무관   주형환

　　　　　　재 무 부 국제금융과장   김창록

　　　　　　　　　　　　은행과장   진영욱

　　　　　　　　　　　　증권정책과 사무관   우기종

　　　　　　　　　　　　보험정책과 사무관   임승태

　　　　　　　　　　　　국제금융과 사무관   최희남

0184

                         법 무 부 국제법무심의관실 검사   정기용

                    ┌ 주 제네바 대표부 관계관
                    │
                    └ 주 영국 대사관 해무관   최낙정

        ㅇ 자   문 : 외환은행   한일석

                     KIEP 연구위원   성극제

                     KDI 연구위원   김지홍

                     (단, 금융.보험분야에 국한된 별도의 양자협상이

                      개최될 경우 재무부 대표중 선임자를 교체

                      수석대표로 함).

        라. 출장기간 : 2.23-3.2

        마. 소요예산 : 해당부처 소관예산

     2. 출장 결과 보고 : 2주일이내.   끝.

수신처 : 경제기획원장관, 재무부장관, 법무부장관, 해운항만청장.

                    외   무   부   장   관

발 신 전 보

분류번호	보존기간

번 호 : **WUK-0325**   920221 1854 BU   종별 : _____

수 신 : 주   영국   대사. //총/영사

발 신 : 장 관 (통 기)

제 목 : UR/서비스 양허협상

연 : WUK-0305

1. 귀관 최낙정 해무관이 2.24-28간 제네바에서 개최되는 UR/서비스 양허협상의 아국
   대표단 일원으로 임명 되었으니 2.23-29간 제네바에 출장토록 조치바람.

2. 상기 UR 협상의 훈령은 본부대표가 지참 예정임.   끝.

(통상국장 대리 최 혁)

앙고재	년월일	기안자성명		과장	심의관	국장		차관	장관	
	통기과	조래			전결				대리	

보안통제	
외신과통제	

0186

발 신 전 보

분류번호	보존기간

번 호 : WGV-0302   920221 1859 FL   종별 : 암호동신

수 신 : 주   제네바   대사. 총영사 , ~~(사본.주영국(안참)~~

발 신 : 장 관 (통 기)

제 목 : UR/서비스 양허협상

　

　92.2.24-28간 귀지에서 개최되는 UR/서비스 양허협상에 참가할 정부대표단이 아래

임명 되었으니 귀관 관계관과 함께 참석토록 조치바람.

- 아　　　　　　　래 -

　

1. 정부대표 :

　　○ 수석대표 : 경제기획원 제2협력관　　　　　　이윤재

　　○ 대　 표 : 경제기획원 통상조정3과장　　　　하동만

　　　　　　　　　　　통상조정3과 사무관　　　　김용준

　　　　　　　　　　　통상조정1과　　　　　　　　주형환

　　　　　　　재 무 부 국제금융과장　　　　　　　김창록

　　　　　　　　　　　은행과장　　　　　　　　　　진영욱

　　　　　　　　　　　증권정책과 사무관　　　　　　우기종

　　　　　　　　　　　보험정책과 사무관　　　　　　임승태

　　　　　　　　　　　국제금융과 사무관　　　　　　최희남

　　　　　　　법 무 부 국제법무심의관실 검사　　　정기용

　　　　　　　주 영국 대사관 해무관　　　　　　　　최낙정

보 안 통 제	(서명)

앙고재	92년 2월 21일	통기과	기안자 성명 조현		과 장 (서명)	심의관 (서명)	국 장 (서명)	차 관	장 관 (서명)

외신과통제

0187

ㅇ 자   문 : 외환은행   한일석

　　　　　KIEP 연구위원   성극제

　　　　　KDI 연구위원   김지홍

　　　　(단, 금융.보험분야에 국한된 별도의 양자협상이 개최될 경우

　　　　재무부 대표중 선임자를 교체 수석대표로 함)

2.　출장기간 : 2.23-3.2

3.　훈   령 :

ㅇ 2.17 제출한 아국의 수정 offer list를 기초로 협상에 임하도록 함.

　- 수정 offer 내용을 충분히 설명토록 함.

　- 상대국으로부터 추가 개방 요구가 있을 경우 동 요구의 우선 순위등

　　그 내용을 명확히 파악, 차기 협상에 대비토록 함.

ㅇ MFN 일탈 ~~신청과~~ 관련 각국의 입장을 파악, 아국의 MFN 일탈 신청에 대비토록

　합.　　　　　　끝.　　　　　(통상국장   김 용 규)

　　　　　　　　　　　　　　　(통상국장 대리 최 혁)

0188

경 제 기 획 원

우 427-760 / 경기도 과천시 중앙동1 정부제2청사 / 전화 503-9149 / 전송 503-9141

문서번호 통조삼 10502-43

시행일자 1992. 2. 24

(경유)

수신 수신처참조

참조

선결			지시	
접수	일자시간	92 : 2. 25	결재·공람	
	번호	6518		
	처리과			
	담당자			

제목 UR/서비스협상관련 자료배포

캐나다의 수정 Offer List를 별첨과 같이 배포하니 업무에 활용하시기 바랍니다.

첨부 : 각국의 수정 Offer List(Ⅴ) 1부.   끝.

경 제 기 획 원 장

통상조정3과장 전결

수신처 : 외무부장관, 내무부장관, 재무부장관, 법무부장관, 교육부장관, 문화부장관,
농림수산부장관, 상공부장관, 보건사회부장관, 건설부장관, 교통부장관,
노동부장관, 동자부장관, 체신부장관, 체육청소년부장관, 과학기술처장관,
환경처장관, 공보처장관, 경찰청장, 특허청장, 해운항만청장, 대외경제정책
연구원장, 한국개발연구원장

0189

외 무 부

종 별 : -

번 호 : GVW-0446

수 신 : 장관(수신처 참조)

발 신 : 주제네바 대사

제 목 : UR/서비스 양자 협상(1)

일 시 : 92 0226 1800

. 2.26(화) 개최된 노르웨이, 뉴질랜드, 핀랜드 등 3개국과의 양자 협상 내용을 하기 보고함.

1. 협의 개요

- UR 협상 전망에 관한 의견 교환, 상대국 수정 OFFER 의 명료화, MFN 일탈문제와 아울러 일부 주요 분야에 대하여 토의하였음.

- 3개국 공히 구체적인 자유화 약속 대상을 요청하지는 않았으나 뉴질랜드의 경우 축산관련 서비스와 교육 서비스 분야에 OFFER 를 기대한다고 하였으며, 노르웨이 및 핀랜드는 통신,금융, 해운 분야에 대하여 질의 하였는바, 특히 금융 분야의 아국 규제 제도에 대하여 많은 관심을 표명 하였음.

- 수정 OFFER 의 설명과 관련, 아국은 기술적인 수정 내용과 아울러 서비스 분야포괄 범위가 확대 되었을 뿐 만 아니라 1차 OFFER 제출 이후의 많은 자유화 조치가반영되어 질적인 면에서도 보다 내실있는 OFFER 가 되었으며,특히 다른 나라의 OFFER와는 달리 미래의 자유화 약속도 포함되어 있다는 점에 상대국의 주의를 환기시키고동수정 OFFER 가 아국이 노력한 최선의 결과임을 강조 하였음.

2. UR 협상 전망에 관한 의견 교환

- 노르웨이등은 UR 전체 협상의 전망이 낙관적이지 못하다고 하는 한편 서비스 협상에 대해서도 각국의 MFN 일탈 움직임, 50 여개국이 OFFER 를 제출하지 않은 점등을 들어 우려를 표명하였으며, 시장접근 분야의 COUNTRY PLAN 제출 시한인 3.1 이후에나 보다 분명한 전망이 가능할 것이라고 함.

- 아국 역시 대체적으로 유사한 견해를 피력하는 한편 농산물중 일부 분야에 극히 민감한 어려운 문제가 있으나 UR 의 성공적 타결에 중요한 비중을 두고 있으며, 합의된 협상 일정에 따라 아국이 해야할 일에 대하여 최선을 다할 것이라고 언급함.

통상국	2차보	통상국	통상국	통상국	외정실	법무부	보사부	문화부
교통부	체신부	경기원	재무부	농수부	상공부	건설부	노동부	과기처
해항정	공보처	분석관	청와대	안기부				

PAGE 1

92.02.27 09:26 DQ

외신 1과 통제관

0190

3. MFN 일탈

- 노르웨이는 다음 사항에 대하여 MFN 이탈을 고려중 이라고 함.

0 육운 : 2개국과 양자 협정이 있음.

0 항공 : CRS 에 상호주의 규정이 있음. ~~~~~~~ 상호개방도 MFN 일탈종?

0 투자보장 협정 : 10 여개 개도국과 협정을 맺고있는바 노르웨이로서는 MFN 적용에 문제가 없으나 상대국이 MFN 일탈을 요구하고 있음.

0 영화 공동생산 협정 : 영국과 협정을 맺고 있으며, 영화 생산에 금융 지원을 하고 있음.

0 북구 인력 공동시장 (스웨덴, 노르웨이, 핀랜드, 덴마크, 아이슬랜드)에 대하여는 동문제가 서비스 협정 적용 범위에 해당하는지 여부가 불분명하기 때문에 MFN 일탈 필요 여부에 대하여 입장이 미정이라고 함.

- 한편, 핀랜드는 지난 1월 밝힌 사항과 변동이 없으나 인력 공동시장, 사회 보장 의료에 관한 국제 협정등은 서비스 협정 적용 범위에 해당하지 않음을 분명히 하거나 적용 범위에 해당한다면 동 협정들은 서비스 무역에 미치는 영향이 미미하므로 체약국 공동으로 MFN 적용대상에서 제외하여야 할 것이라고 하고 이에 관한 토의 문서 (별첨 송부)를 전달하면서 가까운 시일내에 이를 토의하여 결론을 내기를 희망한다고함.

- 아국은 일반적 의무로서의 MFN 원칙 지지입장에 변화가 없다고 전제하고 대외협력위원회 결의안에 따라 해운 분야 정기선화물 유보 제도중 해운 협정체결국에 대한웨이버 면제에 대한 MFN 일탈(95.1 까지)항공분야의 CRS 에 대한 MFN 일탈 입장을밝혔음.

4. 분야별 토의

가. 금융

- 노르웨이 및 핀랜드는 아국 OFFER 가 현존 규제수준을 그대로 반영한 것인지 여부와 인.허가 기준,금융 감독 규제 제도에 대하여 질의 하였는바,아국은 86.9 이후지금까지 많은 자유화 조치가 있었는바, 이를 모두 수정 OFFER 에 반영하였을 뿐 만아니라 전체적인 금융시장 개방 청사진을 마련중에 있다고 설명하는 한편 상대국 수정OFFER 명료화를 위하여 일부 사항을 확인 하였음.

나. 통신

- 패멧 및 서킷 교환 서비스 분야 COMMITMENT 에 관한 아국 REQUEST 에 대하여 노르웨이는 현재 법안이 의회에 계류중이기 때문에 행정부 로서는 확정적인 답변을

PAGE 2

0191

할수 없는 상태라고 함.

  - 핀랜드는 최근 한.미간 봉신 협상 내용 및 동결과의 MFN 적용여 부에 대한
의문을 표시 하였는바, 아국은 동 결과는 모든 국가에 적용될 것이라고 답변 함.

  다. 해운

  - 2.27(수) 노르웨이 주최로 사무국 중재안(91.12.15자)에 대한 일부 국가간 오찬
협의가 있을 예정이기 때문에 구체적 토의는 하지 않았으며, 아국의 화물
유보제도에대하여 설명하였음.

  첨부: 수평적 협정의 MFN 일탈에 대한 토의문서 1부. 끝

  (GVW(F)-134)

  (대사 박수길-국장)

  수신처:봉기,봉일,봉이,봉삼,경기원,재무부,법무부,상공부,건설부,보사부,노동부,교
봉부,체신부,문화부,농수산부,과기처,공보처,항만청

PAGE 3

0192

주 제 네 바 대 표 부

번 호 : GVW(F) - 0/34   년월일 : 20226   시간 : 1800
수 신 : 장   관 (통계.상벌.법이.통상. 경기원. 과정박, 변정박, 상공우, 전오박, 내자박
발 신 : 주 제네바대사   노동부. 교통부. 체신박. 문화석. 농수산석. 공보처. 과기처. 항만청)
제 목 : UR/ 서비스 양자협상 (1)

총   3   매(표지포함)

보 안 통 제	

외신과 통 제	

/34 - 3 -1

0193

UEN 0474/3

Dok. 4704k

Marginal and evident m.f.n.-exemptions or matters falling outside the scope of GATS?

The following are examples of arrangements, the legal status of which under Art. II of the GATS is presently unclear:

- International agreements on social security during permanent or temporary residence

- International agreements on medical care during permanent or temporary residence

- Visa requirements

- International agreements on exemption from entry visas

- International agreements that provide for substantial integration of labour markets

- International agreements on limited movement of persons

- Provisions in international agreements on mandatory and binding dispute settlement through international arbitration.

The Nordic countries have repeatedly sought clarification with regard to the legal status of arrangements of this kind under Article II.

A key question is whether measures contained in the stated arrangements fall under the scope of the GATS at all. In our view, they should fall outside the scope of the agreement.

However, if they are deetermined to fall inside the agreement's scope, i.e. if they are considered to be "measures affecting trade in services", m.f.n.-exemptions would be needed.

134-3-2

0194

Such m.f.n.-exemptions would, in our view, be marginal and evident. Most, if not all, countries would have to seek such exemptions. If not immidiately, then in some year's time when their level of development is higher and they are more integrated into the world economy. Therefore, exemptions of this kind should be treated separately. A solution, that can accomodate both existing and future such measures, should be found, to avoid that each and every country would be required to request specific m.f.n.-exemptions for these measures.

This aim could be achieved by the inscription of an exemption for all Signatories in the Framework as part of Article II, which the Nordic countries have already suggested, or, if more appropriate, in the m.f.n. annex of the GATS.

Whatever the solution it should, however, be achieved rapidly. Valuable time in the ongoing bilateral negotiations is now vasted on inconclusive discussion and speculation regarding the legal status of measures of this kind.

Furthermore, the issue is too important to remain unresolved any longer. Legal certainty with regard to the status of the arrangements referred to above is essential to the credibility of the GATS and to the possibility of countries to make commitments.

134 - 3 - 3

0195

외 무 부

원 본

종 별 :

번 호 : USW-0987

일 시 : 92 0227 1847

수 신 : 장관(봉이, 경기원, 재무부, 경제수석, 사본;주제네바대사-중계필)

발 신 : 주 미 대사

제 목 : 한.미 경제협의회 금융부문 토의결과

2.24 당지에서 개최된 한. 미 경제협의회에서 미측이 우리의 금융시장 개방문제와 관련하여 언급 또는 강조한 내용은 아래와 같은 바, 3.10 한미 금융정책협의회 준비등에 참고 바람.

1. JIM FALL III 재무부 부차관보는 한국정부가 작년말 까지 연지급 수입 신용을 확대하기로 한 약속을 이행하지 않고 있는 데 대해 강한 불만을 표시하고 빠른 시일내 약속을 이행해 줄것을 요청하였음.

2. 동 부차관보는 금번 금융정책협의회에서 한국측이 개별 현안에 대한 단편적인 진전상황이나 절차문제 등을 설명하거나 향후 작업 계획만을 제시함에 그쳐서는 안될 것이며, 포괄적인 금융시장 개방계획의 청사진을 제시하고 내용을 협의할수 있어야 할 것이라고 강조함.

3. 또한 UR 세비스 양자협상과 관련하여 금융서비스(금융, 증권, 보험등)의 중요성을 강조하면서, 이번 협의에서 실질적인 진전이 없을 경우 전체 UR 서비스 협정에서 한국을 제외할 수 밖에 없다고 말하였음.

(대사 현홍주-국장)

92.6.30 까지

통상국 재무부	교환 중계	차관	1차보	2차보	분석관	청와대	안기부	경기원

PAGE 1

92.02.28   09:56

외신 2과 통제관 BX

0196

외 무 부

종 별 :

번 호 : GVW-0469   일 시 : 92 0228 1800

수 신 : 장 관(통기,통일,통이,경기원,재무부,법무부,상공부,건설부,농수부,보사부,

발 신 : 주 제네바 대사   공보처,노동부,교통부,체신부,문화부,과기처,항만청)

제 목 : UR/서비스 양자 협상(3)

2.17 (목) 개최된 EC, 카나다, 스위스와의 양자협상 내용을 하기 보고함.

　1. EC 와의 협상(2.27 오전)

　　가. 협의 개요

　- 아국은 수정 OFFER 에 대한 설명을 통하여 분야별 포괄 범위도 확대되었을 뿐만 아니라 자유화 약속 수준도 제고 되었음을 강조 하였는바, EC 는 아측의 노력을 평가하는 한편 분야별 포괄범위와 관련 다음 사항이 불만족스럽다고함.

　　0 법무 서비스, RENTAL 및 LEASING, 기타 사업 서비스, 운송 보조 서비스

　　0 통신 및 금융 서비스 OFFER 의 실제 포괄범위가 애매함.

　- 한편 EC 는 아국의 수평적 제한 조치와 관련 외국인 토지 취득시 내국민 대우, 외국인 투자인가 기준의 명확화 및 처리 신속화, 인력이동에 있어서 SERVICE SELLER 의 포함 및 SPECIALIST 의범위에 전문자격 소지자의 포함을 요청하였는바

　　0 아측은 토지 문제에 관하여 입장 완화는 불가능하다고 하였으며, 외국인 투자인가에 대하여는 구체적 통계를 적시하여 신속히 처리하고 있음을 설명하고 다만 인력 이동 문제는 추가검토 하겠다고 답변함.

　　나. 분야별 토의

　- EC 측 질의 및 요청 사항(EC 측 요청사항별첨)

　　0 국제여부 해상운송, 해운 대리점, 선박중계업 외국인 지분 제한(50 퍼센트미만)을 3년내에 70 -100 퍼센트 허용, 대표자 국적 요건 폐지

　　0 각 운송 서비스에 있어서 ECONOMIC NEEDS TEST 기준의 명확화

　　0 벌크 화물 유보제도의 폐지

　　0 합자투자 해운 대리점의 업무 범위를 자체화물로 제하는 것은 해운업법 5조 2항과 상충됨.

통상국	2차보	구주국	통상국	청와대	안기부	법무부	보사부	문화부
교통부	체신부	경기원	재무부	농수부	상공부	건설부	노동부	과기처
해항청	공보처							

PAGE 1   92.02.29   21:06 FN

외신 1과 통제관

0197

O 일반 구역 화물 트럭 운송 면허시 트럭 30대이상보유, 세관 범위내 영업 한정등 제한 폐지

- 아측 질의 및 요청 사항

O 불란서의 소매 유통업에 대한 제한 완화

O 이태리의 백화점 설립 제한 완화

O 국경간 도로 운송 서비스의 개방

O 벨지움의 관광 안내업 거주 요건 폐지

2. 카나다와의 협상(2.27 오후)

가. 협의 개요

- 카나다 역시 아국 수정 OFFER 에 자국 관심사항인 지질 조사 및 탐사등 사업 서비스가 포함된점에 긍정적 평가를 하였으며, 아측에 구체적인 자유화 약속 대상을 요 청하지는 않았음.

O 다만, 각종 운송 서비스에 ECOMONIC NEEDS TEST 의기준을 분명히 해줄것을 요청함.

- 아측은 카나다 수정 OFFER 상의 각종 수평적제한 조치중 애매한 사항들을 분명히 해줄 것을 지적하는 한편 명료성 증대 목적의 정보제공란에 기재된 일부 규제에대 하여 시장접근 제한에 기재하여야 할 것이라고 논평함.

나. MFN 일탈

- 카나다는 다음 사항에 대하여 MFN 일탈을 고려중이라고 함.

O 영화 공동 생산 협정

O 영연방하의 영국 선박에 대한 CABOTAGE허용등 우대 제도 (단기간내 폐지 예정)

O 서비스 협정 제 5조(경제통합) 6항에 따른 미.카간 FTA 상의 혜택 부여 결과에 따른 차별 대우

O 미국과의 수로 안내, 해난 구조 서비스(제 2조 3항 국경무역에 해당 여부 검토중)

O 어선의 항구접안 (서비스 협정 적용대상 인지 검토중)

O 멕시코 및 카리브 연안 국가와의 인력 이동협정(주로 농업, 제조업에 단기간 종사하는 인력이므로 서비스 협정 적용대상인지 검토중)

O 규제 제도가 없던 과거에 외국 서비스 공급자가 진입한 사례(협정 제 2조에 ACQUIRED RIGHTS 조항반영 예정)

PAGE 2

0198

다. 금융.보험

- 카나다는 금융분야 MFN 일탈이 각국 금융법에 규정된 상호주의 원칙을 유지하고 서비스 협상의 FREE RIDER 를 막기 위함이 목적이나 다음과 같은 방법이 있다고 함.

O 첫째 금융 분야 전체를 제외하는 것이나 이는 큰 모험이며 실현 가능성이 없으며

O 둘째 기존 상호주의에 대한 MFN 일탈이며 이는 양자 협상 결과를 평가한후 결정할 것임.

- 아국은 금융분야 수정 OFFER 에는 91년 개방조치등이 포함되었으며, 또한 금년말까지 작성예정인 BLUEPRINT 내용을 설명하고 이러한 개방 정책들이 아국 OFFER 평가에 반영되어야 함을 강조하였고 카나다측은 아국 금융 시장 개방정책을 환영하였음.

- 아국은 아국은행의 카나다내에서 영업시 직면하는 가장 큰 문제가 FUNDING 임을 강조하고 아국의 REQUEST 중 이와 관련된 제한조치(외국 은행의 자산 보유한도 규제, 해외로 부터의 영업자금 조달 제한등)

O 카나다도 자국의 관심사항중 은행 복수지점 설치기준이 철폐된것에 만족을 표시하고, SWAP 한도감축/중지, CD 발행한도등 원화/FUNDING문제, 중소기업의 무대출 비율완화등에 우선순위가 있음을 강조하였음.

- 이에 대해 아국은 중소기업 의무 대출 비용은 국내 정책과 관련되며, 이의 완화는 불가함을 설명하고 외국은행의 원화 FUNDING 문제는 아국이 카나다에서 아국 은행이 직면하는 FUNDING 문제를 긍정적으로 검토하는 경우 같이 논의될수 있음을 언급

3. 스위스와의 협상(2.27 오후)

가. 협의 개요

- 스위스 역시 아국에 구체적인 자유화 약속 대상을 요청하지는 않았으며, 상호양국 OFFER 의명료화 작업 수준에 머물렀음.

O 다만 스위스는 운송 서비스 분야의 ECONOMIC NEEDS TEST 철폐를 요청하였으나, 아국은 수용할수없다고 하였음.

나. MFN 일탈

- 스위스는 다음사항에 대하여 MFN 일탈을 고려중이라고 함.

O 영화공동 생산 협정

O 내수로 운송 협정: 19세기부터 라인강 유역국가 및 영구 MFNHEIN CONVENTION 체

PAGE 3

결 시행중

　　0 육상 통과 운송 협정: EC 와 28T 이상트럭의 통과 빈도에 관한 협정

　　0 투자 보장 협정 및 사회보장 협정: MFN 일탈필요여부 검토중

　　0 금융(은행)분야의 상호주의: 상대국의 시장접근 약속 수준에 따라 추후 결정 예
정

　　다. 금융 보험 분야

　　- 아국의 개방 실적과 개방 계획 설명에 스위스는 적극 환영하며, 관심을 표명함.

　　- 스위스는 아국 OFFER 중 금융기관 진출에대한 ECONOMIC NEEDS TEST 의
의무를묻고 이의적용 여부에 관심을 표명

　　0 이에 아국은 금융기관의 과당 경쟁을 막기위한 일종의 안전 장치이며,
현재의여건상 ECONOMIC NEEDS TEST 의 에한 외국 금융기관 진출이 거절되지 않음을
설명

　　- 아국은 금융분야 MFN 일탈이 UR 서비스협상을 무의미하게 할 것이며, 주요국들의
MFN 일탈 동향을 예의 주시하고 있음을 언급

　　0 스위스는 MFN 일탈이 갖는 의미를 정확히 평가해야겠지만 각국이 갖고 있는
상호주의의 점진적인 철폐라 이해하고 있으며, 이에대한 결정은 각국의 약속 내용에
달려 있으며, 서비스협상 평가시 이를 REVIEW 하여 결정할 것임을설명

　　- 스위스측은 보험분야의 CROSS-BORDER 자유화에 관심을 가지고 있다함.

　　첨부: EC REQUEST 1부 끝

　　(GVW(F)-138)

　　(대사 박수길-국장)

PAGE 4

0200

주 제 네 바 대 표 부

번 호 : GVW(F)-0138   년월일 : 20228   시간 : 1800

수 신 : 장   관 (통기.경기원.고법무. 항반정해)

발 신 : 주 제네바대사

제 목 :

GVW 46P 첨부

보 안 통 제	

외신과 통 제	

총 3 매(표지포함)

138-3-1   0201

Geneva, 28 February 1992

EC REQUESTS AND CLARIFICATIONS ON MARITIME TO KOREA

GENERAL : confirm that your understanding is that for shipping on cross-border trade there is no difference between market access and national treatment.

INTERNATIONAL PASSENGER TRANSPORTATION SERVICES :

- clarify on economic needs test under Art. XVI

- raise now to 75% and to 100% within 3 years' time the foreign equity ceiling in joint ventures

- elimination of nationality limitations for representative in joint ventures.

INTERNATIONAL FREIGHT TRANSPORTATION SERVICES :

- confirm that your offer covers all international shipping, covering all trade, all routes and international interport services

- confirm that elimination of cargo preference take place by 1995 (and not from 1995)

- eliminate by the same token the 11 items mentioned

- abolish the waiver system for bulk cargo preferences

- confirm that no bilateral trades will not be further reserved.

CONTAINER FREIGHT STATIONS SERVICES, INCLUDING REPAIR OF CONTAINERS :

- add this sector in your offer.

MAINTENANCE AND REPAIR OF VESSELS :

- raise now to 75% and to 100% within 3 years' time the foreign equity ceiling in joint ventures

- elimination of nationality limitations for representatives in joint ventures.

138-3-2

- 2 -

SHIPPING AGENCY :

- raise now to 75% and to 100% within 3 years' time the foreign equity in ceiling joint ventures

- elimination of nationality limitations for representatives in joint ventures.

MARITIME FREIGHT FORWARDING :

- raise now to 75% and to 100% within 3 years' time the foreign equity in ceiling joint ventures

- elimination of nationality limitations for representatives in joint ventures.

- include customs brokerage/clearance services

- adopt the normal bill of lading procedure for customs clearance by customs authorities.

SHIP BROKERING SERVICES :

- raise now to 75% and to 100% within 3 years' time the foreign equity in ceiling joint ventures

- elimination of nationality limitations for representatives in joint ventures.

TRUCKING SERVICES :

- clarify on economic test

- remove or ease the minimum 30 truck rule for issuance of a bonded transport licence needed in order to contract with Korean railways.

STORAGE AND WAREHOUSES :

- confirm that the offer covers bonded warehouses services

- confirm that the offer will allow acquisition and/or leasehold of land needed for the business.

138-3-3

0203

외 무 부

종 별 :

번 호 : GVW-0470　　　　　　　　　일 시 : 92 0228 1800

수 신 : 장 관(봉기,경기원,재무부,법무부,농수부,상공부,건설부,보사부,노동부,

발 신 : 주 제네바 대사　　　　　고통부,체신부,문화부,과기처,공보처,항만청)

제 목 : UR/GNS 비공식협의

　　2.28(목)　　　　　　　JARAMILLO　　　　　의장　　　　　　주재로
8개국(아국,미국,EC,호주,스웨덴,멕시코,인도,이집트) 비공식 협의가 개최되어 기술적
과제에 대한 토의와 아울러 향후협상일정에 대하여 논의하였는바 주요내용
하기보고함.(동일 오후에는 일본,카나다,스위스,뉴질랜드,홍 콩,싱가폴, 알젠틴등
8개국과 협의)

　　1. 기술적 과제

　　가. FRAMEWORK 34조(용어의 정의)

　　- 갓트 법률국에서 기술적 수정작업을 한초안(별첨 FAX 송부)을 배부하였으나
각국이별도 검토가 필요하다고 하여 본격 토의는 하지않았으며 의견이 있는 국가는
서면 논평을 제시하기로 함.

　　나. 항공부속서

　　- 사무국에서 작성 배부한 초안(별첨 FAX 송부)을 기초로 토의하였는바 제
4항의부수 서비스 이용.접근보장과 관련 이를 지상조업, 공항안전등 공항설비
서비스의이용.접근 보장 규정으로 명확히하려는 EC의 입장과 동 서비스는 제2항의
항공운수권과 직접 연계된 서비스로서 협정적용 대상에서 배제된다는 인도,미국의
입장이 맞서결론을 내리지 못함.

　　다. 통신부속서

　　- 별첨과 같이 사무국에서 5.3항에 대한 수정초안을 배부하였는바 참가국간
이견없었음.(동수정안은 PRIVATE LEASED CIRCUITS 가 공중전기 통신서비스의
일종이라는 견해에 따라 그위치만 변경한것임)

　　- 한편, 인도 및 이집트는 5.2항의 원가 지향요금정책 BEST EFFORTS 조항에 대하여
강한불만을 토로하고 GNS 회의를 소집하여 이를 토의할 것을 요구하여 논의하지못함.

통상국	2차보	구주국	청와대	안기부	법무부	보사부	문화부	고통부
체신부	경기원	재무부	농수부	상공부	건설부	노동부	과기처	해항청
공보처								

PAGE 1　　　　　　　　　　　　　　　　　　　　　　92.03.01　　01:18 FN

　　　　　　　　　　　　　　　　　　　　　외신 1과 통제관
　　　　　　　　　　　　　　　　　　　　　　0204

2. 향후 협상일정

- MFN 일탈 신청목록 제출시한(3.6)과 관련미국은 시장접근분야의 현재의
협상진행사항을 고려시 상당히 민감한 동 목록의 제출시한연기 필요성을 제기하고 EC
도 3.10일 이전에는동 목록 제출이 불가능하는 입장이었음.

- 또한 모든 국가의 MFN 일탈 신청목록이 제시되기 전에는 양자협상 결과의
다자간평가(당초 3.10-11 예정)가 무의미 하게되고 아울러 금주의 양자협상 진행상황
및 제 3차 양허협상일정(3.9-20)을 고려시 3.16 까지 의미있는 NATIONALSCHEDULE
초안의 제출도 어렵다는 견해가 지배적이어서 적정시한으로 3.23.일이 제시되었음.

- 그러나 GNS 단독으로 서비스분야 향후 협상 일정조정을 할수는 없기때문에
GNS의장이 시장접근 분야의 협상일정을 고려하여 TNC의장과 협의조정 하기로함.

첨부: 기술적 과제에 대한 사무국 문서1부(GVW(F)-0139)

(대사 박수길-국장)

PAGE 2

주 제 네 바 대 표 부

번 호 : GVW(F) - 013P　　년월일 : 20228　　시간 : 1800

수 신 : 장　　판 (통가, 경기원, 교통부, 체신부)

발 신 : 주 제네바대사

제 목 : UR/GNS 비공식협의)

총 18 매 (표지포함)

보 안	
통 제	

외신과	
통 제	

배부처	장관실	차관실	一차보	二차보	기획실	의전실	분석관	의전장	아주국	미주국	구주국	중아국	국제기구국	경제국	통상국	문협국	영교국	총무과	감사관	공보국	의연원	청와대	총리실	안기부	공보처	경기원	상공부	교통부	체신부
														①										1				1

13P-18-1

TECHNICAL REVISION TO GATS DEFINITIONS (ART XXIV, XXI AND I)

FINAL ACT	PROPOSED REVISIONS	COMMENTS
Article I		
Scope and Definition		
1. This Agreement applies to measures by Parties affecting trade in services.		
2. For the purposes of this Agreement, trade in services is defined as the supply of a service:		
(a) from the territory of one Party into the territory of any other Party;		
(b) in the territory of one Party to the service consumer of any other Party;		
(c) through the presence of service providing entities of one Party in the territory of any other Party;	(c) by a service supplier of one Party, through commercial presence in the territory of any other Party;	The revised wording brings Article I into conformity with Article XXIV definitions of "commercial presence" and "juridical person".
(d) by natural persons of one Party in the territory of any other Party.	(d) by a service supplier of one Party, through presence of natural persons of a Party in the territory of any other Party.	The revised wording brings Article I into conformity with the Article XXIV definition of "natural person".
3. For the purposes of this Agreement: "measures by Parties" means measures taken by:		

0207

13P-18-2

-1-

FINAL ACT	PROPOSED REVISIONS	COMMENTS
(i) central, regional or local governments and authorities; and		
(ii) non-governmental bodies in the exercise of powers delegated by central, regional or local governments or authorities;		
In fulfilling its obligations and commitments under the Agreement, each Party shall take such reasonable measures as may be available to it to ensure their observance by regional and local governments and authorities and non-governmental bodies within its territory.		
(b) "services" includes any service in any sector except services supplied in the exercise of governmental functions.* *The terms of the exclusion of services supplied in the exercise of governmental functions will be reviewed in the context of the work on Article XXXIV.		

-2-

13f-18-3

FINAL ACT	PROPOSED REVISIONS	COMMENTS
Article XXXI _Denial of Benefits_ 1. A Party may deny the benefits of this Agreement: (a) to the supply of a service, if it establishes that the service originates in the territory of a country that is not a Party to this Agreement, or in the territory of a Party to which the denying Party does not apply this Agreement; and (b) to a service supplier that is a juridical person, if it establishes that <u>ultimate ownership or control</u> of such person is held by persons of a country that is not a Party to this Agreement, or of a Party to which the denying Party does not apply this Agreement.		

0209

13P-18-4

-3-

FINAL ACT	PROPOSED REVISIONS	COMMENTS
Article XXXIV Definitions For the purpose of this Agreement: (a) "measure" means any measure by a Party, whether in the form of a law, regulation, rule, procedure, decision, administrative action, or any other form;		
(b) "supply of a service" includes the production, distribution, marketing, sale and delivery of a service;		
(c) "measures by Parties affecting trade in services" include measures in respect of		
i) the purchase, payment or use of a service,		
ii) the access to and use of, in connection with the supply of a service,		
1. distribution and transportation systems, and		
2. public telecommunications transport networks and services, and		

FINAL ACT	PROPOSED REVISIONS	COMMENTS
iii) the presence, including commercial presence, of persons of a Party for the supply of a service in the territory of another Party;		Clarification.
(d) "commercial presence" means any type of business or professional establishment, including through		
i) the constitution, acquisition or maintenance of a juridical person, or		
ii) the creation or maintenance of a branch or a representative office,		
within the territory of a Party for the purpose of supplying a service.		
	(..) "sector" of a service includes sub-sectors of that service, unless otherwise specified	Simplification. Avoids repeated use in the Agreement of "sectors and sub-sectors". (Secretariat)
	(..) "service of a Party" means a service which originates in the territory of the Party	
(e) "service supplier" of another Party means any person of that Party that supplies a service;	(e) "service supplier" means any person that supplies a service;	Separates origin rule from definition.

0211

131-18-6

FINAL ACT	PROPOSED REVISIONS	COMMENTS
(f) "service consumer" of a Party means any person of that Party that receives or uses a service;	(f) "service consumer" means any person that that receives or uses a service;	Separates origin rule from definition.
(g) "person" of a Party is either a natural or a juridical person of that Party	(g) "person" means either a natural person or a juridical person	Clarification. Separates origin rule from definition.
(h) "natural person" of a Party means	(h) "natural person of a Party" means a natural person who	
i) a natural person who is a national of the Party under the law of that Party, or	i) is a national of the Party or,	
ii) in the case of a Party which does not have nationals, a natural person who has the right of permanent residence under the law of that Party,	ii) in the case of a Party which does not have nationals, or a Party which makes a declaration in its schedule, has the right of permanent residence in the Party	Provides option for Party of having its permanent residents included within scope of Agreement.
and who resides in the territory of that Party or any other Party.	under the law of that Party, and who resides in the territory of that Party or any other Party.	

13P - 18 - 5

0212

FINAL ACT	PROPOSED REVISIONS	COMMENTS
	(..) "juridical person" means any legal entity duly constituted or otherwise organized under applicable law, whether for profit or otherwise, and whether privately-owned or governmentally-owned, including any corporation, trust, partnership, joint venture, sole proprietorship or association.	Mention of "trust" ensures coverage of an important form of juridical person. Mention of "legal entities" ensures that coverage of definition is not exhaustive.
(i) "juridical person" of another Party means any corporation, partnership, joint venture, sole proprietorship or association, whether constituted for profit or otherwise, and whether privately-owned or governmentally-owned, which is	(i) "juridical person of another Party" means a juridical person which is	
i) constituted under the law of that Party, and is engaged in substantive business operations in the territory of that Party or any other Party; or	(i) constituted or otherwise organized under the law of that other Party, and is engaged in substantive business operations in the territory of that Party or any other Party; or	Ensures that definition is comprehensive.
ii) owned or controlled by		
1. natural persons of that Party, or		

FINAL ACT	PROPOSED REVISIONS	COMMENTS
2. juridical persons of that Party as defined under paragraph (i).	2. juridical persons of that other Party identified under subparagraph (i).	Clarity.
(j) A juridical person is		Clarity.
i) "owned" by persons of a Party if more than 50 per cent of the equity interest in it is beneficially owned by persons of the Party;	... the Party;	
ii) "controlled" by persons of a Party if such persons have the power to name a majority of its directors or to otherwise legally direct its actions;		
iii) "affiliated" with another person when it controls, or is controlled by, that other person; or when it and the other person are both controlled by the same person.		
ANNEX ON FINANCIAL SERVICES		
1. Scope and Definition		
1.2 For the purposes of Article I:3(b) of the Agreement, "services supplied in the exercise of governmental functions" means the following:		

13P-18-P

0214

FINAL ACT	PROPOSED REVISIONS	COMMENTS
1.2.1 activities conducted by a central bank or monetary authority or by any other public entity in pursuit of monetary or exchange rate policies;		
1.2.2 activities forming part of a statutory system of social security or public retirement plans; and		
1.2.3 other activities conducted by a public entity for the account or with the guarantee or using the financial resources of the Government.		
1.3 For the purposes of Article I:3(b) of the Agreement, if a Party allows any of the activities referred to in paragraph 1.2.2 or 1.2.3 to be conducted by its financial service providers in competition with a public entity or a financial service provider, "services" shall include such activities.		

0215

DRAFT

27.2.92   -

ARTICLE I:3(B)

(b)   "services" includes any service in any sector, except a service supplied

in the exercise of governmental authority. A service supplied in the

exercise of governmental authority shall not be understood to include

a service supplied on a commercial basis, or in competition with one or

more service suppliers.   *7.5 Annex에서 삭제*

Definition of a "monopoly supplier":

A "monopoly supplier of a service" means any person, public or

private, which in the relevant market of the territory of a

Party is authorized or established formally or in effect by

that Party as the sole supplier of that service.

13P-18구1   0216

Draft
27.2.92

ANNEX ON TELECOMMUNICATIONS

Proposed clarification of paragraph 5.3:

5.3 Each Party shall ensure that service suppliers of other Parties have access to and use of any public telecommunications transport network or service*, **including private leased circuits**, offered within or across the border of that Party, and to this end shall ensure, subject to paragraphs 5.6 and 5.7, that such suppliers are permitted: ...

---

*Definitions 3.2 and 3.3 are relevant to this provision:

3.2 **Public telecommunications transport service** means any telecommunications transport service required, explicitly or in effect, by a Party to be offered to the public generally. Such services may include, _inter alia_, telegraph, telephone, telex, and data transmission typically involving the real-time transmission of customer-supplied information between two or more points without any end-to-end change in the form or content of the customer's information.

3.3 **Public telecommunications transport network** means the public telecommunications infrastructure which permits telecommunications between and among defined network termination points.

0217

/3P — 18 — 12

45-MISC4

Draft
27.2.92

ANNEX ON AIR TRANSPORT SERVICES

1. This Annex applies to measures affecting trade in air transport
services, whether scheduled or non-scheduled, and ancillary services.

2. The Agreement shall not apply to measures affecting:

    (a) traffic rights, however granted;

    (b) the supply of directly related services, when such measures would
    limit or affect the ability of parties to negotiate, to grant or
    to receive traffic rights, or which would have the effect of
    limiting their exercise.

    except as provided in paragraphs 3 and 4 of this Annex.

3. The Agreement shall apply to measures affecting:

    (a) aircraft repair and maintenance services;

    (b) the selling and marketing of air transport services;

    (c) computer reservation services.

4. Each Party shall ensure that access to and use of publicly available
services offered within or from its territory is accorded to air services
providers of other Parties on reasonable and non-discriminatory terms and
conditions where commitments for such publicly available services have been
made and unless otherwise specified in its schedule.*

---

*The content of this paragraph will depend on the outcome of the work
relating to legal clarification of the definitions contained in
Article XXXIV.

13P - 18 - 13

43-MISCS

0218

5. The dispute settlement procedures of the Agreement shall not apply to the rights and activities described in paragraph 2. The dispute settlement procedures of the Agreement may be invoked only where obligations or commitments have been assumed by the concerned Parties and where dispute settlement procedures provided for in bilateral air service agreements or under the Chicago Convention have been exhausted.

6. Air transport services, ancillary services and the operation of this Annex shall be reviewed periodically or at least every five years.

7. Definitions:

    (a) 'aircraft repair and maintenance services' mean activities required at a regular or ad hoc basis in order to guarantee the operational airworthiness of aircraft. These activities do not include aspects of maintenance related to ground-handling.

    (b) 'selling and marketing of air transport services' mean opportunities for the air carrier concerned to sell and market freely its air transport services including all aspects of marketing such as market research, advertising and distribution. These activities do not include tariffs to be charged and their conditions.

    (c) 'computer reservation services' mean services provided by computerized systems that contain information about air carriers' schedules, availability, fares and fare rules, through which reservations can be made or tickets may be issued.

    (d) 'traffic rights' mean the right for scheduled and non-scheduled carriers to operate from, to, within, or over the territory of a Party as well as points to be served, routes to be operated, capacity to be provided, tariffs to be charged and their conditions and number and ownership of airlines to be designated.

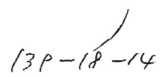

EC

1) POSSIBLE ALTERNATIVE DRAFTINGS OF PARA 4 :

a) "Each Party shall ensure that access and use of publicly available airport services offered within or from its territory is accorded to air service providers of other Parties on reasonable and non discriminatory terms and conditions where additional commitments for such publicly available airport services have been made (end of sentence deleted)."

Comments : 1) draft based on the present drafting with the minimum degree of formal changes; the substantial difference with the previous drafting sent to the GATT secretariat (7/02/92) is that it focusses only on the airport services; the reason is that further examination demonstrate that, given the fact that "sales and marketing" by airlines are covered in the GATS, the issue of "access to and use of" other publicly available services (such as banking or telecoms) is catered for by the ability to trigger directly Article XXXIV as "measures affecting the supply of [sales and marketing services supplied by airlines]" (provided one has been able to secure a commitment on sales and marketing).

2) Since this aspect of the "access to and use of" other publicly available services is not felt any more relevant, the flexibility in scheduling commitments under articles XVI and XVII that was provided by the words "unless otherwise specified in its schedule", terms which were allowing a party, when scheduling a commitment i.e. on telecoms (or on computer and related services), to mention that this commitment was not extending to the supply by or to an airline of this sector's services, is not any more necessary. Indeed, when scheduling at its discretion an additional commitment, a Party remain free to determine the scope of this commitment (for instance, it may decide that its additional commitment will ensure that other parties' airlines will be granted fair and non discriminatory access to and use of airport facilities, but with certain exceptions.

b) "A Party may enter into additional commitments under Article XVIII, to ensure that access to and use of publicly available airport services offered within or from its territory is accorded to air service providers of other Parties under reasonable and non discriminatory terms and conditions."

Comments : Same objective as the above, but with a different drafting cosmeticaly more flexible: the word "ensure" remain used, rather than "provide" as in the third drafting below, wich is the closest from the suggestions informally discussed with the secretariat yesterday; no strong feeling a priori with regard to these two terms, since the most important element would in any case be the terms of the effective additional commitment which would be scheduled.

c) "A Party may enter into additional commitments under Article XVIII, to provide to air service Providers of other parties reasonable and non discriminatory terms and conditions for access to and use of publicly available airport services offered within or from its territory."

/3P-18-15

0220

2

2) DEFINITION OF PUBLICLY AVAILABLE AIRPORT SERVICES :

a) General definition : "Publicly available airport services are services offered at a given airport :

1) by public or private entities,

2) on a commercial or non commercial basis,

3) wich are necessary, as operational facilities, for air service providers to conduct their business activities,

4) to the public defined as the collection of air service providers operating to and from this airport."

Comments : these operational facilities include ground handling facilities insofar as they are provided "publicly", i.e. by a service provider who services potentially all incoming airlines, but it does not encapsulate the self handling of an airline, or any other "self-servicing".

b) illustrative description : "publicly available airport services include in particular :

airport information desk services,
airport security services,
ground handling services,
fire, meteorology, and air traffic control."

Comments : It is to be noted that the suggestion is not meantto invite commitments to liberalise the supply of such services, which in many cases belong to public services responsibilities. Neither does it prevent such possibilities.

3) DEFINITION OF GROUND HANDLING :

"Ground handling services include the following :

-the technical and operational ground handling at airport, such as aircraft pushback, refuelling, cleaning and security;

-the handling of passengers, mail, freight and baggage at airports;

[-services provided for in the provision of in-flight catering.]

13p-18-16

4) OTHER DEFINITIONS :

a) Repair and maintenance : "activities required on a regular or ad hoc basis in order to garantee the operational airworthiness of an aircraft (excuding aspects of maintenance related to ground handling such as water servicing), or to change the image and/or configuration of an aircraft in line with the marketing needs of an air service provider."

Comments : This drafting tries to cater both for the concern expressed not to encompass in the definition ground handling related activities, and for the concern to extend the definition beyond the mere airworthiness requirements.

b) Selling and marketing : "opportunities for [the air carrier concerned] [an air service provider] to sell and market freely its air transport services, including the following aspects of marketing activities (but not the pricing of the air transport services nor the conditions pertaining to fares and tariffs) :

- establishment of retail outlets;
- appointment of agents;
- employment of staff, residents as well as non residents;
- access to the display of flights on CRSs and other distribution systems;
- issuance of own transport documents;
- market research;
- publicity and promotional activities.

Comments : This drafting compiles the previous definition and the one suggested recently by the Community, plus slight technical adjustements recommended by experts.

c) Computerised reservation system : "A computerised system containing information about air carrier schedules, seat availibility, fares and fare rules and related services, through which reservations can be made."

Comments : Slight technical adjustment recommended by experts.

13P-18-17

0222

11.2.2.27 U.S.

7. Definitions:

(a) major aircraft repair/overhaul maintenance: activities, during which an aircraft is withdrawn from service, that are required on a regular or ad hoc basis to maintain the aircraft's major systems in safe and airworthy condition.

(b) media advertising and market research: advertising in public media of air transport services and market research activities connected with air transport services.

(c) computerized reservation system: services provided by computerized systems that contain information about air carriers' schedules, availability, fares and fare rules, through which reservations can be made and tickets issued.

d) _

0223

138 - 18 - 18

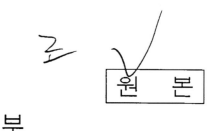

외 무 부

종 별 :

번 호 : GVW-0477 　　　　　　　　　　　 일 시 : 92 0228 2000

수 신 : 장 관(통기, 경기원, 재무부, 법무부, 농수부, 문화부, 상공부, 건설부, 보사부, 　　 m

발 신 : 주 제네바 대사 　노동부, 교통부, 과기처, 체신부, 공보처, 항만청)

제 목 : UR/서비스 해운분아 관련 협의

　　　본직은 2.28 13:00 칼라일 사무차장 초청 해운관련협의 오찬에 참석하였는바, 요지 하기 보고함. (참석국: 아국, 미, EC, 일본, 스웨덴, 카나다, 브라질, 알젠틴 8개국)

　　- 해운분야는 현재 <u>부속서 초안도 없고 남은 협상기간을 고려하여</u> 사무국이 <u>사무국안을 토대로 MODEL SCHEDULE 을 만들어 이를 참가국들이 자국의 NATIONAL SCHEDULE 에 첨부하는 형태로 해운자유화 약속을 하도록</u> 함.

　　- 참석국 대부분은 사무국안이 노르딕안을 기초로하고 미국입장을 어느정도 이해하려고 하는 방향에서 동조하고 이를 지지하는 입장을 표명하였으나, 다만 보조 서비스 분야에서는 일부 문제가 있으나 전체적인 PACKAGE 로서는 이를 지지하였음.

　　- (미국)은 업계의 이해등 때문에 해운 분야의 <u>TOTAL DEROGATION</u> 이 불가피하다고하였으며, (이씨)는 동안을 지지하나 다만 아프리카 국가와의 관계상 <u>U.N LINER CODE관련 협정의 MFN 일탈</u>이 불가피하다고 함. 끝

　　(대사 박수길-국장)

통상국	구주국	법무부	보사부	문화부	교통부	체신부	경기원	농수부
상공부	건설부	노동부	과기처	해항정	공보처			

PAGE 1 　　　　　　　　　　　　　　　　　　　 92.03.01　 01:23 FN

　　　　　　　　　　　　　　　　　　　　　　 외신 1과 통제관

　　　　　　　　　　　　　　　　　　　　　　　 0224

외 무 부

종   별 :

번   호 : GVW-0478   일   시 : 92 0228 2000

수   신 : 장관(봉기,봉일,봉이,경기원,재무부,법무부,농수부,상공부,교육부,건설부,ㅍ

발   신 : 주 제네바 대사   보사부,노동부,교통부,체신부,문화부,과기처,공보처,

제   목 : UR/서비스 양자 협상(4)   항만청)

2.28 (금) 개최된 호주 및 스웨덴과의 양자 협상내용을 하기 보고함.

1. 호주와의 협상(2.28 오전)

- 상대국 OFFER 에 대한 의문사항을 상호확인하는데 많은 시간이 할애되었으며, 호주는 다음사항에 대하여 계속 REQUEST 하거나 관심을 표명하였으나 아국은 아국 수정 OFFER 가 약속할 수있는 최고 수준이며 더이상의 COMMITMENT 는 불가능 하다는 입장을 견지하였음.

0 회계: 국내회계법인과 외국 회계법인과의 FINANCIAL LINK 허용 외국회계사의 자격인정 제도구비

0 법률: 외국법과 국제법 자문을 위한 법률 회사설립 허용

0 국내 일반 구역 화물 운송: 호주 국내시장이 과당 경쟁 상태에 있기 때문에 해외 진출에 많은 관심이 있음.

0 교육 서비스: 정규대학 설립(1,2 학년은 외국에서3,4 학년은 호주에서 수료하도록 하는 체제) 외국어학원 설립

- 한편, 호주는 MFN 일탈과 관련 지난 1월협의시 밝힌바 있는 영화 공동 생산 협정과증권 거래소 회원 자격 부여시 상호주의 요건외에 파푸아뉴기니와의 FTA, 인근도서국가와의 개발원조 협정을 추가 고려하고 있다고 함.

0 또한 2.26 자로 외국은행에 대한 신규면허 제한철폐, 지점 설립 허용 소매 금융허용등 금융개혁방안을 발표했으며, 외국인 투자 제도 역시 상당수준 자유화 조치를 실시키로 했다고 설명함.

2. 스웨덴과의 협상(2.28 오후)

- 스웨덴과의 협상 역시 양국 OFFER 에 대한 명료화 수준에 머물렀으며, 스웨덴은 아국 OFFER가 많이 개선된 점을 궁극적으로 평가함.

통상국	구주국	통상국	통상국	법무부	보사부	문화부	교통부	체신부
교육부	경기원	재무부	농수부	상공부	건설부	노동부	과기처	해항정
공보처								

PAGE 1   92.03.01   01:29 FN

외신 1과 통제관

0225

UR(우루과이라운드)-서비스 분야 양허협상, 1992. 전6권(V.1 1-2월) 231

Prudential

0 한편, 스웨덴은 아국 금융분야의 ECONOMIC NEEDSTEST 기준에 대하여 문의하고동 제도의 남용가능성, 시장접근 기회의 불확실성에 대하여 우려를 표명하였는바, 아국은 동 제도는내.외국인간 무차별적으로 적용되는것이며 설립인가를 거부하기 위한 방편으로 사용되는 것은 아니라고 설명함. 끝

(대사 박수길-국장)

정 리 보 존 문 서 목 록

기록물종류	일반공문서철	등록번호	2020030069	등록일자	2020-03-10
분류번호	764.51	국가코드		보존기간	영구
명 칭	UR(우루과이라운드) / 서비스 분야 양허협상, 1992. 전6권				
생 산 과	통상기구과	생산년도	1992~1992	담당그룹	
권 차 명	V.2 3-5월				
내용목차					

0001

외 무 부

원 본

종 별 :

번 호 : GVW-0532　　　　　　　　　　일 시 : 92 0309 1700

수 신 : 장 관(봉기, 경기원, 재무부, 상공부, 교통부, 항만청)

발 신 : 주 제네바 대사대리

제 목 : UR/서비스 협상

　　3.9(월) 당관에 전달된 스위스의 대 아국 서비스분야 REQUEST 를 별첨 송부함.

　　첨부: 스위스의 REQUEST 1 부.

　　(GVW(F)-168) 끝

　　(차석대사 김삼훈-국장)

통상국	2차보	교통부	경기원	재무부	상공부	해항청

PAGE 1　　　　　　　　　　　　　　　　　　　92.03.10　　08:11 FL

외신 1과 통제관

0002

주 제 네 바 대 표 부

번 호 : GVW(F) - *0168*   년월일 : *20309*   시간 : *1700*

수 신 : 장 관 (*통기, 경기원, 재무부, 상공부, 노동부, 항만청*)

발 신 : 주 제네바대사

제 목 : UR/서비스 협상

총 3 매(표지포함)

보 안 통 제	

외신과 통 제	

168-3-1

0003

Le Chef
de la Délégation Suisse
près
l'AELE et le GATT

Geneva, March 3, 1992

Dear Ambassador Park

We had the honour to meet with representatives of your country on February 27, 1992, for negotiations on initial commitments to be listed in national schedules attached to the services framework agreement (GATS).

We thank you very much for the opportunity to have a fruitful discussion and would like to confirm our strong interest in the item on the attached list. We consider them as key elements which we would appreciate to be reflected in your final schedule.

Yours sincerely

William Rossier
Ambassador

H.E. Mr. Soo Gil Park
Ambassador
Permanent Representative of Korea to GATT
Geneva

168-3-2   0004

Elements for Switzerland to be reflected in the schedule of KOREA

In non financial services area:

- Remove restrictions on freight forwarding services in land transport and maritime transport and take commitments on provision of freight forwarding services in air transport

- Remove need test condition on:
  - distribution services
  - transport services

168-3-3

0005

외 무 부

종 별 :

번 호 : GVW-0515

일 시 : 92 0306 1200

수 신 : 장 관(수신처 참조)

발 신 : 주 제네바 대사대리

제 목 : UR/GNS 회의

1. 갓트 사무국에서는 별첨과 같이 3.16(월) MFN 일탈 및 INITIAL COMMITMENTS협상 현황에 관한 STOCK-TAKING 을 위한 GNS 공식 회의개최를 통보하여 왔음.

2. 상기관련 아국도 3.12(목)까지는 MFN 일탈신청 목록을 제출하여야 할것으로 판단되는바, 동일자에 제출할 수 있도록 지침 통보바람.

3. 3월중 양자 협상은 당초 일정(3.9-3.20) 이 변경되지 않았으나 실제로는 3.16주에 실시될 예정이며 이에따라 당초 3.16로 되어 있던 MFN 일탈 수정목록과 NATIONAL SCHEDULE 초안 제출시기도 3.23주로 연기될 전망 임.(GNS 의장은협상 지연인상을 주지 않기 위하여 각종일자를 공식적으로 변경하지는 않을 예정임)

첨부: 갓트 AIRGRAM 1부(GVW(F)-0161).끝

(차석대사 김삼훈-국장)

수신처:통기,통일,통삼,경기원,재무부,법무부,상공부,농수산부,건설부,보사부,노동부,체신부,문화부,공보처,과기처,항만청) 사본: 박수길대사

통상국	법무부	보사부	문화부	체신부	경기원	재무부	농수부	상공부
건설부	노동부	과기처	해항청	공보처	통상국	통상국	국기국	교통부

PAGE 1

92.03.07   04:54 DS

외신 1과 통제관

0006

주 제 네 바 대 표 부

번 호 : GVⅡ(F) - 0161   년월일 : 20306   시간 : 1520

수 신 : 장   관 (통개, 통영, 통이, 통상, 경기원, 재선부, 민수부, 상공부, 건설부, 내자부

발 신 : 주 제네바대사   노동부, 교통부, 체신부, 문화부, 농수산부, 공보처, 과기처, 항만청)

제 목 :   GVW-STX 전달

총 2 매 (표지포함)

보 안	
통 제	

외신과	
통 제	

161-2-1

0007

GATT/AIR/3299   3 MARCH 1992

SUBJECT: URUGUAY ROUND: GROUP OF NEGOTIATIONS ON SERVICES

1.   THE CHAIRMAN WILL BE CONVENING A MEETING OF THE GROUP OF NEGOTIATIONS
ON SERVICES TO CONDUCT A STOCKTAKING OF THE SITUATION WITH RESPECT TO
M.F.N. EXEMPTIONS AND NEGOTIATIONS ON INITIAL COMMITMENTS AT 10 A.M. ON
MONDAY, 16 MARCH 1992 IN THE CENTRE WILLIAM RAPPARD.

2.   GOVERNMENTS PARTICIPATING IN THE MULTILATERAL TRADE NEGOTIATIONS, AND
INTERNATIONAL ORGANIZATIONS WHICH HAVE PREVIOUSLY ATTENDED THE PROCEEDINGS
OF THIS NEGOTIATING GROUP, WISHING TO BE REPRESENTED AT THIS MEETING ARE
REQUESTED TO INFORM ME AS SOON AS POSSIBLE OF THE NAMES OF THEIR
REPRESENTATIVES.

                                                          A. DUNKEL

OBJET: NEGOCIATIONS D'URUGUAY: GROUPE DE NEGOCIATION SUR LES SERVICES

1.   LE GROUPE DE NEGOCIATION SUR LES SERVICES TIENDRA LE LUNDI
16 MARS 1992, A PARTIR DE 10 HEURES, AU CENTRE WILLIAM RAPPARD, UNE
REUNION, CONVOQUEE PAR LE PRESIDENT, POUR FAIRE LE POINT DE LA SITUATION EN
CE QUI CONCERNE LES EXEMPTIONS NPF ET LES NEGOCIATIONS SUR LES ENGAGEMENTS
INITIAUX.

2.   LES GOUVERNEMENTS PARTICIPANT AUX NEGOCIATIONS COMMERCIALES MULTI-
LATERALES ET LES ORGANISATIONS INTERNATIONALES AYANT PRECEDEMMENT ASSISTE
AUX DEBATS DU GROUPE DE NEGOCIATION QUI DESIRENT ETRE REPRESENTES A CETTE
REUNION SONT PRIES DE ME COMMUNIQUER DES QUE POSSIBLE LES NOMS DE LEURS
REPRESENTANTS.

                                                          A. DUNKEL

ASUNTO: RONDA URUGUAY: GRUPO DE NEGOCIACIONES SOBRE SERVICIOS

1.   EL LUNES 16 DE MARZO DE 1992 A LAS 10 H EN EL CENTRO WILLIAM RAPPARD
SE CELEBRARA UNA REUNION DEL GRUPO DE NEGOCIACIONES SOBRE SERVICIOS,
CONVOCADA POR EL PRESIDENTE, PARA HACER UN BALANCE DE LA SITUACION CON
RESPECTO A LAS EXENCIONES DEL TRATO N.M.F. Y A LAS NEGOCIACIONES SOBRE LOS
COMPROMISOS INICIALES.

2.   RUEGO A LOS GOBIERNOS PARTICIPANTES EN LAS NEGOCIACIONES COMERCIALES
MULTILATERALES Y A LAS ORGANIZACIONES QUE YA HAYAN ASISTIDO A LAS SESIONES
DE ESTE GRUPO DE NEGOCIACION QUE DESEEN ESTAR REPRESENTADOS EN ESTA REUNION
QUE ME COMUNIQUEN LO ANTES POSIBLE EL NOMBRE DE SUS REPRESENTANTES.

                                                          A. DUNKEL

92-0281

0008

161-2-2

경 제 기 획 원

우 427-760 / 경기도 과천시 중앙동1 정부제2청사 / 전화 503-9149 / 전송 503-9141

문서번호 봉조삼 10502- 56

시행일자 1992. 3. 11

(경유)

수신 외무부장관

참조

선결			지시		
접수	일자시간	92 . 3 . 13	결재·공람		
	번호	8651			
처리과					
담당자	〰				

제목 UR/서비스협상관련 MFN일탈사항 제출

1. 봉조삼10502-14('92.2.13) 및 GVW-0515('92.3.6)과 관련입니다.

2. 제14차 대외협력위원회에서 서면결의한 바에 따라 별첨과 같은 내용의 MFN일탈
신청이 UR/GNS에 제출되도록 조치해 주시기 바랍니다.

첨부 : 최혜국대우(MFN) 일탈사항 1부.   끝.

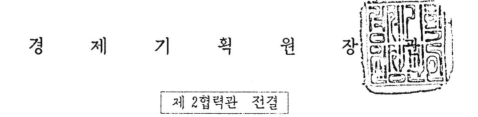

경 제 기 획 원 장

제 2협력관 전결

0009

最惠國待遇(MFN) 逸脫事項

- 韓國은 다음과 같이 MFN逸脫事項을 신청함. 다만 同 MFN 逸脫事項은 잠정적인 것으로써 한국은 그 내용을 追加, 修正, 補完, 撤回할 수 있는 권리를 유보함.

① 콤퓨터 豫約서비스(CRS)

  ○ 韓·美 航空協定('91.6)에 따라 미국에 개방키로 한 SITA를 통한 CRS공급('92.4) 서비스는 美國을 제외한 여타국에 대하여 개방을 유보

② 海運

  ○ 海運産業育成法에 의거 定期外航貨物船의 국적선 우선 이용제도에 대한 웨이버 신청의무 면제대상국은 우리나라와 海運協定을 맺고 있는 국가에 한정(9개국)

  ○ 1995년 1월부터 同 制度 폐지가능

0010

LIST OF MEASURES SEEKING ARTICLE II EXEMPTIONS

The Republic of Korea hereby presents a list of measures seeking Article II exemptions. This list is provisional and Korea reserves its right to extend, modify, reduce or withdraw this list.

① Computer Reservation Services

1) Description of the measures :

Access to foreign CRS through SITA networks are restricted to specified group of persons by the Minister of Communications since such access is considered as third use of international leased lines.

2) Treatment inconsistent with Article II:1 of the Agreement :

Domestic travel agencies are allowed to access SITA when they access CRS designated only by US carriers.

3) Intended duration of the exemption :

Undecided

4) Conditions which create the need for the exemption :

Minister of Communications specifically named "CRS designated by US carriers" for access through SITA, thereby giving benefits only to US carriers.

0011

② Waiver exemption in cargo preference system for liners in international maritime freight transportation

1) Description of the measure :

Waiver should be obtained in order to use non-national flag vessels navigating routes on which Korean liner vessels also navigate. However, if Korea has entered into a bilateral maritime agreement, such waiver is exempted according to Maritime Transportation Industry Fostering Act.

2) Treatment inconsistent with Article II:1 of the Agreement :

Korea has entered into such agreements with nine(9) countries.

3) Intended duration of the exemption :

By the date of entry to January 1, 1995.

4) Conditions which create the need for the exemption :

Korea intends to maintain this cargo preference system for liners by January 1, 1995.

0012

발 신 전 보

분류번호	보존기간

번   호 : WGV-0387   920312 1927 CJ   종별 :

수   신 : 주 제네바 대사. 총영사//

발   신 : 장 관 (통 기)

제   목 : UR/GNS 협상

대 : GVW-0515

대호 UR/GNS 협상의 MFN 일탈 신청과 관련, 콤퓨터 예약서비스 및 정기 외항선 화물선의 국적선 우선 이용제도에 대한 별첨 Waiver 신청을 갓트사무국에 제출바람.

(국영문을 송부하니 영문은 귀관 경제전문가와 협의, 필요시 자의 수정바람)

첨 부(fax) : 상기 Waiver 신청 자료. (WGV55-1) 끝.

(통상국장 김용규)

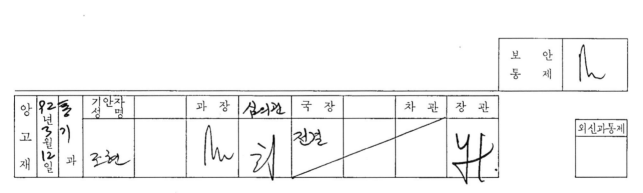

앙고재	92년 3월 12일	통기과	기안자 성명 조현	과 장	심의관	국 장 전결		차 관	장 관

보안통제

외신과통제

0013

외 무 부

종 별 :

번 호 : USW-1271 　　　　　　　　　일 시 : 92 0312 1727

수 신 : 장 관(통이) 사본: 재무부, 경기원

발 신 : 주 미 대사

제 목 : 한국 금융 시장 개방

　　1. 금일 (3.12)자 당지 JOC 에 게재된 아국 금융 시장개방 관련기사를 별첨 팩시 송부함.

　　2. 참고로 동지는 미 재무부관리의 말을 인용, 3.10(화) 개최된 한.미 금융회담에서 <u>한국측은 금융자유화를 위한 작업계획을 제시하였으나</u> 아직 구체성이 결여되어 있다고 평가하고 미측은 한국측이 향후 수주일내에 올해 취할 구체조치를 제시해 줄 것을 희망하고 있다고 보도함.

　　첨부: USWF-1456 (1 매)

　　(대사대리 김봉규-국장)

통상국　　경기원　　재무부

PAGE 1 　　　　　　　　　　　　　　　　　　　92.03.13　　08:56 WG

외신 1과 통제관

0014

South Korea Slow to Open Financial Marts, US Official Says

Knight-Ridder Financial

WASHINGTON — U.S. officials hope they made some progress in talks Tuesday aimed at liberalizing financial markets in South Korea, a senior U.S. Treasury official said.

After the latest in four rounds of meetings with South Korean officials, the United States concluded Tuesday's meetings with little more than a promise by South Korea to prepare plans for change later this year. The official said it was still not certain whether the promise is real.

The talks with South Korean ministers, which have been going on since 1990, are aimed at nudging the country toward broader foreign participation in its financial markets.

High on the list of U.S. goals are lower interest rates, more foreign capital investment and liberalized foreign-exchange trading, said the U.S. official, who asked not to be identified.

"South Korea has got to become less a part of the hermit kingdom and more a part of the global community," the official said after the meetings.

The South Korean delegation presented the United States Tuesday with a "work plan for a blueprint" on reform, the official said. The plan set forth a time frame in which it would study issues and work out changes it might make to open its financial markets. However, it did not include any specific proposals.

The official said a key change would be a loosening of interest rates more in line with international market forces. Currently, the official said, the South Korean financial system is structured to favor domestic companies and to force foreign firms into short-term high-rate borrowings.

"It's the heavy hand of the government that's been propping up a very inefficient system," the official said.

The United States also is pushing South Korea to open its foreign-exchange markets to outside participation. In addition, the official said South Korea needs to liberalize the inflow of capital, ease trade inequities and make its financial markets more transparent for outside participants.

"It is in their interest," the official said.

Reform would widen participation in their markets, the official said, adding it is also in their interest to pursue change because a frustrated Congress is watching the talks and is prepared to retaliate if there is no compliance. "Reciprocity," which is advocated in legislation pending in Congress, threatens to curtail foreign-investment opportunities in the United States for countries that have closed markets.

Officials hope South Korea will outline the first steps it will take this year in the coming weeks. But full reform may not occur until after 1997, if at all, the official said.

(1456 - 1-1)

외 무 부

종 별 : 지 급

번 호 : GVW-0566   일 시 : 92 0313 1800

수 신 : 장 관(통기,통일,통이,통삼,경기원,재무부,법무부,상공부,농수산부,

발 신 : 주 제네바 대사대리   건설부,보사부,노동부,교통부,체신부,문화부

제 목 : UR/서비스 양자 협상   공보처,항만청,과기처,사본:박수길대사

현재까지 합의된 3.16 주 양자 협상일정을 하기보고함.

0 3.19(목) 09:30: EC (금융분야)

0 3.20(금) 09:00 : 중국(아국 요청에 의한 협상임)

10:30 : 일본(금융포함 모든 분야)

15:00 : EC (금융제외 기타 서비스 분야)

0 한편 미국은 3.18(수) 14:30-18:30 양자 협상 개최를 요청하여 왔으나 3.19(목)로 변경하기 위하여 협의중임.

- 카나다는 공식적으로 양자 협상 개최를 요청하지는 않았으나 금융분야 아국 OFFER 및 자국 REQUEST 토의를 위한 아국 대사의 면담 요청등 금융분야에 관심을 표명하고 있음. 끝

(차석대사 김삼훈-국장)

3.17-22

재무, 체신, 교통, 항만, 건설, KIEP

통상국 체신부 공보처	경기원 국기국	통상국 재무부	통상국 농수부	통상국 상공부	법무부 건설부	보사부 노동부	문화부 과기처	교통부 해항정

PAGE 1   92.03.14   04:21 DS

외신 1과 통제관

0016

외 무 부

종 별 :

번 호 : GVW-0567   일 시 : 92 0313 1800

수 신 : 장 관(통기,통일,통이,경기원,재무부,법무부,상공부,농수산부,건설부)

발 신 : 주 제네바 대사대리   보사부,노동부,교통부,체신부,문화부,공보처,

제 목 : UR/GNS 비공식 협의 과기처,항만청,사본:박수길대사

　.3.13(금) 오전 JARAMILLO GNS 의장 주재로 36개국 비공식 협의가 개최되어 3.16(월) 회의 진행계획 및 향후 협상 일정에 대하여 논의하였는바, 주요내용 하기 보고함.

　1. GNS 의장은 3.16 회의 의제로서 다음 3가지를 제시하는 한편 협상 완료 시한 (3.31)은 계속 유지하되 NATIONAL SCHEDULE 초안과 MFN 일괄수정 목록 제출시기는 3.23 주로 연기되는 것이 불가피 하다고 언급함.

　1) 각국별로 자국 OFFER 관련 상황(새로운 사항에 한정) 및 MFN 일탈 계획에 대하여 설명

　2) INTIAL COMMITMENTS 및 MFN 일탈 관련 현재상황에 대한 일반적 논평

　3) 향후 협상 추진 계획에 대한 토의

　2. 의장이 제시한 3.16 회의 의제에 대하여 별다른 이견이 없었으나 현재까지 MFN 일탈 목록이 배부되지 않은 상황에서 (3.13 오후 배부 예정)3.16 회의시 구체적 토의를 하기 어려우므로 STOCK-TAKING 회의가 추가로 필요하다는 의견이 제시되어 3.23 주초에 제 2차 STOCK-TAKING 회의를 개최키로 하였음. (일자는 추후 결정)

　3. 또한, 카나다, 일본, 스웨덴, 스위스 등은 NATIONAL SCHEDULE 작성의 통일을위한 토의가 필요하다고 한바 의장은 3.16 주중에 세미나 형태의 토의를 개최하겠다고 하였으며, 호주 및 스위스는 NATIONAL SCHEDULE 초안 및 MFN 일탈 수정 목록제출이후 추가 양자 협상이 필요하다고 언급함.

　4. 한편, 의장은 3.16 주중에 잔여 기술적 과제(21조, 34조, 항공부속서, 통신 부속서)에 대한 협의를 하겠다고 하였으며, 각국이 양자 협상을 조속히 추진할 것을촉구함. 끝

　(차석대사 김삼훈-국장)

통상국 재무부	농수부	통상국 상공부	통상국 동자부	법무부 건설부	문화부 노동부	교통부 과기처	체신부 해항청	경기원 공보처

PAGE 1

0.03.14   06:17 DS
외신 1과 통제관

0017

경 제 기 획 원

우 427-760 / 경기도 과천시 중앙동1 정부제2청사 / 전화 503-9149 / 전송 503-9141

문서번호 통조삼 10502-55

시행일자 1992. 3. 12

(경유)

수신 수신처참조

참조

선결			지시	
접수	일자시간	92.3.14	결재·공람	
	번호	8799		
	처리과			
	담당자			

제목 제2차 UR서비스 양허협상 회의록 송부

  스위스 제네바에서 '92.2.24부터 2.28간 개최된 제2차 UR서비스 양허협상 결과를 별첨과 같이 송부하니 각부처(기관)는 협상대책추진에 만전을 기해 주시기 바랍니다.

첨부 : UR서비스 양자협상 회의록 1부. 끝.

경 제 기 획 원 장

제 2협력관 전결

수신처 : <u>외무부장관,</u> 내무부장관, 재무부장관, 법무부장관, 교육부장관, 문화부장관,
     농림수산부장관, 상공부장관, 보건사회부장관, 건설부장관, 교통부장관,
     노동부장관, 동자부장관, 체신부장관, 체육청소년부장관, 과학기술처장관,
     환경처장관, 공보처장관, 경찰청장, 특허청장, 해운항만청장, 대외경제정책
     연구원장, 한국개발연구원장

0018

경 제 기 획 원

우 427-760 / 경기도 과천시 중앙동1 정부제2청사 / 전화 503-9149 / 전송 503-9141

문서번호 통조삼 10502-*39*

시행일자 1992. 3.*14.*

선결			지시	
접	일자시간	∵	결재·공람	
수	번호			
	처 리 과			
	담 당 자			

수신 외무부장관

참조 통상국장

제목 : UR/서비스 양허협상 참석

　　　　1. 스위스 제네바에서 개최되는 UR/서비스 양허협상에 다음과 같이 참석코자
하니 협조하여 주기 바랍니다.

- 다　　　　음 -

가. 출장자

　　- 수석대표 : 경제기획원　제2협력관　　　　이윤재

　　- 대　　　표 : 경제기획원　통상조정2과 사무관　신호현
　　　　　　　　　　　　　　　통상조정1과 사무관　주형환

　　- 자 문 관 : K I E P　　연구위원　　　　성극제

나. 출장기간 : '92. 3.17∼3.22
다. 출 장 지 : 스위스 제네바
라. 경비부담 : 경제기획원, KIEP

첨부 : 출장일정 1부.

경 제 기 획 원 장

0019

出 張 日 程

'92. 3. 17(火)   13:50   서울 발 (KE 903)
                  19:00   프랑크푸르트 착
                  21:05   〃   발 (SR 545)
                  22:15   제네바 착

    3. 18(水) ┐
         ~   │   UR/서비스 讓許協商
    3. 20(金) ┘

'92. 3. 21(土)   10:55   제네바 발 (LH 1855)
                  12:15   프랑크푸르트 착
                  13:50   〃   발 (KE 916)

    3. 22(日)   10:20   서울 착

0020

해 운 항 만 청

우 110-410 서울 종로구 인의동 112-2 / 전화 (02)744-4730, FAX 745-9595

문서번호 진흥33700- 241

시행일자 1992.03.16

선결			지시		
접수	일자시간	92'. 3. 18	결제·공람		
	번호	9285			
처리과					
담당자					

수신 외무부장관

참조 통상국장

제목 UR/서비스 협상 정부대표 임명요청

    1. 경제기획원 통조삼 10520-58 ('92. 3.14)의 관련입니다.

    2. 경제기획원으로부터 '92. 3.18부터 제네바에서 개최되는 UR/서비스 협상 회의 참석 요청이 있어 아래와 같이 우리청 직원이 동회의에 참석코자 하오니 조치하여 주시기 바랍니다.

— 아   래 —

    가. 회의기간 및 장소 : '92. 3.18 - 3.20, 스위스 제네바

    나. 출장기간 : '92. 3.18 - 3.22

    다. 우리청 참석자 : 행정사무관 이재균

첨부 기획원 공문사본 1부.   끝.

해 운 항 만 청

0021

경 제 기 획 원

우 427-760 / 경기도 과천시 중앙동1 정부제2청사 / 전화 503-9149 / 전송 503-9141

문서번호 봉조삼 10502-58

시행일자 1992. 3. 14

(경유)

수신 수신처참조

참조

선결	청상		지시		
접수	일자시간	P2 3.14 11:○○	결재공람	차장	대결
	번호	573		국장	
	처리과	진흥과		과장	緩
	담당자			담당	

제목 UR/서비스 양허협상 참여요청

　　　스위스 제네바에서 개최되는 제3차 UR/서비스 양허협상일정이 다음과 같이 확정
되었는 바 귀부처(기관)의 실무책임자가 반드시 참여할 수 있도록 협조해 주시기 바랍
니다.

- 다　　　음 -

1. 협상일정
   - 3.18(수) 14:30～18:30 : 미국
   - 3.19(목) 09:30 　　　 : EC(금융분야)
   - 3.20(금) 09:00 　　　 : 중국
   　　　　　 10:30 　　　 : 일본(금융포함 모든분야)
   　　　　　 15:00 　　　 : EC(금융제외 기타서비스 분야)

2. 협상대표단
   - 경제기획원　　제2협력관(수석대표)
   - 재 무 부　　국제금융과장
   - 건 설 부　　해외협력과장
   - 체 신 부　　봉신협력과장
   - 교통부(항공) 국제항공과장
   - 해운항만청　 진흥과장
   - 대외경제정책연구원 성극제박사(자문관)

"끝"

경 제 기 획 원　장

제 2협력관 전결

수신처 : 재무부장관, 건설부장관, 체신부장관, 교통부장관, 해운항만청장,
　　　　대외경제정책연구원장

0022

우 110-410 서울 종로구 인의동 112-2 / 전화 (02)744-4730, FAX 745-9595

(제 2안)

수신   경제기획원장관

제목   UR / 서비스 양허협상 참여

　　1. 통조삼 10502 - 58 ('92. 3.14)의 관련입니다.

　　2. 표제건 회의참석 대상자를 아래와 같이 통보하오니 조치하여 주시기 바랍니다.

─ 아　　　래 ─

　　가. 소속 및 직급 : 해운항만청 진흥과 사무관

　　나. 성　　　명 : 이 재 균 .

해 운 항 만 청 장

0023

체　　신　　부

110-777 서울 종로구 세종로 100번지　　　/(02)750-2341　　　/Fax (02)750-2915

문서번호 통협 34470- 94

시행일자 1992. 3. 16. (　　　　)

(경 유)

수 신　　외무부장관

참 조

선결			지시		
접	일자시간	1992.　.　.　　：ー	결재・공람		
수	번호				
	처 리 과				
	담 당 자				

제목　　UR/GNS 양허협상 참가

　　　1. 경제기획원 통조삼 10502-58 ('92.3.14) 관련

　　　2. 위 관련 UR/GNS 한.미 양허협상 및 우리나라에 Request를 제출한 EC, 일본 등 기타 국가와의 공식.비공식 협상이 92.3.18(수)~3.20(금) 스위스 제네바에서 개최되는 바 동 협상에 대한 통신분야 전문가를 아래와 같이 참석케 하고자 하오니 적극 협조하여 주시기 바랍니다.

　　　　가. 참가자 및 출장기간

　　　　　o 출 장 자 : 체신부 정보통신국 통신기좌 서광현

　　　　　o 출장기간 : 92.3.17(화) - 3.22(일)(6일간). 끝

체　신　부　장

0024

교   통   부

우100-162 서울 중구 봉래동2가 122   / 전화 (02) 392-4817 / 전송(02)392-9809

문서번호 국항 10502- 271

시행일자 1992. 3. 16. (   )

(경 유)

수   신   외무부장관

참   조

선결			지시	
접	일자 시간	1992. 3. :	결재	
수	번호		재·공	
처 리 과			람	
담 당 자				

제   목   UR/서비스 양허협상 참석대표 추천요청

        스위스 제네바에서 개최되는 UR/서비스 양허협상에 참석할 대표를 아래와

같이 추천요청합니다.

                    "아   래"

        1. 회의기간 : '92.3.18 - 20 (3일간)

        2. 여행기간 : '92.3.17 - 22 (6일간)

        3. 장   소 : 스위스 제네바

        4. 참 석 자 : 항공국 국제항공담당 서기관 김광재

첨   부 1. 관련공문 사본

        2. 협상대책(안) 1부.

        3. 여행일정표. 파견경비내역등 공무여행계획 1부.   끝.

교   통   부   장

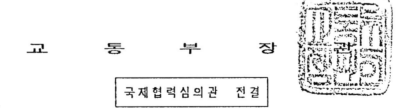

국제협력심의관 전결

0025

교 통 부

우100-162 서울 중구 봉래동2가 122   / 전화 (02) 392-4817 / 전송 (02)392-9809

문서번호 국항 10582-268

시행일자 1992. 3. 16. (   )

(경 유)

수   신   내부결재

참   조

취 급		장 관	
보 존			
차 관			
국 장		기획관리실장	
심 의 관		수송정책실장	
담 당 관		항공정책과장	
기안	김완중		협조

제   목   UR/서비스 양허협상 참석

　　1. 경제기획원 롱조심 10582-58 ('92.3.14)의 관련입니다.

　　2. 스위스 제네바에서 개최되는 제3차 UR/서비스협상에 다음과 같이 참석하고자
합니다.

다　　　　　음

　　1. 회의기간 : '92.3.18 - 20 (3일간)

　　2. 회의장소 : 스위스 제네바

　　3. 의   제 : 중국.일본.EC와의 UR/서비스 양허협상

　　4. 여행기간 : '92.3.17 - 22 (6일간)

　　5. 참 석 자 : 항공국 국제항공담당 서기관 김광재

　　6. 활동계획 : 제3차 UR/서비스 양허협상의 항공분야협상에 참여

　　7. 예   산 : 454(항공)-1011(항공행정)-213(국외여비). 끝.

교 통 부 장 관

0026

검열
1992. 3. 16
통제관

UR/서비스 항공분야 협상 추진

1. 개요

○ UR/서비스협상은 서비스(교통.통신.금융.관광등)의 무역에 적용할 다국
   간 협정을 체결하려는 것
   ● 일반협정(GATS)의 제정, 부문별 부속서(SECTORAL ANNEX)의 제정, 최초
     의 자유화 약속수준(INITIAL COMMITMENTS)의 결정으로 구성
○ 항공, 금융, 통신은 특수성이 있어 일반협정외에 부속서를 제정하기 위한
   논의중에 있음

2. 최근의 추진현황

○ '91.12.20 던켈 GATT사무총장이 UR서비스협상 최종협정문안 및 항공
   부속서등 제시
○ '92.1.13 무역협상위원회(TNC)에서 향후 협상일정 제시(각국가 협상을
   1-3월에 3차례 진행후 마무리할 계획)
   ● 1.20 - 31   제1차 양허협상 개최
   ● 2.17 - 28   제2차 양허협상 개최
   ● 3.9 - 20   제3차 양허협상 개최
                (3.18-20 우리측은 미국.중국.EC.일본과 양허협상)

0027

3. 항공분야 협상(던켈 협정문안 : 별첨)

○ 운수권 및 운수권과 직접 관련된 서비스 : UR협상에서 제외

● 사유 : 시카고협약에 의한 쌍방간 협정에 의함

○ 항공운수보조서비스업 : UR협상 대상 (일반협정 적용)

● 항공기 수선 및 유지서비스

● 항공운송서비스의 판매 및 마켓팅

● 컴퓨터예약시스템(CRS)

● 공공으로 가용한 서비스(PUBLICLY AVAILABLE SERVICES): 대상 업종에 대하여 각국간 논란이 있어 불명확함

4. 우리부 입장

○ 항공분야 협상은 던켈안 수용하되 대외개방은 단계적 시행

● 항공기수선 및 유지서비스, 항공운송서비스의 판매 및 마켓팅

- '97.1부터 외국인 50%미만 투자허용

● 컴퓨터예약시스템

- 공중교환통신망을 사용한 해외에서의 공급은 허용

- 단 SITA(특수공중통신망)를 이용한 해외에서의 공급은 최혜국 대우(MFN)일탈 요청

- 외국인 국내투자는 50% 미만 허용하되 '94.1월부터 완전개방

● 공공으로 가용한 서비스

- 지상조업, 공항안전, 관제등의 서비스는 운수권과 직접 관련된 서비스이므로 협정적용에서 제외

0028

航空運送서비스 附屬書

1. 본 부속서는 航空運送서비스(정기선이던지, 부정기선이던지) 및 補助서비스 교역에 영향을 미치는 조치에 적용한다.

2. 協定文은 본 부속서의 3항 및 4항에 규정된 것을 제외한 다음의 조치에는 적용치 아니한다.

   (a) 運輸權, 양허하였다 할지라도
   (b) 運輸權과 직접적으로 관련된 서비스의 공급이 운수권을 교환하기 위하여 협상하는 締約國의 能力을 제한 또는 영향을 미치거나 운수권 사용을 제한하는 효력을 갖는 경우 運輸權과 직접적으로 관련된 서비스의 공급

3. 協定文은 다음의 조치에 적용한다.

   (a) 航空機修繕 및 維持서비스
   (b) 航空運送서비스의 판매 및 마켓팅
   (c) 컴퓨터 예약시스템

4. 各 締約國은 다른 체약국의 항공서비스 공급자에게 합리적이고 비차별적이고 自國의 讓許表에 달리 명시되지 않았다면 공공으로 가용한 서비스를 양허한 조건으로 자국의 영토내 또는 영토로부터 제공되는 공공으로 가용한 서비스에 대한 接近 및 使用을 보장해야 한다*.

---

* 本項의 내용은 제34조에 포함된 정의의 法的 明確化와 관련된 作業結果에 따름.

0029

5. 協定文의 紛爭解決節次는 제2항에 기술된 권리 및 활동에
   적용되지 아니한다. 협정문의 분쟁해결절차는 오직 義務
   또는 讓許가 關聯締約國에 의해 위배된 경우와 쌍무간 항공
   서비스 협정 또는 시카고협약에 규정된 紛爭解決節次가
   消盡된 경우에만 적용될 수 있다.

6. 航空運送서비스, 補助서비스 및 본 부속서의 운영을 주기적
   으로 또는 최소한 매5년마다 검토되어야 한다.

7. 定義

   (a) 航空機修繕 및 維持서비스 : 항공기의 운항상 내항공성을
       보장하기 위한 정상적 또는 특별한 경우에 요구되는 활동.
       이 활동에는 地上操業과 관련된 維持活動이 포함되지
       않음.

   (b) 航空運送서비스의 판매 및 마켓팅 : 관련 항공운송업자가
       市場調査, 廣告 및 流通과 같은 마켓팅의 제반요소를
       포함 航空運送서비스를 자유롭게 판매 및 마켓팅하는
       활동. 이 활동에는 요금과 요금의 조건이 포함되지 않음.

   (c) 컴퓨터 예약시스템 ; 航空社 運航計劃, 可溶座席, 料金
       및 航路에 대한 정보를 가지고 있으며 이를 통해 예약이
       될 수 있고 티켓이 발매될 수 있는 컴퓨터 시스템에 의해
       提供되는 서비스

   (d) 運輸權 : 운항지점, 운항항로, 제공되는 능력, 요금 및
       요금조건, 指定航空機의 數 및 所有權과 마찬가지로
       체약국의 영토로부터, 영토로, 영토내 또는 영토위로
       운항하는 정기 및 부정기 항공사의 권리

0030

외   무   부

110-760 서울 종로구 세종로 77번지   / (02)720-2188   / (02)725-1737 (FAX)

문서번호 통기 20644-

시행일자 1992. 3.16.(   )

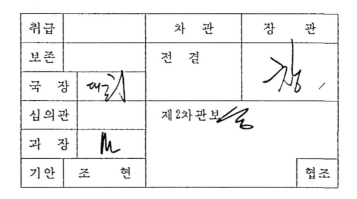

취급		차 관	장 관
보존		전 결	
국 장			
심의관		제2차관보	
과 장			
기안	조 현		협조

수신   내부결재

참조

제목   UR/서비스 협상 정부대표 임명

───

92.3.18-20간 제네바에서 개최되는 UR/서비스 양허협상에 참가할 정부대표단을
"정부대표 및 특별사절의 임명과 권한에 관한 법률"에 의거 아래와 같이 임명코자
건의하오니 재가하여 주시기 바랍니다.

                    - 아   래 -

1. 회 의 명 : UR/서비스 양허협상

2. 회의 개최기간 및 장소 : 92.3.18-20, 스위스 제네바

3. 정부대표 :

      ○ 수석대표 : 경제기획원 제2협력관   이윤재

      ○ 대   표 : 경제기획원 통상조정2과 사무관   신호현

                        통상조정1과 사무관   주형환

            재 무 부 국제금융과 사무관   최희남

            체 신 부 정보통상국 통신기좌   서광현

            교 통 부 국제항공과장   김광재

            해운항만청 진흥과 사무관   이재훈

            주 제네바 대표부 관계관

0031

○ 자   문 : KIEP 연구위원   성극제

　　　　（단, 금융.보험분야에 국한된 별도의 양자협상이 개최될

　　　　경우 재무부 대표중 선임자를 교체 수석대표로 함）

4. 협상일정 （양자협상 대상국）

　　○ 3.18（수） 14:30-18:30 : 미국

　　○ 3.19（목） 09:30　　　　 : EC（금융분야）

　　○ 3.20（금） 09:00　　　　 : 중국

　　　　　　　 10:30　　　　 : 일본（금융포함 모든분야）

　　　　　　　 15:00　　　　 : EC（금융제외 기타서비스 분야）

5. 출장기간 : 3.17-3.22 **（예산 : 해당부처 소관예산）**

6. 훈   령

　　○ 2.17 제출한 아국의 수정 offer list를 기초로 동 수정 offer list
　　　내용을 충분히 설명하는 선에서 양자 협상에 임하도록 하고 상대국으로
　　　부터 추가 개방 요구가 있을 경우 동 요구의 우선 순위등 그 내용을
　　　명확히 파악, 차기 협상에 대비토록 함.　　　　　　 끝.

외 무 부 장 관

0032

외   무   부

110-760 서울 종로구 세종로 77번지   / (02)720-2188   / (02)725-1737 (FAX)

문서번호 통기 20644-

시행일자 1992. 3.17.(   )

취급		장 관	
보존		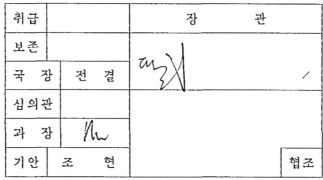	
국장	전결		/
심의관			
과장	🖊		
기안	조 현		협조

수신   내부결재

참조

제목   UR/서비스 협상 정부대표 추가임명

———

    92.3.18-20간 제네바에서 개최되는 UR/서비스 협상에 참가할 정부대표단에
아래 2인을 추가로 임명코자 건의 하오니 재가하여 주시기 바랍니다.

                    - 아   래 -

    1. 정부대표

        ㅇ 건설부 해외협력과 사무관   유윤호

        ㅇ 국토개발연구원 수석연구원   김흥수 (자문)

    2. 출장기간 : 3.18-3.22.   끝.

        외   무   부   장   관

                                                            0033

외 무 부

110-760 서울 종로구 세종로 77번지 / (02)720-2188 / (02)725-1737 (FAX)

문서번호 통기 20644-*105*

시행일자 1992. 3. 17. (   )

취급		장 관
보존		
국 장	전 결	
심의관		
과 장	대 결	
기안	조 현	협조

수신   수신처 참조

참조

제목   UR/서비스 협상 정부대표 임명 통보

1. 92.3.18-20간 제네바에서 개최되는 UR/서비스 양허협상에 참가할 정부대표단이 "정부대표 및 특별사절의 임명과 권한에 관한 법률"에 의거 아래와 같이 임명 되었음을 통보합니다.

- 아   래 -

가. 회 의 명 : UR/서비스 양허 협상

나. 회의 개최기간 및 장소 : 92.3.18-20, 스위스 제네바

다. 정부대표 :

　　　ㅇ 수석대표 : 경제기획원 제2협력관　　　　　　　이윤재

　　　ㅇ 대   표 : 경제기획원 통상조정2과 사무관　　　신호현

　　　　　　　　　　　　　통상조정1과 사무관　　　주형환

　　　　　　　재 무 부 국제금융과 사무관　　　　　최희남

　　　　　　건 설 부 해외협력과 사무관　　　　유훈호

　　　　　　체 신 부 정보통상국 통신기좌　　　　서광현

　　　　　　교 통 부 국제항공과장　　　　　　　김광재

　　　　　　해운항만청 진흥과 사무관　　　　　이재훈

　　　　　　주제네바 대표부 관계관

0034

    ㅇ 자　　문 : KIEP 연구위원　　　　　　　　　　성극제

             (단, 금융.보험분야에 국한된 별도의 양자협상이 개최될

             경우 재무부 대표중 선임자를 교체 수석대표로 함)

  라. 출장기간 : 3.17-22

  마. 소요예산 : 해당부처 소관예산

2. 출장 결과 보고서는 귀국후 2주일이내 당부로 송부하여 주시기 바랍니다.

                                                  끝.

수신처 : 경제기획원장관, 재무부장관, 교통부장관, 체신부장관, 해운항만청장,
                  건설부장관

외　무　부　장　관

발 신 전 보

분류번호 보존기간

번 호 : WGV-0412 920317 1643 CJ 종별 : 암호통신

수 신 : 주 제네바 대사. 총영사/

발 신 : 장 관 (통 기)

제 목 : UR/GNS 양허 협상

대 : GVW-0567

92.3.18-20간 귀지에서 개최되는 UR/GNS 양허 협상에 참가할 정부대표단이 아래 임명 되었으니 귀관 관계관과 함께 참석토록 조치바람.

1. 정부대표

　　　o 수석대표 : 경제기획원 제2협력관　　　　　이윤재

　　　o 대　　표 : 경제기획원 통상조정2과 사무관　　신호현

　　　　　　　　　　　　통상조정1과 사무관　　주형환

　　　　　　재 무 부 국제금융과 사무관　　　최희남
　　　　　　건 설 부 해외협력과 사무관　　　옥윤호
　　　　　　체 신 부 정보통상국 통신기좌　　서광현

　　　　　　교 통 부 국제항공과장　　　　　김광재

　　　　　　해운항만청 진흥과 사무관　　　이재훈

　　　o 자　　문 : KIEP 연구위원　　　　　　　성극제
　　　　　　　　　국토개발연구원 수석연구원　　　김흥수
　　　　　　　　(단, 금융.보험분야에 국한된 별도의 양자협상이 개최될

　　　　　경우 재무부 대표중 선임자를 교체 수석대표로 함)

보안통제 : [서명]

앙 고 재	92년 3월 17일	통기과	기안자성명 조현		과장 [서명]	심의관 전결	국장		차관	장관 [서명]

외신과통제

0036

2. 출장기간 : 3.17-3.22

　　　　　UGV-0147 2　　0517 1645 CJ

3. 훈　령

2.17 제출한 아국의 수정 offer list를 기초로 동 수정 offer list 내용을
충분히 설명하는 선에서 양자 협상에 임하도록 하고 상대국으로부터 추가 개방
요구가 있을 경우 동 요구의 우선 순위등 그 내용을 명확히 파악, 차기 협상에
대비토록 함.　　　　　끝.

　　　　　　　　　　　　　　　　　　　　(통상국장　대리　최　혁)

외 무 부

종 별 :

번 호 : GVW-0581

일 시 : 92 0316 1840

수 신 : 장관(수신처 참조)

발 신 : 주제네바대사대리

제 목 : UR/GNS 회의

3.6(월) JARAMILLO GNS 의장 주재로 개최된 표제공식회의 내용을 하기 보고함.

1. 각국별 OFFER 및 MFN 일탈 신청 목록 제출 상황

가. MFN 일탈

- 의장은 지금까지 18개국이 목록을 제출하였으며 당초 오늘 아침 동 목록을 배부할 예정이었으나 주요 국가가 목록을 제출하기 전에는 배부하지 말것을 요청한 국가가 있어 이를 유보하고 있다고함.(EC 가 3.16 아침 자국 목록을 제출하면서 미국의목록이 제출되기 전에는 배부하지 않도록 요청한 것으로 사료됨)

0 다음 국가들은 수일내에 목록을 제출하겠다고 언급함 : 볼리비아, 콜롬비아, 오지리, 유고, 루마니아, 헝가리, 중국, 가봉, 싱가폴, 베네주엘라, 모로코

0 한편 미국은 금일오후 목록을 제출하겠다고 발언함.(따라서 3.17 중에 MFN 일탈 신청목록이 배부될 것으로 예상됨)

나. OFFER 및 수정 OFFER 제출 현황

- 의장은 총 46개국(EC 를 12개국으로 계산할 경우 57개국)으로 부터 OFFER 가 제출되었으며 총19개국이 수정 OFFER 를 제출하였다고 함.(OFFER및 수정 OFFER 제출 현황 별도 FAX 송부)

0 오지리, 폴란드, 루마니아, 태국, 우루과이, 싱가폴, 페루, 모로코등은 수일내에수정 OFFER 를 제출하겠다고 언급하였으며 나이제리아, 세네갈등이 OFFER 제출 의사를 표명함.

2. INITIAL COMMITMATS 협상 및 MFN 일탈 관련 현재 상황에 대한 논평

- 미국, EC, 카나다, 북구, 스위스등 선진국들은 각국의 자유화 약속 수준과 관련 다음 사항들을 강조함.

0 미국: 일반적으로 금융분야 자유화 약속 수준이 만족스럽지 못함.

통상국	2차보	법무부	보사부	문화부	교통부	체신부	경기원	재무부
농수부	상공부	건설부	노동부	과기처	해항정	공보처		

PAGE 1

92.03.17   07:54 DQ

외신 1과 통제관

0038

많은 국가들이 STANDSTILL 수준에도 못미치는 일부서비스만 OFFER 하였으며 애매하고 개괄적으로 유보(BROADLY WORDED RESERVATION) 하였는바 다음주중에 동 문제들이 해결되어야 함

0 EC: 해운, 항공, 금융, 사업서비스,부가가치통신, 엔지니어링등이 자유화 약속수준의 균형 여부를 판단하는데 있어서 필수 분야임

각국 OFFER 의 분야별 포괄 범위가 확대 되어야하며 모든 분야의 현존 시장접근수준이 OFFER 에 반영되어야 함. 수평적 제한 조치 역시 중대한 무역 장벽임.

0 카나다: 금융분야의 협상 결과가 불만족스러움. 해운분야에 있어서 항구 설비 서비스의 접근 및 사용문제, 최종 지점간 서비스 공급문제가 해결되어야 함.

기본 통신 분야에 확보 가능한 사항을 개발하여야함

0 북구: 해운 분야가 매우 중요함에 불구하고 OFFER하지 않은 나라가 많음.

0 스위스: 금융 엔지니어링 및 FREIGNT FORWARDING 이 극히 중요함.

- 또한 카나다, 북구, 스위스등은 OFFER 수정 및 MFN 일탈 신청 목록 작성 과정에서 서비스협정의 해석상 불분명한 사항이 많이 발견되었다고 전제하고 SCHEDULING 및 서비스협정의 적용 범위(특히 MFN 관련)와 관련 다음과 같은 기술적 문제들에 대한토의가 필요하다고 하였으나 인도, EC등은 의문을 가지고있는 국가는 이를 서면으로사무국에 제출하면 사무국이 대부분 답변할 수 있을 것이며 사무국에서 답변할 수 없는 사항만 토의하면 될것이라고 하여 의장이 동 대안을 수용, 의문이 있는 국가는 그구체적 내용을 사무국에 제출할것을 요청함.

0 비자협정, 인력시장 통합, 의료 및 사회보장관련 협정, 투자보장 협정등이 서비스협정 적용대상인지 여부(사법 및 행정 공조협정과 같이 제2조 MFN 에 대한 FOOT NOTE 제정 필요)

0 4개 서비스 공급 형태 구분등 SCHEDULING 작성 방식의 통일

0 명료성 제공 목적의 정보의 범위

0 MFN 일탈과 COMMITMENT 와의관계(COMMITMENT 한 사항에 대하여 MFN 일탈을 신청한 경우의 효력 문제)

0 서비스 분야별 CPC CODE 기재 문제

0 보조금(15조와 17조의 관계) 및 조세 문제등

- 한편 방글라데시 및 탄자니아는 최저 개발국은INITIAL COMMITMENT 를 하지 않고도 서비스협정 회원국이 되어야 한다고 발언하였으나 EC,카나다등은 서비스 협정

제28조상 NATIONAL SCHEDUL제출이 협정 가입의 필수요건이라고 반박함.

3. 향후 작업계획

- 협상 완료시한(3.31.)은 그대로 유지하되 3.25. 제2차 STOCK-TAKING 회의를 가지기로 하였으며 3.23.주에 NATIONAL SCHEDULE 초안 및 MFN 일탈수정 목록을 제출기로 함.

첨부: OFFER 및 수정 OFFER 제출 현황 1부

(GVW(F)-0184).끝

(차석대사 김삼훈-국장)

수신처:통기,경기원,재무부,법무부,상공부,농림수산부,건설부,보사부,노동부,교통부,체신부,문화부,공보처,과기처,항만청

주 제 네 바 대 표 부

번 호 : GVW(F) - 0184   년월일 : 20316   시간 : 1830

수 신 : 장   관 (총기. 경가헌. 재무부. 명부부. 농수산부. 상공부. 건설부. 보사부. 노동부)
          고통부. 체신부. 문화부. 공보처. 과기처. 총만청

발 신 : 주 제 네 바 대 사

제 목 : Gva   Gvw-581 회의

종 5 매 (표지포함)

보 안 통 제	

외신과 통 제	

184-5-1

0041

16.3.92

LIST OF INITIAL COMMITMENTS

1. MTN.GNS/W/109/Rev.1 21.11.91   Comm. from Switzerland - Conditional
Offer of Switzerland concerning Initial
Commitments

2. MTN.GNS/W/112/Rev.1 21.1.92   Comm. from U.S.A. - Revised Conditional
Offer of the U.S.A. concerning Initial
Commitments - Revision

3. MTN.GNS/W/113/Rev.2 10.2.92   Comm. from Japan - Conditional Offer of
Japan concerning Initial Commitments -
Revision

   MTN.GNS/W/113/Rev.2/Corr.1*
                       17.2.92   Corrigendum (English only)

                       ****

4. MTN.TNC/W/51/Rev.1 8.11.91   Comm. from Australia - Conditional Offer
of Australia concerning Initial
Commitments - Revision

5. MTN.TNC/W/53/Rev.3 1.11.91   Comm. from the EC - Preliminary
Conditional Offer by the EC of Initial
Commitments on Trade in Services -
Revision

6. MTN.TNC/W/54   4.12.90   Comm. from Hong Kong - Conditional Offer
of Hong Kong concerning Initial
Commitments

7. MTN.TNC/W/55/Rev.1 14.2.92   Comm. from Canada - Conditional Offer by
Canada of Specific Commitments in the UR
on Trade in Services - Revision

8. MTN.TNC/W/58/Rev.1 28.1.92   Comm. from New Zealand - Revised
Conditional Offer of New Zealand
concerning initial commitments on Trade
in Serivces under the GATS

9. MTN.TNC/W/59/Rev.1 19.2.92   Comm. from Sweden - Preliminary
Conditional Offer by Sweden on Initial
Commitments
   MTN.TNC/W/59/Add.1 28.4.91   Addendum

10. MTN.TNC/W/61/Rev.1 19.2.92   Comm. from the Republic of Korea -
Conditional Offer by the Republic of
Korea of Initial Commitments on Trade in
Services
   MTN.TNC/W/61/Rev.1/Corr.1
                       28.2.92   Corrigendum

11. MTN.TNC/W/62/Rev.2 14.2.92   Comm. from Finland - Conditional Offer
by Finland Concerning Initial
Commitments - Revision

186-5-2

19-GNMIS   0042

- 2 -

12. MTN.TNC/W/63	24.1.91	Comm. from Norway - Conditional Offer by Norway concerning Initial Commitments in the Services Negotiations
MTN.TNC/W/63/Add.1/Rev.1	21.2.92	Addendum - Revision
13. MTN.TNC/W/64	4.2.91	Comm. from Indonesia - Initial Commitments of Indonesia in the field of Services
14. MTN.TNC/W/65	5.2.91	Comm. from Singapore - Conditional Offer of the Republic of Singapore concerning Initial Commitments
MTN.TNC/W/65/Corr.1	18.2.91	Comm. from Singapore - Conditional Offer of the Republic of Singapore conerning Initial Commitments - Corrigendum
15. MTN.TNC/W/66	6.2.91	Comm. from Austria - Preliminary conditional offer of Austria concerning Initial Commitments in Trade in Services
MTN.TNC/W/66/Add.1	23.5.91	Addendum
16. MTN.TNC/W/67/Rev.2	17.2.92	Comm. from Colombia - Initial Commitments - Revision
17. MTN.TNC/W/70 ** (SEE GNS/W/126)	7.3.91	Comm. from Poland - Preliminary Conditional Offer by Poland concerning Initial Commitments on Trade in Services
18. MTN.TNC/W/71/Rev.2	24.2.92	Comm. from Mexico - Conditional List of Offers of Mexico - Mexico
19. MTN.TNC/W/72/Rev.1	4.3.92	Preliminary Conditional Offer of the Republic of Turkey concerning Initial Commitments
20. MTN.TNC/W/73	25.3.91	Comm. from the Czech and Slovak Federal Republic - Preliminary Conditional Offer by the Czech and Slovak Federal Republic concerning Initial Commitments to Trade in Services
MTN.TNC/W/73/Add.1	16.12.91	Addendum
21. MTN.TNC/W/74/Rev.1	3.92	Comm. from Iceland - Preliminary Conditional Offer by Iceland of Initial Commitments on Trade in Services - Revision
22. MTN.TNC/W/78	3.5.91	Comm. from Romania - Preliminary Conditional Offer by Romania concerning Initial Commitments on Trade in Services
MTN.TNC/W/78/Add.1	12.2.92	Addendum

****

(84-5-)

19-GNMIS   0043

- 3 -

23. MTN.GNS/W/115/Rev.1 17.12.91		Comm. from Chile - Offer of Chile concerning Initial Commitments on Trade in Services
24. MTN.GNS/W/116	14.6.91	Comm. from Brazil - Preliminary, Conditional Offer of Brazil concerning Initial Commitments on Trade in Services
25. MTN.GNS/W/121	15.7.91	Comm. from Yugoslavia - Preliminary Conditional Offer of Yugoslavia concerning Initial Commitments on Trade in Services
26. MTN.GNS/W/122	19.7.91	Comm. from Malaysia - Conditional Offer by Malaysia of Initial Commitments on International Trade in Services
27. MTN.GNS/W/123	19.7.91	Comm. from Venezuela - Declaration by the Government of Venezuela to the Group of Negotiations on Services
MTN.GNS/W/123/Add.1/Rev.1 5.3.92		Comm. fm Venezuela - Initial Commitment - Revision
28. MTN.GNS/W/124	19.7.91	Comm. from China - Conditional Offer of the People's Republic of China concerning Initial Commitments
29. MTN.GNS/W/125	19.7.91	Comm. from Argentina - Conditional Offer of the Rep. of Argentina concerning Initial Commitments
MTN.GNS/W/125/Add.1 25.11.91		Addendum - Comm. Argentina - Financial
** MTN.GNS/W/126 (SEE TNC/W/70)	23.7.91	Comm. from Poland - Preliminary Conditional Offer of Poland concerning Initial Commitments
30. MTN.GNS/W/127	25.7.91	Comm. from Costa Rica - Declaration to submit offer for Initial Commitments
MTN.GNS/W/127/Add.1 27.9.91		Comm. fm Costa Rica - Initial Commitments
31. MTN.GNS/W/128	25.7.91	Comm. fm Uruguay - Initial Commitments
32. MTN.GNS/W/129	25.7.91	Comm. fm Peru - Initial Commitments
33. MTN.GNS/W/131	7.8.91	Comm. fm Philippines - Intention to submit Preliminary Conditional Offer
MTN.GNS/W/131/Add.1 8.11.91		Comm. fm Philippines - Initial Commitments - Addendum

184-5-4

- 4 -

34. MTN.GNS/W/132	9.8.91	Comm. from Thailand - Intention to submit Preliminary Conditional Offer
MTN.GNS/W/132/Add.1/Rev.1	28.2.92	Comm. fm Thailand - Initial Commitments Revision to Addendum 1
MTN.GNS/W/132/Add.2	12.3.92	Comm. fm Thailand - Initial Commitments Addendum 2
35. MTN.GNS/W/133/Rev.1	3.3.92	Comm. fm Hungary - Initial Commitments Revision
36. MTN.GNS/W/136	27.9.91	Comm. fm South Africa - Initial Commitments
37. MTN.GNS/W/137	27.9.91	Comm. fm Egypt - Initial Commitments
38. MTN.GNS/W/141	17.10.91	Comm. fm Morocco - Initial Commitments
39. MTN.GNS/W/142	25.10.91	Comm. fm El Salvador, Guatemala, Honduras and Nicaragua - Initial Commit.
40. MTN.GNS/W/143	1.11.91	Comm. fm Cuba - Declaration of intent to submit offer for Initial Commitments
MTN.GNS/W/143/Add.1	10.3.92	Comm. fm Cuba - Initial Commitments Addendum
41. MTN.GNS/W/144	22.11.91	Comm. fm India - Initial Commitments
42. MTN.GNS/W/147	26.2.92	Comm. fm Bolivia - Initial Commitments
43. MTN.GNS/W/148	3.3.92	Comm. fm Sri Lanka - Initial Commitments

19-GNMIS   0045

외 무 부

종 별 :

번 호 : GVW-0583　　　　　　　　　　일 시 : 92 0316 1900

수 신 : 장 관(통기, 경기원, 재무부, 상공부, 건설부, 교통부)

발 신 : 주 제네바대사대리　　　　　　　Copy : 동북아2과

제 목 : UR/서비스 협상

　　　3.16(월) 당관에 전달된 중국의 대아국 서비스분야 REQUEST 를 별첨 송부함.

　　　첨부: 중국의 REQUEST 1 부. 끝

　　　(GVW(F)-185)

　　　(차석대사 김삼훈-국장)

통상국　　교통부　　경기원　　재무부　　상공부　　건설부　　오희정

　　　　　　　　보사부, 노동부, 아주국

　　　　　　　　　　　　　　　　92.03.17　07:42 WH

　　　　　　　　　　　　　　　　　　외신 1과 통제관

　　　　　　　　　　　　　　　　　　　0046

주 제 네 바 대 표 부

번 호 : GVW(F) - 0185   년월일 : 20316   시간 : 1830

수 신 : 장   관 (통기. 경기형. 재무부. 상공부. 건설부. 교통부)

발 신 : 주 제네바대사

제 목 :　　　GVW-583 관 5

종　 5 매 (표지포함)

보 안 통 제	

외신과 통 제	

185-5-1

0047

MISSION PERMANENTE DE LA RÉPUBLIQUE POPULAIRE DE CHINE

A GENÈVE

11, CHEMIN DE SURVILLE - 1210 PETIT-LANCY, GENÈVE
TÉL. (022) 92 25 48

16 March, 1992

Dear Mr. Lee,

Enclosed please find a initial list of requests, general and specific, for initial commitments with respect to your country in accordance with the procedures agreed by the Group of Negotiations on Services.

My delegation would appreciate the opportunity of discussing with your delegation on the issue of initial commitments on 20 March.

Sincerely Yours

He Ning
Second Secretary
Permanent Mission of P.R. China

Mr. Jong Wah Lee
Attache
Permanent Mission of Korea
Route de Pre-Bois 20
1216 Cointrin

0048

PEOPLE'S REPUBLIC OF CHINA REQUEST LIST ON SERVICES

(TO THE REPUBLIC OF KOREA)

The People's Republic of China is submitting to the Republic of Korea a two-part request list regarding the negotiations on initial commitments on trade in services in the framework of the GNS. The first part is a general request for a minimum level of binding and liberalization in the service negotiations. The second part contains specific requests to the Republic of Korea for commitments to remove or reduce existing restrictive measures, in respect of commercial presence , cross-border supply and movement of personnel, in certain sectors or sub-sectors in which China has significant interests.

China reserves its right to modify, add to, or correct this request list in the course of negotiations.

Part I

The first part of this list constitutes a general request to the Republic of Korea for commitments as follows:

1. To bind a standstill of all existing measures inconsistent with Articles XVI and XVII of the draft Agreement, in the sectors as described in the Services Sectoral Classification List (MTN. GNS/W/120) at the level actually applied on 31 December 1991, whether through legislation , administrative regulation or by any other administrative method, and not to introduce any new restrictions, and,

2. To apply Articles XVI and XVII of the draft Agreement (as

0049

set out in Annex II of MTN.TNC/W/FA of ,20 Dec. 1991) to the temporary movement of natural persons providing services to the fullest extent not inconsistent with existing mandatory legislation. Natural persons include not only managers, executives and specialists, but also skilled workers.

3. This commitment would apply from the date of entry into force of the General Agreement on Trade in Services.

Part II

The second part of this list constitutes a specific request to the Republic of Korea.

1. Financial services

-- To make a binding commitment on the present level of market access and national treatment in the financial sector including banking, insurance and securities.

-- To eliminate restrictions which disadvantage foreign financial service providers in establishing banks and other financial institutions.

-- To allow foreign financial service providers to compete on equal terms with the domestic financial service providers in any markets.

-- To allow foreign banks to purchase properties on the basis of national treatment.

-- To allow cross-border transfer of information and equipments necessary for the conduct of ordinary business of foreign service providers.

0050

-- To grant foreign financial service providers national treatment as regards the scope of activities necessary for ordinary business.

-- To ease visa formalities for entering the Republic of Korea.

2. Tourism services

-- Chinese chefs should fall within the category of specialists if the Republic of Korea has a specific commitment regarding the movement of personnel in the future.

-- Restrictions on travel and tourism of Koreans to China should be further relaxed.

3. Construction and Related Engineering Services

-- to ensure that the Chinese natural persons providing services such as graduate workers be granted the same opportunity and payment as that granted to domestic service providers with similar capability.

-- to relax restrictions on labour market.

0051

재 무 부

우 427-760 경기도 과천시 중앙동 1 / 전화 503-9266 / 전송 503-9324

문서번호 국금 22251- 2

시행일자 '92. 3. 17 ( )

수신 외무부장관

참조 통상국장

선결			지시	
접	일자시간	92·3·17	결재·	
수	번호	9156	공람	
	처리과			
	담당자			

제목 카나다와의 금융분야 양자협의 결과

1. GVW-0566('92.3.13)과 관련입니다.

2. 지난 2월 스위스 제네바에서 개최된 카나다와의 제2차 서비스 양자협의 결과를 아래와 같이 송부하오니 주제네바 대표부로 전달될 수 있도록 협조하여 주시기 바랍니다.

아 래

- 지난 2월 회의시 '91년 시장개방 조치까지 포함한 아국 offer에 대한 설명을 하였는 바, 카측은 구체적인 의견제시가 없이 종결되었고, 아국의 금융자율화 및 시장개방에 대해 만족을 표명함.

- 카나다의 Request에 대하여 아국의 입장을 다음과 같이 설명

  o 은행의 branching와 관련, 외국은행의 복수지점 인가기준이 국내은행과 동일하게 적용되고 있으며, 이에 따라 2월초 카나다계 은행(Royal Bank of Canada)의 복수지점 설치가 인가에 대해 카측은 사의를 표명함.

  o 외국은행의 funding 문제는 CD 한도 확대, SWAP 한도 감축 정지 등을 통하여 해결되고 있음.

0052

o 중소기업 의무대출비율은 대기업의 경제력 집중을 막기 위하여 유지하는
   것으로 오히려 대출비율에 있어서 외국은행이 특혜를 받고 있음.

   (국내은행 : 대출 증가율의 45%, 외국은행 : 대출증가율의 35%)

o 카나다은행의 신탁업무 가능 여부는 카나다내에서 본점이 신탁업무가 가능한
   경우 인가가 가능하므로, 이에 대한 자료 제공시 검토하겠음.

- 아측 Request에 대해 카측은 외국은행의 자산한도를 카나다내 총은행자산의
   12%로 제한하는 규제조치 철폐를 검토키로 약속함.

- 양국은 앞으로 각국 은행의 funding 애로에 대해 상호 검토키로 하였는 바,
   양국은 UR 관련 금융현안은 없음.   끝.

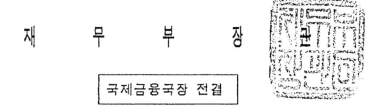

재 무 부 장

국제금융국장 전결

0053

발 신 전 보

번   호 : WGV-0435   920320 1841 BU종별 : _____

WUS -1280

수   신 : 주   제네바   대사. /총/영사 (사본 : 주미 대사)

발   신 : 장 관 (통 기)

제   목 : UR/서비스 협상

2.24-28간 개최된 UR/서비스 2차 양자 협상에서 미국, 카나다등은 아국에 대해 Service Seller의 양허를 요구 하였는바, 동 요구사항 검토에 참고 코자하니 아래 사항을 파악, 보고바람.

1. 미국, 카나다, EC, 호주등이 요구하는 Service Seller의 개념, 구체적 예

2. EC가 요구하는 Sole representative의 개념, 구체적 예

3. Service Seller 및 Sole representative의 예상 활동 영역

4. 상기 국가들이 현행 출입국관계법상 이들 인력에 대한 입국과 활동에 대한 제한 조치를 취하고 있는지 여부.   끝.

(통상국장 김 용 규)

보안통제	⟨서명⟩

앙고재	92년 3월 20일	통기과	기안자 성명	조현	과장 ⟨서명⟩	심의관 ⟨서명⟩	국장 전결	차관	장관 ⟨서명⟩

외신과통제

0054

외 무 부

종 별 :

번 호 : GVW-0625

수 신 : 장 관(통기),통이, 경기원, 재무부, 법무부, 상공부, 농수산부, 건설부, 보사부,

발 신 : 주 제네바 대사　　　　　　노동부, 교통부, 체신부, 공보처, 과기처, 항만청)

제 목 : UR/서비스 양자 협상(1)

일 시 : 92 0320 1720

. 3.19(목) 개최된 미국과의 표제 양자 협상 내용을 하기 보고함.

1. 미측 관심사항에 대한 토의요지

가. 회계 및 법무서비스 분야의 AFFILIATION 허용

- 회계 및 법무서비스 분야의 AFFILIATION 허용

- 회계분야의 AFFILIATION 허용문제와 관련 미국이 서면으로 제시한 내용 (별첨 FAX 송부)에 대하여 아측은 1차적 논평임을 전제로 당초 미국이 REQUET 했던 FINANCIAL LINK 보다 훨씬광범위 내용으로서 수용하기 어렵다고 함.

0 미측은 자국이 제시한 내용중에 부자문제이외의 다른 사항에도 문제가 있는지 질의한바 아측은 검토후 추후 답변하겠다고 함.

- 한편, 미측은 동 AFFILIATION 이 법무서비스분야에도 매우 유용한 개념이라고 하면서 모든 법무서비스 제공에 한국 변호사 자격취득을 전제조건으로 하는 아국의 규제는 그대로 유효한 상태에서 국제법무법인과의 AFFILIATION (국제법무법인의 명칭사용, 수입분배) 허용을 제휴계약의 구체적 내용등에 대한 정보 제공을 요청함.

나. 기본통신 개방에 관한 '96년까지의 지속적협상에 참여 여부

- 아측은 지난 2월 협상시 밝힌바와 같이 동협상에 참여할 용의가 없다고 하는 한편 동복수국간 협상 결과의 법적 구성 형태 (GATS더하기 로서 별도의 규범 제정 여부 등)에 대하여 질의한바

0 미측은 MULTILATBRAL COMMITMENTS 로서 각국의 NATIONAL SCHEDULE 에 반영될 것이라고 함.

다. 금융분야 OFFER 개선

- 미측은 아국의 금융분야 수정 OFFER 의유보 내용이 너무 애매하고 개괄적이다고 전제하고 조속한 시일내에 보다 구체적으로 명확화 되어야한다고 강조함.

통상국 농수부	2차보 상공부	통상국 건설부	법무부 노동부	보사부 과기처	교통부 해항정	체신부 공보처	경기원	재무부

PAGE 1

92.03.21　09:56 WG

외신 1과 통제관

0055

0 아측은 미국의 금융분야 수정 OFFER 가제출되지 않았음을 지적하는 한편 미국의 금융분야 MFN 일탈 계획의 구체적 내용에 대하여 질의하였는바

0 미측은 현재 입법중인 법률 (가속적 법률이될것임)에 따라 모든 외국 금융기관의 신규진입, 확장, 영업 모두에 대하여 당해 국가의양허 수준에 따라 대우를 달리하는 것이라고함. (MFN 일탈 대상국가 및 대상조치가 모든 OPEN-ENDED 임 TOTAL DEROGATION 임)

0 이에 대하여 아측은 금융분야를 사실상 서비스협정 적용 범위로 부터 제외하는 것이라고 지적한바 미측은 이는 최대한도의 MFN 일탈이며 각국의 자유화 약속 수준에 따라 변경될 수 있다고 함.

　라. 보험분야의 신상품 인가 및 보험업 협회회원 자격 문제

- 미측은 신상품의 인가와 관련 보다 다양한 종류, 장기간, 다른 이율의 무배당 상품의 허용과 기타신상품의 인가 절차를 보다 명료화 해줄것을 요청함. (별도의 양자 협상이 진행중인 사항임)

0 또한 외국 보험사는 보험업 협회의 준회원자격만이 인정됨으로서 규정당국에 대한 정책건의 과정에서 의견 반영이 어려운 문제점이 있다고 한바 아측은 그와 관련한 문제는 없다고 해명함.

　마. SERVICE SELLER 에 대한 COMMITMENTS 문제

- 아측은 미측제안을 유용한 접근 방법이라고 평가하고 계속 검토중이라고 함.

　2. 아측 관심사항에 대한 토의 요지

　가. 보험분야의 영업인가 문제

- 캘리포니아주의 아국 현대 해상 화재보험사 지점설치 인가지연 사유에 대하여 미측은 상당기간이 경과 되었음을 인정하는 동 보험사가 탈세, 부당해위등의 이유로 한국정부의 조사대상이 되고있기 때문이라고 답변함.

0 아측은 동조사는 당해 보험사에 대한 조사가 아니라 현대그룹에 대한 조사일뿐만 아니라 한편 인가신청사가 향후 어떤 조치를 취해야 할 것인지 정보제공을 요청함.

　나. 금융분야의 인력입국 허용 문제

- 미국내에 설립된 아국 금융기관에 파견되는 임직원의 입국허용 제한 완화 요청에 대하여 미측은 동임직원의 배우자 및 미혼 자녀는 동반입국이 허용되나 부모는 방문 비자를 별도로 받아야한다고 함.

　다. 관광안내업 설립인가 문제

PAGE 2

'0056

- 로드 아일랜드주의 제한 조치에 대하여 미측은 거주요건이나 국적요건, 서비스공급업체수 제한등이없다고 해명함.

3. 양자협상 회의록 작성문제

- 미측은 그간의 양자협상에서 토의된 세부내용의 기록 작성 문제를 제기하였는바, 아측은 입장 표명을 유보하는 한편 기록작성시 동문서 의법적 지위에 대하여 질의함. (미측은 추후답변하겠다고 함)

첨부: 미국의 AFFILIATION 에 대한 정의 1부

(GVW(F)-0198).끝

(대사 박수길-국장)

PAGE 3

0057

주 제 네 바 대 표 부

번 호 : GVW(F) - **0118** 년월일 **20320** 시간 : **1750**

수 신 : 장   관 (총기, 총이), 경가원, 재무부, 법무부, 상공부, 농수산부,

발 신 : 주 제네바대사 건설부, 보사부, 노동부, 교통부, 체산부, 문화부, 홍보처,

제 목 : GVW - 0625 첨부   과기처, 항만청)

총 **3** 매 (표지포함)

보 안	
통 제	

외신과	
통 제	

UNITED STATES TRADE REPRESENTATIVE

1-3 AVENUE DE LA PAIX

1202 GENEVA, SWITZERLAND

TELEPHONE: 732 09 70

'82. 3. 16

Dear Mr. Han:

During our February bilateral negotiation on services, the U.S. delegation agreed to provide the Korean delegation with some written information regarding our interest in a commitment in the accounting sector which allowed international affiliation of accounting firms.

The following are key elements in the concept of "international affiliation" with respect to the accounting profession:

1. Right to use the international name independently or in connection with a local name, as business needs or strategy dictate.

2. Right for internationally affiliated firms to provide the full range of services that national regulation permits local firms which do not have international affiliations to provide, including the presumption that other services may be provided and new services introduced unless explicitly prohibited for all firms. Includes access on an equal basis to all appropriate licenses, permits, and certifications to practice.

3. Right to make international payments and transfers, including inward and outward investments, between the local entity and worldwide entity and between the local entity and other similar affiliated entities in other countries. This include the ability to pay the international affiliate for propriety goods and services necessary to provide quality client service, such a technical support, technology transfer, methodology transfer, marketing aids, professional liability insurance for work within Korea, and manuals and reference materials.

4. Right to move managerial and technical personnel into the country as needed, and the right for all employees to travel abroad for purposes of training.

5. Right to transfer proprietary date, software, technology and training into and out of the country, with the expectation that
it will receive full and adequate protection from piracy.

I look forward to our next round of negotiations later this week.

1f8 - 3 - 2

0059

UNITED STATES TRADE REPRESENTATIVE

1-3 AVENUE DE LA PAIX

1202 GENEVA, SWITZERLAND

TELEPHONE: 732 09 70

'82. 3. 16

Dear Mr. Han:

During our February bilateral negotiation on services, the U.S. delegation agreed to provide the Korean delegation with some written information regarding our interest in a commitment in the accounting sector which allowed international affiliation of accounting firms.

The following are key elements in the concept of "international affiliation" with respect to the accounting profession:

1. Right to use the international name independently or in connection with a local name, as business needs or strategy dictate.

2. Right for internationally affiliated firms to provide the full range of services that national regulation permits local firms which do not have international affiliations to provide, including the presumption that other services may be provided and new services introduced unless explicitly prohibited for all firms. Includes access on an equal basis to all appropriate licenses, permits, and certifications to practice.

3. Right to make international payments and transfers, including inward and outward investments, between the local entity and worldwide entity and between the local entity and other similar affiliated entities in other countries. This include the ability to pay the international affiliate for propriety goods and services necessary to provide quality client service, such a technical support, technology transfer, methodology transfer, marketing aids, professional liability insurance for work within Korea, and manuals and reference materials.

4. Right to move managerial and technical personnel into the country as needed, and the right for all employees to travel abroad for purposes of training.

5. Right to transfer proprietary date, software, technology and training into and out of the country, with the expectation that it will receive full and adequate protection from piracy.

I look forward to our next round of negotiations later this week.

0060

118-3-3

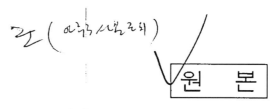

원 본

외 무 부

종   별 :

번   호 : GVW-0633   일   시 : 92 0323 1530

수   신 : 장 관(봉기)봉일,봉삼,경기원,재무부,법무부,교육부,상공부,건설부,

발   신 : 주 제네바 대사   보사부,노동부,교통부,체신부,문화부,공보처,과기처,

제   목 : UR/서비스 양자협상(2)   항만청,관세청)

    3.20(금) 개최된 중국, 일본, EC 와의 양자협상 내용을 하기 보 고함.

    1. 중국과의 양자 협상가. 중국의 REQUEST

    - 중국은 별첨과 같이 자국이 관심을 가지고 있는 인력의 범위를 전달하고
한편식당의 요리사, 건설인부, 연수생에 대한 동등 대우등을 요청하였으나 아측은 동
문제 대부분이 서비스 협정적용 대상이 아니며, 적용대상에 포함되는 경우에도
상업적주재에 따른 기업내 인력이동에 한하여 COMMITMENT 한 것이라고 답변함.

    0 또한 중국은 아국 관광객의 중국여행 제한(중국내 어떤 기관으로부터
초청장을받은 경우에만 중국 입국 허용) 완화를 요청한바 아측은 동 문제 역시
정치.외교적사항으로서 서비스 협상에서 다루기에 부적절하다고 답변함.

    나. 아국의 REQUEST- 유봉, AUDIOVISUAL 분야에 COMMITMENT 를 요청한 아국
REQUEST 에 대하여 중국은 동분야의 사업은 중국인에 한하여 허용되며 봉신분야에
있어서는 부가가치 봉신 서비스에 한하여 COMMITMENT 할 것을 긍정적으로
검토하겠다고함.

    0 합작 투자의 경우 외국인 지분 25 퍼센트 이상요건에 대하여 중국은 진실한 합작
투자에 한하여 조세 감면 혜택을 향유할수 있도록 동 기준을 운영하고 있다고 함.

    0 아측은 또한 한국기 게양 선박의 중국 입장이 금지되고 있음을 지적한바 중국은
검토하겠다고답변함.

    2. 일본과의 양자 협상

    가. 해운 분야

    - 일본은 아국의 해운분야 MFN 일탈과 관련LINER CODE 회원국에 대한 WAIVER
자동부여,지정화물에 대한 WAIVER 제도 운영시 양자 협정체결국에 대한 혜택부여
여부등에 대하여 질의한바 아측은 그와 같은 차별 조치가 없다고 하는 한편 일본

| 통상국 | 통상국 | 통상국 | 법무부 | 보사부 | 문화부 | 교통부 | 체신부 | 교육부 |
| 경기원 | 재무부 | 상공부 | 건설부 | 노동부 | 과기처 | 해항청 | 관세청 | 공보처 |

PAGE 1   92.03.24   04:46 DS

                                                          외신 1과 통제관

                                                              0061

선박(정기선 및 부정기선)에 대하여도 WAIVER 가 주어진 사례가 있음을 설명함.

- 또한 일본은 자국업체의 FREIGHT FORWARDING분야 투자와 관련 한국, 중국, ASEAN 등국가에 있어서 많은 문제에 직면하고 있으며, 동분야의 49 퍼센트 지불 제한이매우 중요한 제한이라고 한바, 아측은 일본 기업이 이미 투자한 실적(2건)이 있다고전제하고 아국의 경우 '89년부터 동 분야 시장개방을 시작했기 때문에 단시일내에 또다른 자유화 약속을 하기는 어렵다고 답변함.

0 또한 아국은 일본의 동 분야 상호주의 적용에 대한 MFN 일탈과 관련 현존 법규에 규정되어 있다고 해서 이를 그대로 반영한다면 협상의 의미가 없게 되는 것이라고 지적함.

(나) 건설분야

- 일본은 아측의 면혀 발급제도, 해외공사 실적인정, 건설 엔지니어의 자격 인정에 관한 기준, 업체별 도급한도 계산 방법, 건설공제조합 출자의무 금액등에 대하여문의하는 한편 업체별공사 계약당 도급한도 제도와 관련 동 제도가 비록공사 1건당제한이라 하더라도 건설 시장의 분할때문에 사실상 서비스 협정 16조에 규정된 총서비스 공급가액 제한과 같은 무역 왜곡효과가 있다고 지적함.

0 또한 일본은 자국의 경우 정부공사 이외에 민간발주 공사에는 그와 같은 제한이 없다고함.(발주자 개인의 문제임)

- 아국은 일본이 미국에 개방키로 합의한 35 개공사중 제 3섹터가 발주하는 공사에 대하여 아국에도 동일한 혜택을 부여해 줄것을 요청한바, 일본은 원칙적으로 동의하나 서비스협정 제 13조에 정부 조달은 제외되어 있으며, 제3 섹터가 정부기관은 아니라 하더라도 이를 대신하여 정부 사용 목적의 공사를 발주하는 것이므로 정부조달협정에 해당하는 사항이라고 함.

0 이에 대하여 아국은 서비스 협정 13조에 따라 제외되는 것은 정부 사용 목적을 위하여 정부기관 스스로가 구매하는 경우만 해당하므로 제3섹터가 정부기관을 대신하여 발주하는 공사는 MFN 적용대상이라고 지적함.

다. AUDIO VISUAL

- 일본은 동 분야에 아국이 MFN 일탈 신청을 하지 않은 점을 환영하고 일본 영화 수입금지조치에 대하여 자국 업계가 많은 불평을 하고 있다고 하였으나 아측은 논평을 유보하였음.

3. EC 와의 협상

PAGE 2

0062

가. 금융분야

- 아국은 최근 발표된 금융 자율화 및개방계획(BLUEPRINT)을 설명하고 EC 의 관심 사항인 금융기관 자회사 설립,부자신탁업등도 장기계획으로 검토될 것임을 언급함.

0 이에 대해 EC 는 아국의 개방계획등 부자신탁업, 외국인 부자한도등이 당초계획(장기계획)보다 앞당겨 질수 있는지 여부와 이중 시장 접근 관련 내용을 OFFER 에 BINDING할 것인지를 문의한바, 아국은 BLUEPRINT내용이 거시경제 변수를 고려한 단계적 작업으로 경제 여건 변화에 따라 달라질수 있으므로 이를 BINDING 하기가 어렵다고 설명함.

0 또한 EC 는 ECONOMIC NEED TEST 개념의 명료화, EC 증권사인가, 외국인 주식 부자한도 MONITOR 방법, 외국 보험사 면허 갱신제도,자동차 보험인가 요건등에 관심을 표명함.

- EC 는 아국 REQUEST 사항인 복수 점포장제도,영란은행의 창구지도등에 추가적인 설명을 하고,최종입장은 아니지만 EC 로서는 금융분야에 대한 MFN 일탈 의사가 없음을 밝히고 미국의 금융분야 MFN 일탈도 여타 국가들의 OFFER수준이 개선된다면 철회할 가능성이 있다고 언급함.

나. 해운분야

- EC 는 해운분야 사무국 문서('91.12.15 자)의 각요소별로 아국입장을 문의하였는바 아국은 기존입장에 따라 기본적으로 동 접근 방법에 별문제가 없으나 일부 보조서비스에 문제가 있으며제한 조치 폐지 기간에 신축성이 있어야 한다고 언급함.

- 한편, EC 는 동 문서상의 각 요소별로 다음사항을 강조함.

0 항국 설비 서비스의 접근 및 사용에 관하여 부속서 제정 필요

0 각 해운 보조서비스의 공급은 단계별로 단절되어있는 것이 아니라 수송 서비스공급과정의 일부이므로 외항선사 또는 운송 주선 업자에 의한 일관된 서비스 공급이이루어져야 함.

- 또한 EC 는 위와 같은 전제하에 지난 2월협의시 추가 요청한 각 해운 보조 서비스 공급제한조치의 3년 내 폐지를 재차 요청하였으며, 통관서비스에 대하여는 대체적으로 모든 나라가 전직세관 공무관의 독적 공급체제이나 운송 주선업자에 의한 관세사의 고용 또는 CUSTOMSBROCKERAGE 의 허용을 요청함.

0 아측은 해운 보조서비스의 시장 개방이 불과 3년전부터 시작되었고, 아국 산업이

PAGE 3

0063

유치단계에 있음을 들어 추가 자유화 약속이 곤란하다고 하는 한편 관세사에 대하여는 OFFER 에 포함하기 곤란할뿐만 아니라 변호사, 공인회계사등과 같이 타인에의고용을 금지하는 법규정의 유무부터 검토하여야 한다고 언급함.

　다. 기타 분야

　- EC 는 다음 사항들에 대하여 개속 아국의검토를 요청함.

　O 인력이동 약속범위에 SERVICE SELLER 및 SOLEREPRESENTATIVE 포함

　O CRS 에 MFN 일탈은 심각한 차별 조치이며, 동서비스는 항공회사가 공급하는 것이 아니므로 항공운수권과의 관계도 희박함.

　O 유통분야에 일반 무역업 및 무역 중개업 포함.

　O 법무 서비스의 포함 및 회계 서비스에 대한 ECREQUEST 반영

　O RENTAL/LEASING 서비스, 광업관련 서비스,시험검사 및 분석 서비스, 교육 서비스(직업훈련 및외국어 훈련), FRANCHISING 의 포함

　④ 관찰 및 건의

　- 당초 GNS 에서 합의된 양자 협상 일정은 3.20까지 완료하도록 되어 있으나 UR전체 협상의 지연 가능성, 서비스 분야 MFN 일탈 문제 협상의 방대한 작업량, 선진국들이 기대하는 서비스분야 INITIAL COMMIMENTS 수준의 미흡등을 고려할때 4월이후 추가 양자 협상이 개최될 것으로 전망됨.

　- 향후 지속될 협상에 대비하여 아국 OFFER 및MFN 일탈 관련 다음 사항에 대한 검토가 필요한 것으로 판단됨.

　O AUDIO VISUAL 분야의 MFN 일탈 신청(일본영화의 수입금지, 영화 배급 업체 설립 금지등)

　O 해운 및 항공 보조 서비스 OFFER 내용재검토(일괄 작업 체제로의 수송 서비스체계변환 추세 고려)

　첨부: 중국의 인력이동 관심분야 1부. 끝

　(GVW(F)-202)

　(대사 박수길-국장)

주 제 네 바 대 표 부

전 보 : GVR(F) - 0202   년월일 : 20323   시간 : 1530

수 신 : 장   관 (총리, 경기원, 재무부, 법무부, 농수산부, 상공부, 건설부, 보사부, 노동부)
           교통부, 체신부, 문화부, 공보처, 과기처, 청안청

발 신 : 주 제 네 바 대 사

제 목 : UR/GNS 협의

보 안	
통 제	

외신과	
통 제	

송   유   면 (프지프합)

Informal Note of China

'92. 3. 2o

Natural persons providing services as mentioned in China's request list include, in particular, the following categories of personnel in certain sectors and subsectors:

Maritime Transport Services

√ 1. Crew members:

-- master; chief engineer

-- chief officer; second engineer

-- second officer; third engineer

-- third officer; engineer

-- radio operator; electrician

-- purser

-- other ordinary seamen

2. Port management officer and staff

3. Shipping company management officer and staff

Education Services

-- post graduate teacher

-- laboratory assistants

Architectural Services

-- architect

Accounting, Auditing and Book Keeping

-- cost auditor

-- cost accountant

-- cashiers

0066

Engineering Services

-- electrical engineer

-- electronics engineer   ,

-- mining engineer

-- geological engineer

Integrated Engineering Services
-- maintenance engineer

-- design engineer

-- lab technician

Operation and Maintenance of Railways

-- station master

-- ticket collectors

-- cook

-- fireman

-- electric assistant

-- loco drivers

computer and related services

-- system analyst

-- programmer

-- field engineer

-- data entry operator

Health Related Services

-- physician, surgeon

-- laboratory technician (pathology, bio-chemistry,

   microbiology, electron microscopy, radiology)

-- chemists

-- nurses

-- mid-wives

Hotel and Restaurant Services

    -- housekeeper

    -- chef (including executive chef and sous chef)

    -- restaurant hostess

    -- lobby hostess

    -- steward/waiter

Construction and Engineering

    -- machine tool operators

    --painters

    --labourers

외 무 부

종 별 :

번 호 : GVW-0635   일 시 : 92 0323 1530

수 신 : 장관(통기, 경기원, 재무부, 상공부, 건설부, 보사부, 교통부, 체신부, 문화부,

발 신 : 주 제네바 대사   과기처, 항만청

제 목 : 카나다 대사 면담결과

    3.20.4:30 당지 카나다대사가 서비스 협상등 관련 의견교환을 위해 본직을
방문하였는바 면담결과를 하기 보고함.

    1. 서비스 협상- 카나다 대사는 아국의 수정 OFFER(특히 통신, 엔지니어링,
건설등)에 대해 긍정적인 평가를 하고, 보험 및 금융분야에 일부 추가관심을 표명함

    0 보험사 설립에 대한 제한 및 차별 여부의 질의에 대해 아무런 제한적
조치가없다고(MFN 원칙적용) 설명하고 보험의 경우 카나다계 영품 MANULIFE 보험사가
기설립 영업중임을 부연함.

    0 OFFSHORE LENDING 에 대한 문의에 대해 OFFSHORE 계정에 의한 대출의 경우
아무런 제한이 없음을 설명하였으나 카대사는 외국은행이 국내에서 내국인에의 외화
대출에 대한 제한을 언급함.

    - 카나다는 영화 공동생산협정 및 미국과의 FTA협정에 의한 금융분야의 MFN
일탈신청을 하였는바 미국, EC등 일부 국가가 우려를 표명하고 있다고 하였으며 또한
해운자유화와 관련 일부국가(미국의 MFN 일탈 신청)의 소극적 입장에 대해 관심을
표명하고 아국의 협조를 요청함. 본직은 해운분야에 대해 지난번 칼라일사무차장과의
오찬협의 결과를 설명하고 사무국안을 원칙적으로 지지하는 방향에서 검토하고
있다고말함.

    2. UR 협상전망

    - 카나다대사는 지난번 필리핀 ESCALIER 대사 송별 케언즈그룹 만찬에 던켈
사무총장이 동석하였는바 던켈총장은 미.EC간 농산물에 관한 타협이 조만간 이루어질
가능성이 많으며 그경우 금년 6월까지 협상 타결이 가능할 것이라고
언급하였는바, 카나다 대사는 미의회의 승인시기등을 감안시 금년 타결은 반듯이는
낙관할수 없다는 견해를 표명함.

| 통상국 | 보사부 | 문화부 | 교통부 | 체신부 | 경기원 | 재무부 | 상공부 | 건설부 |
| 과기처 | 해항정 | | | | | | | |

PAGE 1   92.03.24   04:55 DS

                                        외신 1과 통제관

                                        0069

- 미국 및 케언즈그룹은 아직 입장 변화가 없으며, EC의 경우 프랑스등의 입장은오히려 강경화되고 있고 최근 GREEN BOX 문제이외에 REBALANCING, 수출 보조금 및 최소시장 접근문제를 다시 제기하고 있음.

이러한 점에 비추어 7월 개최 예정인 G7 회의시까지 어떠한 진전도 없을 경우에는 내년초로 협상 연기가 불가피할 것이라는 우려를 표명함.

- 카나다 대사의 금번 방문은 다음주(3.25)에 있게될 서비스 협상 분야 다자간 평가 회의와 관련 자국의 MFN 일탈 분야에 대한 이해를 구하고 미국의 해운분야 MFN일탈에 대한 우려에 갑은 입장을 취해줄 것을 요구하기 위한 것으로 보임. 끝

(대사 박수길-국장)

외 무 부

원 본

암호수신

종 별 :

번 호 : GVW-0668　　　　　　　　　　　일 시 : 92 0326 1000

수 신 : 장관(봉기,봉일,봉이,경기원,재무부,법무부,상공부,농림수산부,건설부,

발 신 : 주 제네바대사　　　　보사부,노동부,교통부,체신부,문화부,공보처,

제 목 : UR/GNS 회의　　　　　　　　　　　　　　과기처,항만청)

　　　3.25.(수) 개최된 표제회의 주요내용을 하기 보고함.(본직, 이경협관, 한경협관보

참석)

　　　1. 각국별 OFFER 및 MFN 일탈 신청목록 제출상황

　　- 세네갈, 자메이카, 카메룬등이 OFFER 를 제출하겠다고 함.

　　- 세네갈, 모로코, 베네주엘라, 자메이카등이 수일내에 MFN 일탈신청 목록을

제출하겠다고 하였으며 멕시코는 MFN 일탈 신청사항이 없다고 밝힘.

　　　2. INITIAL COMMITMENTS 협상 및 MFN 일탈 관련 현재 상황에 대한 평가

　　- 각국의 MFN 일탈 신청사항을 구체적으로 토의하지는 않았으며 호주, EC,

뉴질랜드, 알젠틴, 카나다, 일본, 스웨덴, 스위스, 인도, 우루과이, 한국,

페루, 헝가리, 멕시코, 브라질, 홍콩, 터키등 많은 나라가 주로 미국의 4 개

주요분야(해운, 항공, 기본통신, 금융)에 있어서 MFN TOTAL DEROGATION 에 대해

다음과같은 이유를 들어 집중 비판함.

　　O 4 개분야 전부를 협정적용 대상에서 배제하는 것으로서 서비스협정을 무의미하게

함과 동시에 일방주의 및 양자체제의 계속을 의미함.

　　O MFN 일탈을 양허 교섭수단(NEGOITATING CHIP)으로 활용하는 것은 수용할 수

없음.

　　O MFN 일탈은 구체적 조치에 한정하여야 하며 자유재량적인 국내법규 및 조치를

대상으로 하여서는 안됨.

　　- 미국은 지금까지 제출된 각국의 OFFER 내용 특히 금융, AUDIO VISUAL,

기본통신분야의 약속 수준이 실망스러운 것이었으며, MFN 은 자유화 약속 수준의

균형과 분명한 연계관계에 있다고 하는 한편

　　O 미국은 타국에 비하여 보다 명확하고 공개적으로 MFN 일탈을 신청하였으며

통상국 법무부 건설부	장관 보사부 노동부	차관 문화부	1차보 교통부	2차보 체신부	통상국 경기원	통상국 재무부	외정실 농수부	분석관 상공부

PAGE 1　　공보처. 과기처. 항만청　　　　　　　92.03.27　　04:17

외신 2과　통제관 FK

0071

다른나라들이 금융, 기본봉신분야에서 자유화 약속 수준을 높인다면 MFN 일탈을 철회하겠다고 함.

  - 주요국가의 발언요지는 다음과 같음.

  0 호주: 충실한 내용의 OFFER 를 제출하였으나 현재와 같은 상황이 지속된다면 OFFER 에서 몇몇 분야를 제외할 수 밖에 없음.

  일부 국가의 MFN 일탈 신청 내용은 평가하기에 충분한 정보가 제공되지 않았으며 광범위하고 경제적 영향이 큰 사항들이 있음.

  0 EC: 3.16. 이후 협상이 후진하고 있으며 이와같은 상황이 지속된다면 서비스협상 결과를 수락할 수 없음.

  투자정보협정에 대한 MFN 일탈은 동협정에 포함된 서비스분야가 모두 제외되고 되므로 매우 위험함.

  FTA 에 대한 예외신청은 협정 제 5 조(경제통합)을 우회하는 것임.

  해운분야 MFN 일탈 신청은 현재 확보된 자유화 수준까지 잠식하는 내용을 담고 있음.

  0 카나다: 서비스 협정적용 범위에 대하 오해로 인하여 불필요한 사항에 대한 MFN 일탈을 신청한 사례가 있음.

  조세문제 및 SCHEDULING 관련 기술적 사항을 명확히할 필요가 있음.

  0 스웨덴: MFN 일탈 관련 국내법규의 내용, 일탈기간, MFN 일탈의 수혜국가, 미래의 조치에 대한 MFN 일탈 여부등 추가정보가 필요함.

  상호주의 조치에 대한 MFN 일탈 신청은 협상수단으로 활용코자 하는 것으로서 수용하기 곤란함.

  - 본직은 MFN 일탈관련 그경제적 영향 및 협정의 기본원칙 침해 가능성등 현상황에 대하여 우려를 표명하고 아국은 타국과는 달러 INITIAL COMMITMENTS 에있어서도 '86.9 이후 추진한 많은 자발적 자유화 조치와 추가 자유화 계획까지OFFER 에 반영하였음을 상기시키고 다른 국가들로 부터 이에 상응하는 기여가 없을 경우 자유화 약속수준의 축소와 MFN 일탈의 추가 신청까지 고려하겠다고 함.

  0 또한 상호주의 조치에 대한 MFN 일탈이 억제되어야 한다는 점과 항공부속서, 협정 제 34 조(정의)에 대한 작업이 조속히 마무리 되어야 한다고 하는 한편UR 협상의 성공을 위하여 각국이 자유화약속의 최대화와 MFN 일탈의 최소화를 위해 노력하여야 할것이라고 함.

(발언문 별첨)

3. 향후 작업계획

- 의장은 금일회의 결과에 대하여 방대한 서비스분야 배제 및 MFN 일탈 신청내용에 대하여 많은 나라가 우려를 표명하는등 부정적 측면이 많이 부각되었으며 개인적으로 최근의 협상진전상황이 실망스러운 것이라고 평가한다고 하는 한편 다음주까지 INITIAL COMMITMENTS 와 MFN 일탈에 관한 집중적인 양자협상을 계속하고 4.3(금) 최종평가회의를 개최하자고 제의함.

O 그러나 EC 가 현상황에서 차기 GNS 회의 일정을 정하는 것을 부적절하다고 강력히 반발하였으며 의장은 원칙적으로 4.3(금)로 정해놓고 추가협의를 거쳐확정하겠다고 함.

- 또한 의장은 지금까지 기술적 과제에 대한 충분한 협의를 진행하지 못했다고 밝히고 향후 수일간 동과제(21 조, 34 조, 항공부속서, 통신부속서, SCHEDULING)에 대한 협의를 추진하겠다고 함.

4. 관찰 및 평가

- 각국의 MFN 일탈 신청내용을 취합한 결과 일부국가의 신청사항은 그내용이 불명확하여 이를 구체화하는 작업이 필요할 뿐만 아니라 상호 연계되어 있는 미국의 4 개분야에 대한 TOTAL DEROGATION 과 다른 국가의 자유화 약속수준문제를 해결하기 위하여는 상당한 시일이 소요될것으로 예상되며 우선 협상진행의 MODALITY 를 정하는 것도 어려운 과제로 등장할 것으로 전망됨.

첨부: 아국발언문 1 부

(GVW(F)-0214). 끝

(대사 박수길-국장)

주 제 네 바 대 표 부

번 호 : GVW(F) - 0214 년월일 : 2-0326 시간 : 1600

수 신 : 장 관 (통기. 경기원. 재무부. 법무부. 농수산부. 상공부. 건설부. 보사부. 노동부. 교통부. 체신부. 문화부. 공보처. 과기처. 항만청)

발 신 : 주 제네바대사

제 목 : '첨부'

보 안 통 제	

총 5 매 (표지포함)

외신국 통 제	

214-5-1

0074

This morning I listened with great interest and attention to the statements by many delegations, in particular, those fascinated by the humorous, but friendly clashes of two titans. Although I have no intention of taking sides, I feel compelled to offer an assessment.

Services, as we are well aware, is among the most successful areas of the Uruguay Round negotiations. We are hopeful that this will remain so, despite the possible negative influence stemming from other negotiating areas, in particular agriculture.

However, when I looked at the list of MFN derogations submitted to the Secretariat thus far, I could not help but feel that even the services negotiations have been adversely affected by developments in other fields. In terms of the infringement of the basic principle of MFN, and the significant economic impact those derogations could have on world trade in services in general, I am worried at what would happen if those derogations are left intact.

Today's meeting has a special importance because we are here not only to conduct a multilateral stock-taking of the negotiations on initial commitments and MFN exemptions, but also to consolidate the basis for the successful conclusion of the Round.

Mr. Chairman, since the 13 January TNC Meeting, my delegation has actively participated in bilateral negotiations on initial commitments. Despite some progress in these negotiations, my delegation is not encouraged by the results of the negotiations on initial commitments, and the recent developments in MFN exemptions.

0075

I would also like to draw your particular attention to the fact
that since September 1986 when the Uruguay Round negotiations
were launched, Korea has continuously pursued the unilateral
liberalization of its services sector. In particular, Korea has
undertaken a great number of liberalization measures in its
financial services sector. All of these measures are reflected
in Korea's revised offer as binding commitments.

Korea believes that initial commitments should not merely be a
transplant of current regulatory regimes into offers. For this
reason, Korea has made a number of advanced liberalization
commitments, with specific time schedules. While most of the
participants' offers merely reflect existing levels of market
access, Korea is offering more than just standstill, it is
offering a roll back in substantial terms.

Moving to the issue of MFN exemptions, I share the concern
expressed by other speakers over the consequences of unregulated
MFN exemptions. It is easy to foresee the difficulty of applying
MFN in areas where multilateral disciplines have not operated.
In this regard, MFN exemptions of a limited nature, both in terms
of their scope and duration, may be inevitable for certain
measures. However, unlimited derogation from MFN for a whole
service sector would significantly undermine the multilateral
mechanism for trade in services. Any exemptions from MFN should
be confined to specific measures.

It will be difficult for any country to maintain an initial
commitment in any service sector where total derogation from MFN
is sought by other participants. Specifically, Korea doubts
whether it could accept a total derogation from MFN in maritime
transport, air transport, basic telecommunications and financial
services.

Seeking MFN exemptions for reciprocity measures should also be
discouraged. They are mainly based on commercial considerations
imposed to balance trade, rather than on strong historical

2

216-5-3

reasons and geographical specificities. I appreciate that a number of participants have refrained from seeking MFN exemptions for these measures. Korea is one of those countries.

However, my delegation will reconsider its contributions, and may reduce the level of it commitments and increase its request for MFN exemptions, if equivalent contributions are not matched by its trading partners.

On the measures presumed by some participants to fall outside the scope of the General Agreement on Trade in Services, my delegation encourages the parties concerned to submit the precise content of these measures to the Secretariat as soon as possible. While these measures are largely supposed to be outside the scope of the GATS, it is necessary to examine their exact nature and content, and their implications on trade in services.

Concerning the matters for which technical work is still needed, it is urgent that we resolve the remaining issues, particularly with respect to the Annex on Air Transport, and the Article 34 Definitions.

Due to the lack of a common understanding among trading partners on the issues before us, we have had great difficulty in preparing our revised offer and engaging in bilateral negotiations on initial commitments. Nevertheless, I would like to stress that the Korean government places great importance on bringing the services negotiations to fruition.

Unfortunately, in light of developments that have or have not taken place in the past few weeks, we feel compelled to put ourselves, at least at this moment, on the side of the pessimists concerning the prospects for the Round. However, it is not too late to restore our optimism. In this regard, let me emphasize the following suggestions.

3

2-14-5-4

Now is the moment for constructive action from all participants. Not one of us is interested in seeing the failure of the Round, and no one is ready for the serious consequences of such a failure.

As the Australian delegate pointed out, the package we seek must be the maximum one, and derogations should be limited to the necessary minimum.

Our offers should be credible and substantial in both content and scope. This is one of the most convincing means to contribute to the success of the Round.

4

외 무 부

종 별 :

번 호 : GVW-0694   일 시 : 92 0327 1900

수 신 : 장 관(통기)

발 신 : 주 제네바 대사

제 목 : UR/GNS 회의

    연: GVW-0668

    연호 보고한 아국 발언문안에 3.25(수) GNS 회의시 본직 발언 내용과 일부 상이한
점이있어 수정안을 보고하니 참고 바람.

    첨부: 3.25 GNS 회의시 아국 발언문 1부

    (GVW(F)-224)

    (대사 박수길-국장)

통상국

PAGE 1   92.03.28   06:04 DS

외신 1과 통제관

0079

주 제 네 바 대 표 부

번 호 : GVW(F) - 0224   년월일 : 20327   시간 : 1800

수 신 : 장 관 (통기)

발 신 : 주 제네바대사

제 목 :

GVW-6PX 회복

총 5 매(드지프함)

보안 통제	

외신과 통제	

（도표 영역）

224-5-1

0080

1992-03-27 19:42 KOREAN MISSION GENEVA 2 022 791 0525 P.01

This morning I listened with great interest and attention to the statements by many delegations, in particular, I was fascinated by the clashes of two titans, the two major trading countries, if in a friendly and humorous manner. Although I have no intention of taking sides, I feel compelled to offer an assessment from the point of principle.

Services, as we are well aware, is among the most successful areas of the Uruguay Round negotiations. We are hopeful that this will remain so, despite the possible negative influence stemming from other negotiating areas, in particular agriculture.

However, when I looked at the list of MFN derogations submitted to the Secretariat thus far, I could not help but feel that even the services negotiations have been adversely affected by developments in other fields. In terms of the infringement of the basic principle of MFN, and the significant economic impact those derogations could have on world trade in services in general, I am worried at what would happen if those derogations are left intact.

Mr. Chairman, since the 13 January TNC Meeting, my delegation has actively participated in bilateral negotiations on initial commitments. Despite some progress in these negotiations, my delegation is not encouraged by the results of the negotiations on initial commitments, and the recent developments in MFN exemptions.

I would also like to draw your particular attention to the fact that since September 1986 when the Uruguay Round negotiations were launched, Korea has continuously pursued the unilateral liberalization of its services sector. In particular, Korea has

0081

undertaken a great number of liberalizati   measures in its
financial servic   sector. All of these measures are reflected
in Korea's revised offer as binding commitments.

Korea believes that initial commitments should not merely be a
transplant of current regulatory regimes into offers. For this
reason, Korea has made a number of advanced liberalization
commitments, with specific time schedules. While most of the
participants' offers merely reflect existing levels of market
access, Korea is offering more than just standstill, it is
offering a roll back in substantial terms.

Moving to the issue of MFN exemptions, I share the concern
expressed by other speakers over the consequences of unregulated
MFN exemptions. It is easy to foresee the difficulty of applying
MFN in areas where multilateral disciplines have not operated.
In this regard, MFN exemptions of a limited nature, both in terms
of their scope and duration, may be inevitable for certain
measures. However, unlimited derogation from MFN for a whole
service sector would significantly undermine the multilateral
mechanism for trade in services. Any exemptions from MFN should
be confined to specific measures.

It will be difficult for any country to maintain an initial
commitment in any service sector where total derogation from MFN
is sought by other participants. Specifically, Korea doubts
whether it could accept a total derogation from MFN in maritime
transport, air transport, basic telecommunications and financial
services.

Seeking MFN exemptions for reciprocity measures should also be
discouraged. They are mainly based on commercial considerations
imposed to balance trade, rather than on strong historical
reasons and geographical specificities. I appreciate that a
number of participants have refrained from seeking MFN exemptions
for these measures. Korea is one of those countries.

2

224-5-3

1992-03-27   19:42   KOREAN MISSION GENEVA   2 022 791 0525   P.03

0082

314   우루과이라운드 서비스 분야 양허 협상 1

However, my delegation will reconsider its contribution, and may reduce the level of it commitments and increase its request for MFN exemptions, if equivalent contributions are not matched by its trading partners.

On the measures presumed by some participants to fall outside the scope of the General Agreement on Trade in Services, my delegation encourages the parties concerned to submit the precise content of these measures to the Secretariat as soon as possible. While these measures are largely supposed to be outside the scope of the GATS, it is necessary to examine their exact nature and content, and their implications on trade in services.

Concerning the matters for which technical work is still needed, it is urgent that we resolve the remaining issues, particularly with respect to the Annex on Air Transport, and the Article 34 Definitions.

Due to the lack of a common understanding among trading partners on the issues before us, we have had great difficulty in preparing our revised offer and engaging in bilateral negotiations on initial commitments. Nevertheless, I would like to stress that the Korean government places great importance on bringing the services negotiations to fruition.

Unfortunately, in light of developments that have or have not taken place in the past few weeks, we feel compelled to place ourselves, at least at this moment, on the side of the pessimists concerning the prospects for the Round. However, it is not too late to restore our optimism. In this regard, let me emphasize the following.

Now is the moment for every participant to be constructive. None of us is interested in seeing the failure of the Round. We all have a great stake in the success of the Round. No one is ready for the serious consequences of a failure.

3

0083

As the Australian delegate pointed out, the package we seek must be the maximum one, and derogations should be limited to the necessary minimum.

Our offers should be credible and substantial in both content and scope. This is one of the most convincing means to contribute to the success of the Round.

0084

외 무 부

종 별 :

번 호 : GVW-0697 일 시 : 92 0327 1930

수 신 : 장 관(통기,통이,통삼,경기원,재무부,체신부)

발 신 : 주 제네바 대사

제 목 : UR/서비스협상

　　3.26(목) 배부된 미국의 금융분야 수정 OFFER 와 스웨덴의 통신분야 수정 OFFER 를 별첨송부함.

　　첨부: 1. 미국의 수정 OFFER 1부

　　2. 스웨덴의 수정 OFFER 1부,(GVW(F)-226).끝

　　(대사 박수길-국장)

통상국　　통상국　　통상국　　체신부　　경기원　　재무부

‖

주 제 네 바 대 표 부

| 번 호 | GVW(F) - 226 | 년월일 : 20324 | 시간 : 1400 |

수 신 장   관 (통기.통이.통산.경기원.재무부.체신부)

발 신 주 제네바대사

제 목

Gvw-6P7 전방

송 9 매 (포지프합)

브 안 봉 제	

의신과 통 제	

226-P-1

0086

MULTILATERAL TRADE
NEGOTIATIONS
THE URUGUAY ROUND

RESTR**IIII**D
MTN.GNS/W/112/Rev.1/Add.1
26 March 1992
Special Distribution

Group of Negotiations on Services

Original: English

COMMUNICATION FROM THE UNITED STATES OF AMERICA

Revised Conditional Offer of The United States
in Banking and Other Financial Services (Excluding Insurance)
Based on the Understanding in Financial Services

Addendum

The following pages replace and cancel pages 22-23 of
MTN.GNS/W/112/Rev.1.

This offer is based on the Articles of Agreement to the General Agreement on Trade in Services (the Framework), the Annex on Financial Services (the Annex), and the Understanding on Commitments in Financial Services (the Understanding) contained in the 20 December 1991 document MTN.TNC/W/FA. Pursuant to these documents, the market access obligations of the Understanding have been adopted as an alternative to the market access obligations of the Framework. The cross-border, movement of consumer, commercial presence, and movement of personnel obligations of the Understanding thus substitute for the corresponding obligations of the Framework.

This offer is intended to represent a standstill with respect to federal, state, and local measures in the United States banking and securities sectors pursuant to the Understanding. Non-governmental organizations and associations are bound only to the extent set out in paragraph 2 of the Understanding's national treatment provisions.

This revised offer should be read in conjunction with the U.S. exemption from Article II with respect to financial services, and is conditional on receiving adequate liberalization commitments from other Parties. The offer is also subject to technical changes, in particular changes needed to conform reservations to the obligations in the Understanding with the provisions of the Framework. Consistent with paragraph 2 of the Annex, future and existing prudential measures do not constitute restrictions on market access or national treatment and are thus not scheduled as such.

GATT SECRETARIAT
UR-92-0051

0087

228-A-2

SERVICE SECTOR	TERMS, LIMITATIONS AND CONDITIONS OF MARKET ACCESS[1]	CONDITIONS AND QUALIFICATIONS ON NATIONAL TREATMENT[2]
COMMERCIAL BANKS	**Federal Measures - Subsidiaries**	
	The National Bank Act generally requires that all the directors of a national bank be citizens unless a national bank is an affiliate or subsidiary of a foreign bank, in which case only a majority of the board need be citizens.	
	The Bank Holding Company Act of 1956 and the International Banking Act of 1978 require a potential host state to expressly authorize a foreign bank with a bank subsidiary or domestic deposit-taking branch in another State to own additional bank subsidiaries within the host state. Under this authority, some states do not permit foreign banks to own subsidiaries in their territory on the same basis as domestic bank holding companies from the foreign bank's "home state".	
	A majority of the shares of an Edge corporation (specialized international banking companies chartered under Federal law) can be owned by domestically owned banks and domestically owned non-bank companies willing to restrict their business activities to those closely related to banking. Majority ownership of an Edge corporation by a non-U.S. person is limited to foreign banks and U.S. subsidiaries of foreign banks. Other foreign persons may directly or indirectly own only a minority of the shares of an Edge corporation.	
	Federal Measures - Branches and Agencies	
	The International Banking Act defers to express state law prohibitions on the establishment of a Federal branch or agency.	
	Under the International Banking Act, foreign banks that are engaged directly or indirectly in taking domestic deposits in one state through a subsidiary or branch, can expand directly into another host state only through limited branches or agencies, and only as expressly permitted by the host state laws. State-chartered bank subsidiaries that are not members of the Federal Reserve System are not subject to this prohibition (all other U.S. bank subsidiaries are).	

226(-9-)

1992-03-27 20:21 KOREAN MISSION GENEVA   2 822 ... .   P.04

0089

SERVICE SECTOR	TERMS, LIMITATIONS AND CONDITIONS OF MARKET ACCESS[1]	CONDITIONS AND QUALIFICATIONS ON NATIONAL TREATMENT[2]
COMMERCIAL BANKS (continued)		Federal Measures - Branches and Agencies
		Under the Federal Deposit Insurance Corporation Improvement Act of 1991, foreign bank branches are prohibited from taking insured deposits unless they were engaged in that activity on 19 December 1991.
		Foreign bank branches and agencies in the United States are required to register under the Investment Advisers Act of 1940, while domestic banks are exempt from registration.
		Foreign banks with branches and agencies in the United States cannot be members of the Federal Reserve System, and may thus not vote for board members of local reserve banks. Foreign-owned subsidiaries in the United States can be members.
		The United States internal Revenue Service does not permit stand-by letters of credit issued by foreign bank branches and agencies to be used as security for tax liabilities for cross-border insurance activities.
	Other Federal Measures	
	Corporations owned by foreign governments are not exempt from the Bank Holding Company Act, while corporations owned by the Federal or state governments are exempt.	

221-P-4

0090

SERVICE SECTOR	TERMS, LIMITATIONS AND CONDITIONS OF MARKET ACCESS[1]	CONDITIONS AND QUALIFICATIONS ON NATIONAL TREATMENT[2]
COMMERCIAL BANKS (continued)	State Measures - All Forms of Commercial Presence Certain states prohibit foreign ownership of state-chartered subsidiaries either through interpretation, express bar, or definition of eligible holding company. Certain states maintain terms, limitations and qualifications on market access by foreign bank branches and agencies through: (1) expressly prohibiting any state or Federal license for those offices in their territory; (2) not providing for state licensing of such offices; (3) limiting the location or deposit-taking activities of such offices on terms less favourable than those applicable to state bank subsidiaries; or (4) application of a reciprocity test on establishment. Certain states do not provide representative offices in their territory. Other existing state measures may impose terms, limitations and conditions of market access.	Certain state measures impose conditions and qualifications on national treatment, including the ineligibility of foreign banks for an exemption from state broker-dealer registration statues.
LENDING SERVICES	Foreign-owned firms are not entitled to extend credits backed by guarantees backed by the Overseas Private Investment Corporation.	
SECURITIES AND COMMODITIES SERVICES[4]	Federal law prohibits the offering of futures on onions, options on onions, and options on futures on onions.	The Primary Dealers Act of 1988 prohibits a foreign firm from being designated as a primary dealer in U.S. government debt obligations if U.S. firms are denied the same competitive opportunities as domestic firms in the underwriting or distribution of government debt instruments in the firm's home country.
ALL OTHER FINANCIAL SERVICES	No terms, limitations and conditions.	No conditions and qualifications.

NOTES

1. Because the Understanding is adopted as an alternative approach to Part III of the Framework, the terms, limitations and conditions of market access listed in this offer relate to provisions of the Understanding; the provisions of Article XVI of the Framework are not addressed.

It is understood that the institutional framework of a Party's financial sector relating to the separation of financial activities does not constitute a market access restriction per se.

2. It is understood that the Framework's national treatment obligation, including "conditions of competition", has the following meaning:

(a) Each Party shall grant to financial service providers of any other Party, in the application of all measures, treatment no less favourable than that accorded to its financial service providers in like circumstances.

(b) A measure of a Party, whether such measure accords different or identical treatment, shall be deemed to be consistent with paragraph (a) only if it provides to financial service providers of any other Party equal competitive opportunities as are available to financial service providers of the Party in like circumstances. Equal competitive opportunities shall be deemed to exist where a measure does not disadvantage financial service providers of any other Party in their ability to compete as compared with the Party's financial service providers in like circumstances. In assessing equal competitive opportunities a principal factor will be the effect of a Party's measures. The absence of a significant market share in the territory of a Party by financial service providers of any other Party shall not in itself constitute denial of equal competitive opportunities.

It is further understood that certain language in Article XVII(3) of the Framework, (i.e. "modifies the conditions of competition") does not (1) exempt from the national treatment commitment any measure existing at the time of entry into force of the Agreement, even if no change is made in the measure, or (2) prevent a party from adopting a measure that alters in any way the conditions of competition, so long as such measure does not deny to financial service providers of another Party national treatment, as defined in paragraphs (a) and (b) of this note.

3. This offer is based on the assumption that it is not necessary to achieve non-discriminatory interstate banking restrictions in the United States. National treatment under the International Banking Act's application of interstate banking to foreign banks is determined according to a foreign bank's "home state". A foreign bank's home state is generally the first state in the United States where a foreign bank takes domestic deposits (either through a subsidiary or branch). National treatment is provided where a foreign bank from a particular home state is accorded no less favourable treatment than that accorded a domestic bank or bank holding company from the foreign bank's home state. A different approach to national treatment will require revisions to this offer.

4. The following illustrative prudential requirements are applicable to the regulation of commodities and securities services, and are provided for transparency purposes only: (1) instruments meeting the definition of futures and options under the Commodity Exchange Act must generally be offered on a recognized exchange; (2) service providers transacting securities or commodities business in the United States must generally be registered under United States laws; (3) securities must generally be registered before being offered in the United States.

MULTILATERAL TRADE NEGOTIATIONS
THE URUGUAY ROUND

RESTRICTED

MTN.TNC/W/59/Rev.1/Add.1
23 March 1992

Special Distribution

Trade Negotiations Committee

Original: English

COMMUNICATION FROM SWEDEN

Revised Conditional Offer by Sweden concerning Initial Commitments on Telecommunication Services

Addendum

The following communication is circulated at the request of the permanent delegation of Sweden to the members of the Group of Negotiations on Services.

This Addendum contains the revised offer by Sweden on telecommunications services.

This offer is very comprehensive. It covers all telecommunications services, including basic. Sweden offers to bind full market access and national treatment without limitations.

./.

GATT SECRETARIAT
UR-92-0055

226-P-8

0093

The following text shall replace the text on "telecommunications services" on page 14 of Sweden's revised offers, contained in document MTN.TNC/W/59/Rev.1:

	Article XVI (market access)	Article XVII (national treatment)
Telecommunications Services(*)	No limitations. BOUND	No limitations. BOUND

(*) New legislation, in accordance with this offer, under preparation and expected to enter into force in 1993.

주 제 네 바 대 표 부 '92 3. 27

20, Route de Pre-Bois, POB 566 / (022) 791-0111 / (022) 791-0525(FAX)

문서번호 제네(경) 20644-339

시행일자 1992. 3. 27.

수신 장관

참조 통상국장,

경제기획원장관 (대외경제조정실장)

제목 UR/서비스 협상(MFN)

선 결			지 시		
접	일자 시간		결 재		
수	번호	18623	공		
	처리과		람		
	담당자	(서명)			

3.18 배부된 21개국의 MFN 일탈 신청 목록에 이어 3.24 배부된 베닌과 중국의 MFN 일탈 신청 목록을 별첨 송부합니다.

첨부 : 베닌과 중국의 MFN 일탈 신청 목록 1부.   끝.

주 제 네 바 대 사

0095

In accordance with the Informal Note by the Chairman of the GNS
circulated on 30 January 1992, the secretariat circulated a draft list of
intentions in respect to m.f.n. exemptions for individual participants on
18 March 1992. As indicated in the note of 30 January 1992, these lists
are being made available on a confidential basis to all those participants
who have presented offers.

Since the circulation of the list on 18 March 1992, the following
additional draft lists on m.f.n. exemptions have been received:

Benin
China

These draft lists are also being made available on a confidential basis to
those participants that have made offers.

In addition, a corrigendum to the Canadian draft list of m.f.n.
exemptions as contained in the document of 18 March 1992 is being
circulated at the request of the Canadian Government.

Also attached is an additional request from the Delegation of Uruguay.

50-MISC4
0096

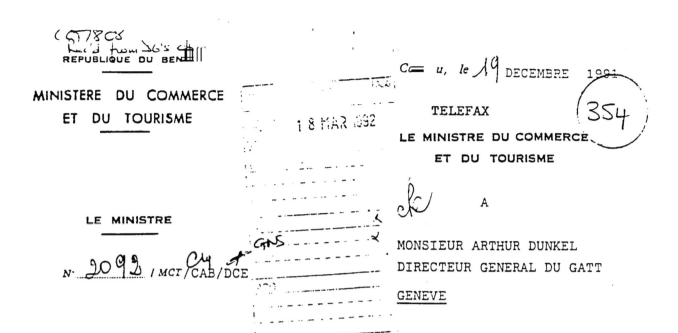

RÉPUBLIQUE DU BÉNIN

MINISTÈRE DU COMMERCE
ET DU TOURISME

1 8 MAR 1992

C= u, le 19 DECEMBRE 1991

TELEFAX

LE MINISTRE DU COMMERCE
ET DU TOURISME

(354)

LE MINISTRE

N° 2093 / MCT / CAB / DCE

GNS

A

MONSIEUR ARTHUR DUNKEL
DIRECTEUR GENERAL DU GATT

GENEVE

Monsieur le Directeur Général,

Le Secrétariat du GATT a souhaité connaître les besoins des Etats
membres, en termes de dérogations, à l'application de la Clause de
la Nation la plus favorisée, dans le cadre du projet d'accord GATS su
les services.

J'ai l'honneur de porter à votre connaissance que la politique de la
République du Bénin en matière de transports maritimes, repose sur
l'application du Code de Conduite des Conférences Maritimes.

Cette Convention de l'Organisation des Nations Unies, signée le 6
Avril 1974 et entrée en vigueur en 1983, constitue l'instrument indispensable permettant aux pays en voie de développement de participer
aux trafics maritimes générés par leur commerce extérieur. Elle constitue aussi un moyen irremplaçable de coopération Nord-Sud puisque,
tout en privilégiant les compagnies maritimes nationales des pays
importateurs, elle ne néglige pas la participation des armements des
pays tiers à ce trafic.

En ce domaine, l'application mécanique de la Clause de la Nation la
plus favorisée remettrait en cause la possibilité, pour les pays en
voie de développement, d'accéder aux activités des transporteurs maritimes.

Afin de ne pas écarter, de manière sûre et définitive, les pays en
voie de développement du secteur du transport maritime, il faut admet-
tre que le Code de Conduite des Conférences Maritimes soit une dérogation à la Clause de la Nation la plus favorisée.

. . . / . . .

0097

Est-il nécessaire de rappeler que la portée, l'intérêt et la validité
du Code, en son entier, ont été réaffirmés dans une Résolution du
7 Juin 1991, à l'issue d'une Conférence de Révision qui s'est tenue
à GENEVE pendant plusieurs mois et à laquelle un certain nombre de
parties non contractantes ont participé.

Je souhaite donc vivement que la demande de dérogation que je présen-
te, au nom du Gouvernement du BENIN soit retenue. Elle conditionne
l'existence même de nos armements nationaux et la réalisation de la
politique maritime que mon pays s'est fixée.

Je vous prie de croire, Monsieur le Directeur Général, à l'assurance
de mes salutations distinguées.

AMPLIATION

M. JIRAMILLO
Président du Groupe de Négociations
sur les Services.

BERNARD HOUEGNON.-

0098

MISSION PERMANENTE DE LA RÉPUBLIQUE POPULAIRE DE CHINE
A GENÈVE

11, CHEMIN DE SURVILLE - 1213 PETIT-LANCY, GENÈVE
TÉL. (022) 92 25 48

23 March, 1992

Dear Ambassador,

In accordance with the procedures agreed by the GNS, I submit herewith to you China's draft list of intentions with respect to MFN exemptions.

The draft list is a non-exhaustive list due to variety of service sectors and complexity of measures affecting trade in services. China reserves its right to modify and add to this draft list of intentions with respect to MFN exemptions in the course of negotiations.

Please accept the renewed assurances of my highest consideration.

Wang Tiance
Minister-Counsellor
Deputy Permanent Representative
Permanent Mission of P. R. China

H. E. Mr. Felipe Jaramillo
Chairman
Group of Negotiations on Services
GATT
Centre William Rappard
154, rue de Lausanne
1211 Geneva 21

0099

DRAFT LIST OF INTENTIONS WITH RESPECT TO MFN EXEMPTIONS OF THE PEOPLE'S REPUBLIC OF CHINA

Measures adopted relating to trade in services to which Article II of the GATS is not applicable

A. Bilateral agreements on the promotion and reciprocal protection of investments

1.Description of Measure

As of February 1992, China has signed thirty-three agreements on the promotion and reciprocal protection of investments with foreign countries, twenty-three of which have come into effect. These agreements provides that one contracting party shall recognize subrogation of the other contracting party to the rights of the investors and the litigation rights. Such subrogation rights are normally not accorded to countries without agreements on the promotion and reciprocal protection of investments with China.

2. Intended Duration of Exemptions

Subject to the effective duration of the agreements concerned.

B. Bilateral agreements for the avoidance of double taxation and the prevention of fiscal evasion

1. Description of Measure

0100

As of August 1991, China has signed thirty-two agreements for the avoidance of double taxation and the prevention of fiscal evasion with respect to taxes on income, twenty-six of which have come into effect. The favourable taxation treatment under these agreements are normally not accorded to countries without such taxation agreements with China. These favourable taxation measures include that both contracting parties adopt limited rates of withholding tax imposed in the contracting states in which income arises, that income of service providers from both contracting parties shall be favorably taxed, that reduced or exempted taxes by one contracting state in which income arises shall be credited as paid taxes in calculation of income taxes in the other contracting state of residence, and also that both contracting states accord mutually to each other's nationals or permanent establishments no less favourable treatment than that accorded to their own nationals or permanent establishments in respect of income tax.

2. Intended Duration of Exemptions

Subject to the effective duration of the agreements concerned.

C. Bilateral memorandum of consultation on shipping

1. Description of Measure

The party concerned may establish entities in China either as joint ventures or wholly-owned subsidiaries subject to the Chinese laws on joint and sole ventures for ships owned or operated by the carriers of the party concerned or for cargo moving under the carriers' bill of lading or tariff. The party concerned may engage in direct business activities including: to solicit and book cargo; prepare, authenticate, process and issue bills of lading; assess, collect, remit freight and other charges; negotiate and enter into services contracts; and contract for

0101

handling and ancillary services.

2. Intended Duration of Exemptions

Unforeseeable at present stage.

3. Justification

According to present state of trade transport between signatories.

D. Bilateral agreements on maritime transport

1. Description of Measure

   (i)   Agreements on exemption granted from tax.

   (ii)   Agreements on 50% Cargo sharing

   (iii)   Agreements on no less than one third cargo sharing

2. Intended Duration of Exemptions

Subject to the effective duration of the agreements concerned.

3. Justification

According to present state of trade transport between signatories.

0102

March 12, 1992

Exemptions for the Most-Favoured-Nation Treatment Obligation

. Attached is Canada's preliminary list of necessary
exemptions from the obligations of Article II:1, as
provided for under Article II:2. Canada reserves the
right to add, amend or delete entries.

. There are, in addition, some other areas where further
discussion would be warranted as to whether and how the
most-favoured-nation treatment obligation would apply.
This could include activities which might be outside
the scope of the multilateral trade negotiations or of
the GATS, for example access to maritime port services
by fishing vessels, or where work in the legal
rectification process ("track three") may have
implications. Canada reserves the right to modify its
proposed exemptions list in light of such further
consideration.

. The final list of MFN exemptions is conditional upon a
balanced and equitable overall package, comprising:

(a) general acceptance of the GATS as negotiated,
including its sectoral annexes and its
relationship to the new Multilateral Trade
Organization;

(b) appropriate market access commitments by other MTN
participants; and,

(c) an acceptable set of MFN exemptions by other MTN
participants.

. In addition, it will be necessary to consider whether
exemptions may be required pertaining to air
transportation services (air traffic rights and
directly related services including marketing and
selling services and computer reservations services)
and financial services (including reciprocity
provisions of Canadian legislation, and other
discriminatory measures, concerning financial
services), in the light of the final disposition of
negotiations in these sectors.

0103

The Permanent Mission of Canada
to the United Nations

La Mission Permanente du Canada
auprès des Nations Unies

1, rue du Pré-de-la-Bichette
1202 Geneva

March 20, 1992

Mr. Gary Sampson
Director
Negotiating Group on Services
GATT
Centre William Rappard
154, rue de Lausanne
1211 Geneva 21

Dear Mr. Sampson,

     Please substitute the attached as replacement for the first page of our submission.

     I would be grateful if it could be recirculated as soon as possible.

Yours sincerely,

François Nadeau
Counsellor

0104

Ginebra, 17 de marzo de 1992

La Delegación del Uruguay presenta sus más atentos saludos al Señor Presidente del Grupo de Negociaciones de Servicios y tiene el placer de referirse a la comunicación que le fue cursada el pasado 6 de marzo del corriente con respecto a la intención del Gobierno del Uruguay de invocar el artículo II:2 del Acuerdo sobre Servicios relativo a las exenciones a la cláusula de Nación Más Favorecida.

En tal sentido la Delegación del Uruguay desea hacer las siguientes precisiones a la lista de Acuerdos de Promoción y Protección de Inversiones indicada en la referida comunicación.

Debe adicionarse a la lista el Acuerdo suscrito con Polonia en agosto de 1991. Por otra parte los acuerdos con Francia y España aún se encuentran en proceso de negociación por lo que deben figurar como en negociación.

La Delegación del Uruguay aprovecha la oportunidad para reiterar al Señor Presidente las seguridades de su más distinguida consideración.

Embajador Felipe Jaramillo
Presidente del Grupo de Servicios
GINEBRA

0105

외 무 부

종   별 :

번   호 : GVW-0714   일   시 : 92 0331 1600

수   신 : 장 관(통기,통이,통삼,경기원,재무부,법무부,상공부,농수부,공보처,과기처

발   신 : 주 제네바 대사   건설부,보사부,노동부,교통부,체신부,문화부,항만청)

제   목 : UR/서비스 협상

   . 3.31.(화) 당관에 전달된 카나다 및 아이슬랜드,스리랑카의 대 아국 서비스분야
REQUEST 를 별첨송부함.

     첨부: 1. 카나다의 REQUEST 1 부

     2. 아이스랜드의 REQUEST 1부

     3. 스리랑카의 REQUEST 1부, 끝

     (GVW(F)-234)

     (대사 박수길-국장)

첨부물 필요시 원본부서에 요청 바람

통상국	통상국	통상국	보사부	문화부	교통부	체신부	경기원	재무부
농수부	상공부	건설부	노동부	과기처	해항청	공보처	법무부	

PAGE 1   92.04.01   01:26 FN

외신 1과 통제관

0106

주 제 네 바 대 표 부

종 30   매 (표지포함)

보 안
등 재

의 신 부
등 재

GVW-114 의 첨부

The Permanent Mission of Canada
to the United Nations

La Mission Permanente du Canada
auprès des Nations Unies

1, rue du Pré-de-la-Bichette
1202 Geneva

March 27, 1992

H.E. Mr. S. G. Park
Ambassador
Permanent Representative to GATT
Permanent Mission of the Republic of Korea
20, route de Pré-Bois
1216 Cointrin

Excellency,

I refer to the exchange of views we had on March 20 concerning the Uruguay Round initial commitments negotiations in Services, which has served to foster a better understanding of our mutual positions.

As I underlined in our meeting it is now urgent for a number of participants, in the interest of a successful Round, to improve the existing package of services commitments. My government has made a major effort in the form of the revised Canadian offer of February 14, which includes extensive coverage and a high level of bindings for sectors, coverage of the regulatory regimes of the Canadian provinces and a general commitment on temporary movement of service providers.

The revised Korean offer is more in keeping with the importance of Korea's services economy and international trade. Given the effect of this offer on other countries' offers, we think further improvements, particularly in financial services and temporary movement of service providers, would have an important overall effect. With respect to financial services, we request:

234-30-2

0108

- 2 -

—   a commitment to secure and improve the access of foreign
    banks to local currency funding. In this regard, Korea
    should maintain the recent suspension of the swap reduction
    plan, ensuring equitable access to all foreign banks, and
    should consider further increases of ceilings on the
    issuance of Certificates of Deposits. We are also concerned
    that domestic banks of certain countries are permitted to
    engage in trust activities (another source of funding) in
    Korea while others, such as Canadian banks, are not.

—   the removal of measures which require foreign banks to
    channel a high percentage of loans to higher risk categories
    of companies (eg. the rule that 35% of total lending be
    allocated to designated small and medium-sized companies.
    Moreover the 20% limit on the amount of lending to a single
    borrower further raises the cost of doing business.

—   commitment that authorization for multiple bank branching
    within the Korean market and the licencing of foreign
    insurance companies be based on clear criteria and
    transparent procedures.

    Further, as a result of discussions during the
bilateral meeting of our delegations on February 27, we
understand that, while there is no prohibition on US dollar loans
outside Korea, there are still extreme constraints on US dollar
loans to Korean entities in Korea and, for practical purposes, a
prohibition on new US dollar loans to Koreans in Korea. I would
request that this additionnal information be examined and, as the
case may be, that an appropriate commitment be made to lift those
restrictions.

    With respect to Korea's requests of Canada on financial
services, I understand that most of those have been clarified
during the last bilateral meeting of our negotiators. Our
negotiating team will be prepared to respond to the outstanding
requests when our two countries next meet.

    With respect to the temporary movement of service
providers, I note the significance of your revised offer but wish
to stress the following: (1) that the binding apply across the
board as is the case in our offer, not only for those sectors
where commercial presence commitments are made; (2) that Korea
make an offer on entry for service sellers.

0109

234-30-3

- 3 -

On business services, we would like to see the
following sub-sectors on offer: services incidental to
agriculture and forestry, fishing and mining (CPC 881, 882, 883).

On maritime transportation, you will be aware that
Canada and a number of other countries are working to encourage a
critical mass of participants to make commitments on maritime
transport along the substantive lines of the Nordic paper. We
would hope that Korea will make similar commitments.

I trust that the above will be useful for your
consideration.

Yours sincerely,

Gerald E. Shannon
Ambassador
Permanent Representative

236-30-X

0110

Tel. Nos.: 734 93 40
734 93 49
Telex No: 14188
Telefax : 734 90 04

My ref.: UN/GATT/18/11
Yr ref.:

CONSULATE GENERAL OF THE DEMOCRATIC SOCIALIST REPUBLIC OF SRI LANKA IN SWITZERLAND.

56, rue de Moillebeau
1211 Geneva 19

19 March 1992

H.E. Mr. Soo Gil Park
Ambassador/Permanent Representative to GATT
Permanent Mission of the Rep. of Korea
Rte de Pré-Bois 20
1216 Cointrin

Dear Ambassador,

In accordance with procedures agreed upon by the Group of Negotiations on Services, Sri Lanka submits herewith its Initial Requests to all participants in the Uruguay Round negotiations on Trade in Services. These requests are for liberalization commitments in sectors and sub-sectors of particular interest to Sri Lanka and removal of barriers to trade by way of restrictions on movement of relevant categories of personnel in these specific sectors and sub-sectors.

These requests may be modified or amended and additional requests may be made in the light of the negotiations.

Sri Lanka would appreciate the opportunity to discuss these requests with your Delegation at your earliest convenience.

Sri Lanka has already presented its Conditional Offer on Initial Commitments on Trade in Services in document No.MTN.GNS/W/148.

Yours sincerely,

L.P. Douglas Pemasiri
Permanent Representative to GATT

234-30-5

0111

Sri Lanka's Initial Requests on Trade in Services

Sri Lanka requests from all participants in the Uruguay Round commitments in the sectors and sub-sectors indicated below :

I.   Business Services

  1. Professional services
       (a) Accounting, auditing and book-keeping services
       (b) Architectural services
       (c) Engineering services

  2. Computer and related services

       (a) Software implementation services
       (b) Data processing services

  3. Other business services
       (a) Placement and supply services of personnel
       (b) Services incidental to agriculture, hunting and forestry
       (c) Services incidental to fishing
       (d) Services incidental to mining
       (e) Services incidental to manufacturing
       (f) Services incidental to maintenance and repair of equipment
       (g) Building-cleaning services
       (h) Packaging services
       (i) Printing and publishing services

II.   Construction and related engineering services

III. Environmental services
  1. Refuse-disposal services
  2. Sanitation and similar services

IV.   Tourism and travel-related services

      Hotel and restaurants, including catering, services

V.   Transport services
  1. Services auxiliary to all modes of transport
      Storage and warehouse services

234-20-6

0112

PERMANENT MISSION OF ICELAND

9-11, RUE DE VAREMBÉ - CH-1211 GENÉVE 20

Geneva, 26 March 1992

Dear Mr. Ambassador,

In accordance with the procedures agreed upon in the GNS, Iceland submits herewith its Initial General Requests to participants in the Uruguay Round negotiations on Trade in Services.

While we are fully aware of the fact that these requests are addressed to participants at a very late stage in the negotiations, we expect that due account be taken of Iceland's interests as reflected in this request list, in the preparation of final schedules of commitments.

Yours Sincerely,

Kjartan Jóhannsson

Permanent Representative
of Iceland to GATT

H.E. Ambassador Soo Gil Park
Permanent Mission of the Republic
of Korea to GATT
Route de Pré-Bois 20
1216 Cointrin

236-30-17   0113

March 24, 1992

ICELAND'S REQUESTS IN THE SERVICES NEGOTIATIONS

Attached is an initial list of Iceland's general requests in the services negotiations to complement initial offers as presented by negotiating partners in the GATS-Uruguay Round. Following is a description of the approach used to draft the requests:

1.   GENERAL REQUESTS

    Under the above mentioned heading Iceland requests all participants in the services negotiations to establish a minimum-level of liberalization in the horizontal-specific regulations that are stated under this item. It is also requested that all participants bind their commitments on national as well as sub-national levels.

2.   GENERAL SECTOR REQUESTS

    This part contains sector-specific requests which Iceland considers necessary in addition to any horizontal regulation mentioned under general requests (para 1).

    These requests consist mainly of two categories:

A.   Requests to other participants to eliminate "all sector-specific restrictions on commercial presence, cross-border supply and consumption abroad" as well as with regard to "full national treatment".

    This implies that any sector-specific restriction should be abolished.

B.   Requests where Iceland asks for "a binding commitment on the present level of Market Access on National Treatment in the sectors concerning commercial presence, cross-border supply and consumption abroad".

    This implies that any existing sector-specific restriction, should be bound at the present level.

234-30-8

0114

ICELAND'S GENERAL REQUESTS

APPLICABLE TO ALL SECTORS

Make a binding commitment, on national as well as sub-national levels, on your present level of Market Access and National Treatment concerning:

* foreign investment in commercial presence of a service supplier,
* foreign investment in real estate auxiliary to the free provision of services
* foreign exchange control (including profit remittances)

Bind your commitments on national as well as sub-national levels.

Furthermore, we are making the following additional sector-specific requests:

SECTOR	REQUEST

1. BUSINESS SERVICES

A. Professional services

a. Legal Services CPC 861

concerning advice on international law and for foreign legal consultance provided the legal adviser fulfils the home country's professional qualification conditions:

- eliminate all sector-specific restrictions on commercial presence, cross-border supply and consumption abroad
* provide full national treatment

234-30-A

2

Sector	Commitments
b. Accounting, auditing and book-keeping services CPC 862	concerning accounting, auditing and book-keeping services for foreign accounting firms/accountants, provided the accountant fulfils the host country's professional qualification conditions. * eliminate all sector-specific restrictions on commercial presence, cross-border supply and consumption abroad. * provide full national treatment (including removal of nationality requirements)
d. Architectural services, CPC 8671 e. Engineering consulting services CPC 8672	* eliminate all sector-specific restrictions on commercial presence, cross-border supply and consumption abroad * provide full national treatment (including removal of nationality requirements)
f. Integrated engineering services CPC 8673 g. Urban planning and landscape architectural services CPC 8674	* eliminate all sector-specific restrictions on commercial presence, cross-border supply and consumption abroad * provide full national treatment (including removal of nationality requirements)

3

h. Medical and dental services

* eliminate all sector-specific restrictions on commercial presence, cross-border supply and consumption abroad
  * provide full national treatment (including removal of nationality requirements)

i. Veterinary services

* provide full national treatment (including removal of nationality requirements)

B. Computer and Related Services
(including categories a,b,c,d,e,)

CPC 841-844,

* eliminate all sector-specific restrictions on commercial presence (except for processing of personal data), cross-border supply and consumption abroad
  * provide full national treatment (including removal of nationality requirements)

C. Research and Development Services
(including categories b,c,)

Make a binding commitment to eliminate all sector-specific restrictions in this sector concerning:

* commercial presence,
* cross-border supply and consumption abroad,
  and to:
* provide full national treatment (including removal of nationality requirements).

234-30-11

0118

D. Real Estate Services

a. Real estate services involving own or leased property

Make a binding commitment on the present level of Market Access and National Treatment in this sector concerning:

* commercial presence,
* cross-border supply and
* consumption abroad

b. On a Fee or Contract basis (822)

Make a binding commitment on the present level of Market Access and National Treatment in this sector concerning:

* commercial presence,
* cross-border supply and
* consumption abroad

E. Rental/Leasing Services without Operators

a. Relating to ships CPC 83103

Eliminate all sector-specific restrictions on

* commercial presence,
* cross-border supply and
* consumption abroad.

b. Relating to aircraft CPC 83104

Eliminate all sector-specific restrictions on

* commercial presence,
* cross-border supply and
* consumption abroad.

23K - 30 - 12

5

c. Relating to other transport equipment

Eliminate all sector-specific restrictions on

- commercial presence,
- cross-border supply and
- consumption abroad.

d. Relating to other machinery and equipment

Eliminate all sector-specific restrictions on

- commercial presence,
- cross-border supply and
- consumption abroad.

e. Other

Eliminate all sector-specific restrictions on

- commercial presence,
- cross-border supply and
- consumption abroad.

F. Other Business Services

a. Advertising services, CPC 871

- eliminate all sector-specific restrictions on commercial presence, cross-border supply and consumption abroad.
- provide full national treatment (including removal of nationality requirements)

23K~30~13

b. Market research
and public opinion
polling services
CPC 864

- eliminate all sector-specific restrictions on commercial presence, cross-border supply and consumption abroad
- provide full national treatment (including removal of nationality requirements)

c. Management consulting, CPC 865
d. Services rel. to man. consulting CPC 866

- eliminate all sector-specific restrictions on commercial presence, cross-border supply and consumption abroad
- provide full national treatment (including removal of national requirements)

d. Management consulting services

- eliminate all sector-specific restrictions on commercial presence, cross-border supply and consumption abroad
- provide full national treatment (including removal of national requirements)

e. Technical testing and analysis services

- eliminate all sector-specific restrictions on commercial presence, cross-border supply and consumption abroad
- provide full national treatment (including remmoval of national requirements)

0121

f. Consulting services incidental to agriculture, hunting and forestry CPC 881

" eliminate all sector-specific restrictions on commercial presence, cross-border supply and consumption abroad
" provide full national treatment (including removal of nationality requirements)

i. and j. Consulting services incidental to manufacturing CPC 884.

" eliminate all sector-specific restrictions on commercial presence, cross-border supply and consumption abroad
" provide full national treatment (including removal of nationality requirements)

k. Placement and supply services of Personnel

" eliminate all sector-specific restrictions on commercial presence, cross-border supply and consumption abroad
" provide full national treatment (including removal of nationality requirements)

m. Related scientific and technical consulting services

" eliminate all sector-specific restrictions on commercial presence, cross-border supply and consumption abroad
" provide full national treatment (including removal of nationality requirements)

234-30-15

8

n.   Maintenance and repair of equipment (i.e. 633+8861-8866; not incl. maritime vessels, aircraft or other transport equipment)

* eliminate all sector-specific restrictions on commercial presence, cross-border supply and consumption abroad
* provide full national treatment (including removal of nationality requirements)

o. Building services

* eliminate all sector-specific restrictions on commercial presence, cross-border supply and consumption abroad
* provide full national treatment (including removal of nationality requirements)

p. Photographic Services

* eliminate all sector-specific restrictions on commercial presence, cross-border supply and consumption abroad
* provide full national treatment (including removal of nationality requirements)

r. Printing, publishing

* eliminate all sector-specific restrictions on commercial presence, cross-border supply and consumption abroad,
* provide full national treatment (except fro news papers and magazines, including removal of nationality requirements)

234-30-16

0123

9

s. Convention services
- eliminate all sector-specific restrictions on commercial presence, cross-border supply and consumption abroad
- provide full national treatment (including removal of nationality requirements)

2. COMMUNICATION SERVICES

B. Courier Services (7512)
- eliminate all sector-specific restrictions on commercial presence, cross-border supply and consumption abroad.
- provide full national treatment (including removal of nationality requirements)

C. Telecommunication Services

e. Telegraph services (7522)
- eliminate all sector-specific restrictions on commercial presence, cross-border supply and consumption abroad.
- provide full national treatment (including removal of nationality requirements)

234-30-17

10

0124

g. Facsimile services
- eliminate all sector-specific restrictions on commercial presence, cross-border supply and consumption abroad.
- provide full national treatment (including removal of nationality requirements)

h. Electronic mail (7523)
- eliminate all sector-specific restrictions on commercial presence, cross-border supply and consumption abroad.
- provide full national treatment (including removal of nationality requirements)

i. Voice mail (7523)
- eliminate all sector-specific restrictions on commercial presence, cross-border supply and consumption abroad.
- provide full national treatment (including removal of nationality requirements)

j. On line information and data base retrieval
- eliminate all sector-specific restrictions on commercial presence, cross-border supply and consumption abroad.
- provide full national treatment (including removal of nationality requirements)

k. Electronic data interchange (EDI)
- eliminate all sector-specific restrictions on commercial presence, cross-border supply and consumption abroad.
- provide full national treatment (including removal of nationality requirements)

234-30-18

0125

m. Code and protocol Conversation
* eliminate all sector-specific restrictions on commercial presence, cross-border supply and consumption abroad.
* provide full national treatment (including removal of nationality requirements)

n. On-line information and/or data processing (incl. transaction processing)
* eliminate all sector-specific restrictions on commercial presence, cross-border supply and consumption abroad.
* provide full national treatment (including removal of nationality requirements)

D. AUDIO VISUAL SERVICES

a. Motion picture and video tape production and distribution services.
* eliminate all sector-specific restrictions on commercial presence, cross-border supply and consumption abroad.
* provide full national treatment (including removal of nationality requirements)

b. Motion picture projection services
* eliminate all sector-specific restrictions on commercial presence, cross-border supply and consumption abroad.
* provide full national treatment (including removal of nationality requirements)

234-30-1A

c. Radio and television services

• eliminate all sector-specific restrictions on commercial presence, cross-border supply and consumption abroad.
• provide full national treatment (including removal of nationality requirements)

d. Radio and television transmission

Make a binding commitment on the present level of Market Access and National Treatment in this sector.

e. Sound recording services (7524)

- eliminate all sector-specific restrictions on commercial presence, cross-border supply and consumption abroad
• provide full national treatment (including removal of nationality requirements)

3. CONSTRUCTION AND RELATED ENGINEERING SERVICES (including A, B, C, D, E)

CPC 512-518

• eliminate all sector-specific restrictions on commercial presence, cross-border supply and consumption abroad
• provide full national treatment (including removal of nationality requirements); especially concerning
  - requirements of association with a domestic company or of local participation
  - discriminatory duties and charges, including taxes

234 -30 -20

13

0127

4. DISTRIBUTION SERVICES (including A, B, C, D, E)

CPC 621, 622, 631, 632, 6111, 6113, 6121, 8929

Make a binding commitment on the present level of Market Access and National Treatment in this sector concerning:
* commercial presence,
* cross-border supply and
* consumption abroad.

5. EDUCATIONAL SERVICES

A. Primary education — Make a binding commitment on the present level of Market Access and National Treatment in this sector concerning:
* commercial presence,
* cross-border supply and
* consumption abroad.

B. Secondary education — Make a binding commitment on the present level of Market Access and National Treatment in this sector concerning:
* commercial presence,
* cross-border supply and
* consumption abroad.

236 - 30 - 21

14

0128

C. Higher education

Make a binding commitment on the present level of
Market Access and National Treatment in this sector
concerning:
* commercial presence,
* cross-border supply and
* consumption abroad.

D. Adult education

Make a binding commitment on the present level of
Market Access and National Treatment in this sector
concerning:
* commercial presence,
* cross-border supply and
* consumption abroad.

E. Other education

Make a binding commitment on the present level of
Market Access and National Treatment in this sector
concerning:
* commercial presence,
* cross-border supply and
* consumption abroad.

234-30-22

15

0129

6. ENVIRONMENTAL SERVICES
(including A, B, C, D,)
CPC 9401-9403)

- eliminate all sector-specific restrictions on commercial presence, cross-border supply and consumption abroad
- provide full national treatment (including removal of nationality requirements)

7. FINANCIAL SERVICES

A. All Insurance and insurance relataed services

a. Life, accident and health insurance services

Make a binding commitment on the present level of Market Access and National Treatment in this sector concerning:
- commercial presence
- cross-border supply and consumption abroad

a. Non- life insurance services

Make a binding commitment on the present level of Market Access and National Treatment in this sector concerning:
- commercial presence
- cross-border supply and consumption abroad

23K-30-23

0130

16

c. Reinsurance and retrocession

Make a binding commitment on the present level of Market Access and National Treatment in this sector concerning:
* commercial presence
* cross-border supply and consumption abroad

7. FINANCIAL SERVICES (cont.)

d. Services auxiliary to insurance (incl. broking and agency services)

Make a binding commitment on the present level of Market Access and National Treatment in this sector concerning:
* commercial presence
* cross-border supply and consumption abroad

B. Banking and other financial services (excl. insurances)

All

Make a binding commitment on the present level of Market Access and National Treatment in this sector, based on the understanding on commitments in Financial Services (cf. MTN.TNC/W/FA).

a. Acceptance of deposits and other repayable funds

Make a binding commitment on the present level of Market Access and National Treatment concerning:
* commercial presence
* cross-border supply and consumption abroad

234-30-24

b. Lending of all types, incl. inter alia, consumer credits, mortgage credit factoring and financing of commercial transaction

Make a binding commitment on the present level of Market Access and National Treatment concerning:
- commercial presence
- cross-border supply and consumption abroad

7. FINANCIAL SERVICES (cont.)

c. Financial leasing

Make a binding commitment on the present level of Market Access and National Treatment concerning:
- commercial presence
- cross-border supply and consumption abroad

d. All payment and money transmission services

Make a binding commitment on the present level of Market Access and National Treatment concerning:
- commercial presence
- cross-border supply and consumption abroad

e. Guarantees and commitments

Make a binding commitment on the present level of Market Access and National Treatment concerning:
- commercial presence
- cross-border supply and consumption abroad

f. Trading for own account or for account of customers, whether on an exchange in an over-the-counter market, or otherwise, the following:
- transferable securities,

Make a binding commitment on the present level of Market Access and National Treatment concerning:
- commercial presence
- cross-border supply and consumption abroad

234-30-25

0132

18

- other negotiable instrum.
and financial assets, incl.
bullion

g. Participation in the
issues of all kinds of
securities, incl. under-writing
and placement as agent
(whether publicly or privately)
and provision of services to
such issues

Make a binding commitment on the present level of
Market Access and National Treatment concerning:
* commercial presence
* cross-border supply and consumption abroad

7. FINANCIAL SERVICES
(cont.)

i. Asset management, such as
portfolio management, all forms
of collective investment
management, pension funds
management, custodial deposit.
and trust services

Make a binding commitment on the present level of
Market Access and National Treatment concerning:
* commercial presence
* cross-border supply and consumption abroad

k. Advisory and other auxiliary
financial services on all the
activities listed in Art. 1B of
MTN.TNC/W/50, incl. credit ref.
and analysis, investment and
portfolio reasearch and advice,
advice on acquisitions and on
corporate restructuring and
strategy

Make a binding commitment on the present level of
Market Access and National Treatment concerning:
* commercial presence
* cross-border supply and consumption abroad

234-30-26

19

0133

l. Provision adn transfer of
finacial information and
finacial data processing and   Make a binding commitment on the present level of Market
related software by poviders   Access and National Treatment (excluding personal data)
of other financial services

9. TOURISM AND TRAVEL RELATED SERVICES
(including C)

**Tourist guides
services
CPC 7472**

* eliminate all sector-specific restrictions on commercial
presence, cross-border supply and consumption abroad,
* provide full national treatment (including removal of nationality
requirements) especially concerning
- requirements of association with a domestic company or of local participation,
- discriminatory duties and charges, including taxes

10. RECREATIONAL
CULTURAL AND
SPORTING SERVICES
(incl. A, B, C and E)

* eliminate all sector-specific restrictions on commercial
presence, cross-border supply and consumption abroad,
* provide full national treatment (including removal
of nationality requirements)

2 36 - 30 - 27

11. TRANSPORT SERVICES

A. Maritime Transport Services

International shipping services

Bind all measures that effect
a) the crossborder supply of international shipping services,
b) the purchase abroad by national consumers of international shipping services and
c) the commercial presence of providers of international shipping services
at the existing level of market access and national treatment.

Make a binding commitment to eliminate all measures that restrict market access or condition national treatment for
a) the crossborder supply of international shipping services and
b) the purchase abroad by national consumers of international shipping services
within three years after the entry into force of the Agreement.

Maritime transport auxiliary services

Bind all measures that effect
a) the crossborder supply of maritime transport auxiliary services,
b) the purchase abroad by national consumers of Maritime transport auxiliary services and
c) the commercial presence of providers of maritime transport auxiliary services
at the existing level of market access and national treatment.

<u>Definition of terms, used above:</u>

<u>International shipping services:</u>

transportation of passengers or goods between ports located in different states, including passenger cruise traffic outside a Party's territorial waters.

11. TRANSPORT SERVICES
   {cont}

Maritime transport auxiliary services:

all maritime transport related services within the confines of the port or sea environment, limited to those which provide an immediate, interactive, supporting role to the primary function of the maritime transport industry, which is the transportation of goods and/or passengers between ports.

C. Air Transport Services

Make a binding commitment on the present level of Market Access and National Treatment in this sector concerning:
- commercial presence
- cross-border supply and
- consumption abroad.

234-30-2A

22

F. Road Transport Services

Make a binding commitment on the present level of Maret Access and National Treatment in this sector

concerning:
* commercial presence
* cross-border supply and
* consumption abroad.

234-30-30

경 제 기 획 원

우 427-760 / 경기도 과천시 중앙동1 정부제2청사 / 전화 503-9149 / 전송 503-9141

문서번호 통조삼 10502-66

시행일자 1992. 3. 31

(경유)

수신 수신처참조

참조

선결			지시	
접수	일자시간	9o : 4.1	결재·공람	
	번호	10906		
	처리과			
	담당자	*(서명)*		

제목 제3차 UR/서비스 양자협상 회의록 송부

　　　스위스 제네바에서 '92.3.19~3.20간 개최된 제3차 UR/서비스 양자협상 결과를
별첨과 같이 송부하니 해당부처(기관)은 향후 협상대책추진에 만전을 기하여 주시기
바랍니다.

첨부 : UR/서비스 양자협상 회의록 1부. 끝.

경 제 기 획 원 장

제 2협력관 전결

수신처 : 외무부장관, 내무부장관, 재무부장관, 법무부장관, 교육부장관, 문화부장관,
　　　　농림수산부장관, 상공부장관, 보건사회부장관, 건설부장관, 교통부장관,
　　　　노동부장관, 동자부장관, 체신부장관, 체육청소년부장관, 과학기술처장관,
　　　　환경처장관, 공보처장관, 경찰청장, 특허청장, 해운항만청장, 대외경제정책
　　　　연구원장, 한국개발연구원장

0137

외 무 부

종 별 :

번 호 : GVW-0762   일 시 : 92 0407 1830

수 신 : 장 관(통기, 경기원, 체신부)

발 신 : 주 제네바 대사

제 목 : UR/서비스협상(통신분야)

연: GVW-0684

연호 3.26 11개국 비공식 협의에서 논의한바 있는 미국의 기본통신 분야 MFN 일탈계획에 대하여 EC 는 자국의 입장을 서면으로 당관에 송부해 왔는바, 별첨 송부하니참고 바람.

첨부: 미국의 기본 통신분야 MFN 일탈에 대한 EC 의 입장 1부

(GVW(F)-0246).끝

(대사 박수길-국장)

통상국   2차보   체신부   경기원

PAGE 1   92.04.08   05:47 DS
외신1과 통제관

0138

주 제 네 바 대 표 부

번 호 : GVW(F) - 0246　　년월일 : 20407　　시간 : 1030

수 신 : 장　　관 (통기. 경기원. 체신부)

발 신 : 주 제네바대사

제 목 : UR/서비스협상 (통신분야)

　　　　　　　　　　　송　　　　매 (르지프함)

보 안	
통 제	

의신과	
통 제	

246-5-1

0139

TELECOM SERVICES: US PROPOSAL ON MFN EXEMPTION

The essence of the proposal launched by the US for resolving the issue of MFN is that they would be prepared to drop their request for a derogation from MFN for basic[1] telecom services providing that other countries open up their markets in this sector. If a sufficient number of other countries do not make a commitment then the US will maintain its derogation.

The US has now finalised its list of MFN exemptions, including basic telecommunications, and it can now be seen that the proposal of December is somewhat misleading, since it can be seen from the exemption list that the US wishes to exclude not just long-distance but all basic telecom services, including local telephony, mobile and satellite services.

In addition, there are a number of reasons why the US proposal appears to be rather unreasonable:

1. It is based on sectoral reciprocity, which is unacceptable in a global negotiation.

2. To state that the US market is "open" and that therefore other countries should open their markets is deceptive - parties are interested in real, rather than theoretical market opening possibilities. It is simplistic to argue that just because any voice market has been opened it can be entered freely: significant competition in this area is mainly for large, rich companies.

3. The proposal would involve other Parties having to measure up to a US benchmark of what constitutes liberalisation.

These arguments are expanded over-page.

---

1   Long-distance and international voice, both facilities-based and resale

Background

1. The US approach to basic, as opposed to enhanced, telecom services is that they should be excluded from the Uruguay Round negotiations on services, on the grounds that, unlike the US, most other countries do not have open competition in such services, so that it would be "unfair" for the US to be the only country to bind itself unilaterally.

2. There are a number of general objections to this approach:

- the US market is not as open as they say it is (eg local telephony is essentially a monopoly);

- the US's main concern is not to protect its market but to retain leverage to press for future market opening bilaterally;

- the US derogation seeks to exclude what other Parties have already opened or are in the process of opening (such as mobile);

- many other Parties' regulatory situations are changing rapidly in the direction of liberalisation of basic services, and although this will not result in a system which exactly resembles the US model, nevertheless the market access opportunities for US companies in particular will be considerable;

- it is vital to ensure that market access negotiations for such an important market are multilateral, and that the main part of this market is not dealt with completely outside of the GATT through a patchwork of bilateral deals in which the US may be able to exert pressure, or from which some Parties may be excluded.

3. In December 1991 the US launched a proposal for resolving the issue of MFN, the essence of which is that they would be prepared to drop their request for a derogation from MFN for basic telecom services providing that other countries open up their markets in this sector according to certain criteria and within a certain period of time.

Shortcomings of the US proposal

4. The US proposal of December, which assumes that once the US has bound itself in GATT to opening its market for long-distance voice, foreign companies will freely be able to enter, and therefore other countries should do the same, is overly simplistic. Real competition (ie competition with the major carriers, not just niche markets) is accessible only by the world's major carriers.

Although long-distance voice is open to competition in the US, and there is already some market entry by foreign firms (eg some firms have entered this market via the provision of fibre-optic cables), it must be recognised that there is a difference between real competition and potential competition, as the economic barriers to entry and exit remain considerable.

The provision of large-scale mass market telecommunications services is a highly capital intensive business, with a very high (and increasing) proportion of fixed as opposed to variable costs. Entry frequently requires access to public rights of way that may be difficult or time-consuming to obtain from state and municipal authorities. Moreover, considerable time is required to design, engineer, acquire, construct and install a new system. Innovative new technologies cannot be relied upon to confer a cost advantage on the start-up company, since the established carriers also utilise the

246-5-3

0141

newest technologies, and do so at a lower unit cost because of their larger size and ability to build upon existing facilities.

Thus in the US the main competitor, on the basis of its recent monopoly position, is AT&T, with MCI and Sprint (both of which developed out of existing networks used by public utilities) both with a less than 10% share each, and Cable & Wireless with less than 1% of the market.

Moreover, there are well-known regulatory obstacles in the US which hinder market entry (eg Section 310, which limits foreign ownership of a common carrier requiring a radio licence).

5. For the above reasons, the proposal's demand for sectoral reciprocity in any commitments made by a Party in long-distance voice would mainly benefit major US companies.

The argumentation about the difficulties of entering the long-distance market applies to all markets, not just that of the US. However, the bottom line is that US access by the powerful BOCs[1] and AT&T to third country markets which have not yet re-balanced their tariffs is a viable proposition[2], while significant access to the US market by many non-US companies does not seem likely in the short term.

It should be noted that not only are US companies already doing very well in a number of Parties' value-added and data services markets, but also the fact remains that AT&T and the RBOCs are among the largest and wealthiest telephone companies in the world at present, and access to the basic telecom market is to a large extent on a first-come-first-served basis, often by those with the deepest pockets. Many of the BOCs, for example, have access to significant funds from their non-regulated activities, which they are able to use to enter markets outside the US. Indeed, it needs to be underlined that these companies are prohibited from competing in the long-distance market in the US.

6. The US proposal of December 1991 is misleading. It can be seen from the US exemption list the US wishes to exempt not just long-distance but all basic telecom services, including local telephony, mobile and satellite services, whereas the proposal refers only to long-distance and international services.

7. So far there has been no discussion of local telephony, mobile and satellite services. It is understood that the US would exempt from MFN any service which it would not bind in its offer. Since the US appears to have no intention to bind local telephone services, this means that the US local services market, which is largely closed to competition, and which represents some 60% of the US telecom market in revenue terms, will be excluded. Yet BOCs are major participants in a number of cable TV companies outside the US which also provide local telephone service. Similarly there is no mention of access to the mobile services market in the US, which is currently made difficult by ownership restrictions linked to radio licences, and where BOCs automatically receive a licence, while BOCs are shareholders in many mobile telephone consortia around the world.

---

1. Bell Operating Companies

2. Tariff rebalancing: Although changes are under way, it is still generally public policy that long-distance and international calls, which tend to be relatively high-priced, incorporate a cross-subsidy to pay for local calls, which tend to be relatively low-priced. In the US some cross-subsidisation still takes place but the subsidy has been greatly reduced over a period of time, so that the price of local calls and telephone rental has risen, while the price of long-distance calls has fallen.

246 - 5 - 4

8. The US proposal does not take into account the realities of other countries' present state of regulation, and the terms of reference would involve other Parties having to measure up to a US benchmark of what constitutes liberalisation. The US focus for market opening by other parties is mainly on long-distance and international services, as these are in its own interests. Yet it is these services which according to current public service policy of many governments around the world are used to cross-subsidise local services. The US is in a stronger position than many other countries in that it has re-balanced its tariffs between long-distance and local services.

20

UR 서 비 스 협 상
노동력 이동분야 대응방향 검토

1992. 4. 14.

노 동 부

0144

목   차

Ⅰ. 인력이동 범위에 대한 我國 Offer 내용 검토

Ⅱ. 주요 대응방안 검토

    1. 서비스 판매자의 Offer 문제

    2. 단독대표자의 Offer 문제

    3. 전문가의 개념 정의

    4. 노사관계와 관련 인력이동에 대한 약속 부적용 문제

첨 부 : 중국의 서비스분야별 노동력 이동분야 관심사항.

0145

UR/노동력이동에 대한 대응방향

I. 인력이동 범위에 대한 我國 Offer 내용 검토

　o 我國 Offer상 인력이동 허용범위

　　- 『상업적 주재가 약속된 분야의 기업에 필수적인 인력은 일시적 이동을
　　　허용함』

　　　. 상급관리자,임원,전문가로서 당해기업에 1년이상 고용되고 있는자

　　　. 출입국관리법,노사관계법 준수의무 부여, 단 노사분쟁시에는 적용되지 않음

　o 최근 3차에 걸친 국가별 양허협상 과정에서 제시된 주요국의 Request 내용과
　　我國 Offer 내용의 명료화 필요성 대두

　〈 주요국의 Request 〉

　- 서비스 판매자 (Service Seller)의 추가 양허요청
　　(미국, EC, 캐나다, 스웨덴, 뉴질랜드, 핀랜드)

　- EC는 단독대표자 (Sole representative)의 추가 양허요청

　〈 我國 Offer의 명료화 〉

　- 전문가 (Specialist)의 범위에 자격소지자 포함여부
　　(EC, 미국등은 자격소지자를 전문가에 포함하고 있음)

　- 전문가의 구체적 확인방법

　- 노사관계와 관련되는 인력이동 제한 (일본)

1

0146

ㅇ 인력이동 범위에 대한 노동부의 기본입장

  - 국내 노동시장의 여건과 전망,노동력 이동에 따른 부정적 측면에 대한 고려
    등으로 서비스 업종별로 필수인력에 한해 제한적으로 이동 허용

  - 현재 아국 출입국관리법상 입국이 허용되어 실제로 활동하고 있는 인력에
    대해서는 현지 협상 분위기에 맞추어 점진적으로 허용

  - 전문가의 범위를 엄격하게 제한하여 단순인력의 유입을 억제하고 전문인력
    이동의 자유화에 따른 해당분야 서비스의 수출의 이익과 수입의 비용을 비교
    하여 전체적으로 우리나라에 이익이 큰 경우에는 이를 점진적으로 허용

2

Ⅱ. 주요 대응방안 검토

1. 서비스 판매자의 Offer 문제

ㅇ 사업상의 상담,회의참석,시찰을 위한 입국자는 현재 단기종합 비자를 받아 입국하여 사실상 서비스판매자의 역할을 하고 있으므로 양허불허의 실익이 없고 주요 선진국이 모두 Offer 하고 있는 사항이므로 관계부처의 의견을 종합하여 다음과 같이 Offer

---

〈 서비스 판매협상, 계약체결을 위한 인력의 이동 〉

『서비스판매자』라 함은 한국내에서 보수를 받지 않는 사람으로서 한국내에 사업적 기반이 없는 서비스 공급자를 대표하여 해당 서비스판매를 위한 협상 또는 계약을 체결하기 위하여 일시적으로 입국하고자 하는 사람을 말함

- 이들은 한국내에서 해당 서비스를 직접 판매하거나 제공할수 없으며 체류 기간은 90일을 초과할수 없음

※ 서비스판매자 추가양허에 대한 관계부처의 의견은 1개부처 (문화부)만을 제외하고는 별다른 문제가 없다고함

3

0148

2. 단독대표자의 Offer 문제

ο EC의 단독대표자의 개념

> 상급관리자 및 중역의 범주에 속하는 자로서 EC 국가내에서의 서비스제공을 위한 상업적 주재 설립의 책임을 맡은 자.
>
> - 이러한 대표자는 일반대중에게 직접 서비스를 제공하는 업무에 종사 하거나 직접서비스를 제공하여서는 안되며 서비스공급자가 EC국가내에 사무소,지점,자회사 등이 없어야 함

ο 아직 미국,카나다 등이 Offer 하지 않고 있고 동 개념이 불명료하므로 일단 우리의 Offer에서는 계속 제외

- 상업적 주재의 설립을 위한 서비스 공급기업의 상급관리자 및 중역이 일시적으로 입국하는데는 현행 단기종합비자(90일)가 발급되고 있기 때문에 동 업무수행에는 지장없음

- 다만 이것을 법적으로 양허 (legal binding) 하는것은 우리의 출입국 관리법상 정확히 부합되는 규정이 없기때문에 곤란함을 설득

4

0149

3. 전문가의 개념정의

① 전문가에 공인된 자격의 소지자를 포함할 것인지 여부

- 각국마다 자격제도가 상이하기 때문에 일률적으로 모든 종류의 공인된 자격의 소지자를 전문가의 범위에 포함시킬수는 없으나 제도운영상 특수자격증 소지자는 전문가의 범위에 들수있을 것으로 해석 가능

- 다만 중국등 개도국들로 부터의 다양한 자격소지자들이 전문가의 범위에 포함되어 입국할 우려가 있으므로 자격소지자를 전문가에 포함시키는 것은 곤란

② 전문가 여부의 구체적 판단

Offer에 기재한 전문가의 개념정의는 매우 일반적인 내용이기 때문에 동 개념정의에 따라 전문가 여부를 판단하기는 곤란

- 따라서 서비스 협정발효후 양허표에 약속한 내용의 실천과정에서 구체적인 사례를 중심으로 전문가의 범위를 구체화시키는 것이 필요

- 전문가 여부의 판단기준은 국내인력으로 대체할수 없는 당해 서비스 분야의 고도의 전문적이고 독점적인 경험과 지식을 가진자로 하되, 양허표에 등재된 개별 서비스 업종별로 소관부처가 노동력 이동범위를 명백히 하여 전체적인 인력수급 정책과 상충됨이 없도록 노동부와 협의

5

- 개별서비스 업종별로 소관부처는 첨부와 같은 『중국의 서비스분야별 노동력 이동분야 관심사항』을 참고하여 업종별 전문가의 요건 및 범위를 설정

- 노동부는 수정 Offer에 양허한 업종별 전문가의 요건 및 범위를 소관 부처로 부터 취합 작성하여 경제기획원, 법무부와 협의

- 업종별 전문가의 구체적 판단은 현재 수정 양허표에 등재된 회계사, 세무사, 건축사 등과 같이 국내 자격취득을 요건으로 하거나 기술계의 경우는 국가기술자격법에 의한 『기술사』의 자격취득 요건과 경력의 소지여부로 판단함이 타당할것임

4. 노사관계와 관련 인력이동에 대한 약속부적용 문제

- 동 조항은 다음의 사유가 발생할 경우를 대비하여 기재
  ① 사용자는 파업등 근로자의 쟁의기간중 쟁의에 관계없는 자를 채용 또는 대체할수 없다는 노동쟁의조정법 제15조 『사용자의 채용제한』규정 준수 보장
  ② 노사교섭의 결과로 노.사간에 인력이동에 대하여 특별한 제한을 가하는 단체협약이 성립될 경우 이를 준수
  ③ 인력이동의 허용이 노사분규에 직·간접적으로 영향을 미치게될 경우 인력 이동을 제한 (인력이동부속서에서 논의되었던 사항)

6

0151

- ③의 경우에는 노사분쟁의 소지를 줄일수 있는 안전장치로서 동 조항의 존치필요

- 따라서 동 조항은 현행대로 유지

  ※ 일본은 동 조항이 인력이동이 약속된 외국인의 출국정지 근거로 활용될
  우려가 있지 않느냐는 의문을 표시하였는바 이에 대하여는 출입국관리법상
  별도의 출국정지 기준이 적용되는 것으로서 이 조항이 그러한 의도를 갖고
  있지 않다고 대응

Informal Note of China

'92. 3. 20

Natural persons providing services as mentioned in China's request list include, in particular, the following categories of personnel in certain sectors and subsectors:

Maritime Transport Services

1. Crew members:

-- master; chief engineer

-- chief officer; second engineer

-- second officer; third engineer

-- third officer; engineer

-- radio operator; electrician

-- purser

-- other ordinary seamen

2. Port management officer and staff

3. Shipping company management officer and staff

Education Services

-- post graduate teacher

-- laboratory assistants

Architectural Services

-- architect

Accounting, Auditing and Book Keeping

-- cost auditor

-- cost accountant

-- cashiers

0153

Engineering Services

-- electrical engineer

-- electronics engineer

-- mining engineer

-- geological engineer

Integrated Engineering Services

-- design engineer

-- lab technician

Operation and Maintenance of Railways

-- station master

-- ticket collectors

-- cook

-- fireman

-- electric assistant

-- loco drivers

computer and related services

-- system analyst

-- programmer

-- field engineer

-- data entry operator

Health Related Services

-- physician, surgeon

-- laboratory technician (pathology, bio-chemistry,

   microbiology, electron microscopy, radiology)

-- chemists

    -- nurses

    -- mid-wives

Hotel and Restaurant Services

    -- housekeeper

    -- chef (including executive chef and sous chef)

    -- restaurant hostess

    -- lobby hostess

    -- steward/waiter

Construction and Engineering

    -- machine tool operators

    --painters

    --labourers

주 제 네 바 대 표 부

20, Route de Pre-Bois, POB 566 / (022) 791-0111 / (022) 791-0525(FAX)

문서번호 제네(경) 20644-391

시행일자 1992. 4. 16.

수신 장 관

참조 통상국장, 경제기획원장관,
재무부장관

선결			지시		
접수	일자시간		결재공람		
	번호	22954			
	처리과				
	담당자				

제목 UR/서비스협상

     표제 협상 관련 당관에 전달된 EC의 금융분야 수정 Offer 초안을 별첨
송부합니다.

     첨부 : EC의 금융분야 수정 Offer 1부.   끝.

92 4. 16

        주 제 네 바 대

0156

CONDITIONAL EC OFFER - CHAPTER ON FINANCIAL SERVICES

10.04.1992

EC OFFER (*)

1) Cross border supply; 2) Consumption abroad; 3) Commercial presence; 4) Presence of natural persons

FINANCIAL SERVICES SECTOR *

BANKING AND OTHER FINANCIAL SERVICES (excluding insurance)**

NOTE: Unlike foreign subsidiaries, branches established directly in a Member State by a non-Community company are not subject to prudential regulations at Community level which enable such subsidiaries to benefit from enhanced facilities to set up new establishments and to provide cross border services throughout the Community. Therefore, such branches receive an authorisation to operate in the territory of a Member State under conditions equivalent to those applied to domestic companies of that Member State, and may be required to satisfy a number of prudential requirements such as separate capitalisation and other solvency requirements, and reporting and publication of accounts requirements.

The relative importance of the restrictions contained in this offer needs to be assessed in the context of the functioning of the Community internal market. By virtue of Article 58 of the EEC treaty (cf.remark for "all sectors" offer, under "limitations on national treatment" - commercial presence), as far as primary establishment is concerned, companies formed in accordance to the law of a Member State and having their registered office, central administration or principal place of business within the Community shall be treated as nationals of Member States; such companies benefit from the right of secondary establishment and free provision of services throughout the Community and shall be treated as Community nationals regardless of the country of ownership or control.

Thus, Member States may apply the restrictions indicated in this schedule only with regard to the direct establishment from a third country of a commercial presence or to the provision of cross-border services from a third country; consequently, a Member State may not apply these restrictions, including those concerning establishment, to third country subsidiaries established in other Member States of the Community, unless these restrictions can also be applied to companies or nationals of other Member States in conformity with Community law.

* The Community intends to bind all the financial services sector in accordance with the provisions contained in the "understanding on commitments on financial services"; as regards movement of essential personnel, the Community intends to apply No 9 of the "understanding" only insofar as consistent with the section of the Community offer concerning all sectors. As regards cross-border financial services, this offer only covers those transactions indicated in Nos 3 and 4 of the "understanding".

This offer only refers to the relations between the Community and its Member States on the one hand, and non-Community countries on the other, and is without prejudice to the obligations of Member States under Community law.

** Establishment, cross-border provision of financial services and operating conditions within the Community are subject to normal prudential considerations of a non-discriminatory nature, such as capacity to provide financial services, reporting requirements and application of various solvency and liquidity requirements, residence requirements for managers, directors or representatives, trading rules governing dealing in securities, etc.; among these conditions, the Community and its Member States require, as a general rule and in a non-discriminatory manner, that financial institution incorporated in a Member State of the Community must adopt a specific legal form. As regards new financial services or products, their admission to the market may be subject to the existence of, and consistency with, a regulatory framework aimed at achieving the objectives indicated in Article 2.1 of the Financial Services Annex.

2.

3.

BANKING (cont.)

1) None

1) None other than:

B: establishment in Belgium is required for the provision of portfolio management services and investment advisory services.

I: the offer and marketing of services concerning the distribution to the public, through telecommunication or other information means, of information concerning prices, the volume of transactions, the offer and demand conditions relating to the negotiation of securities dealt in the Italian regulated market, or in other recognised markets, requires prior authorisation by the Stock Exchange Commission (Consob). This authorisation may not be granted if the authorities determine that there is a risk that the data provided may induce the public to error.

I: an establishment (a securities investment company incorporated in Italy or a bank subsidiary or branch) is needed in order to provide investment research and advice relating to securities (dealing, issue, underwriting) and asset management, securities custody, and services regarding mergers, acquisitions, corporate restructuring, management buy-outs and venture capital.

2) None

2) None other than:

D: issue of securities denominated in Deutschemarks can be lead managed only by a bank of independent legal status domiciled in Germany.

BANKING (cont.)

2) (cont.)

GR: establishment is required for the provision of custodial and depository services involving the administration of interest and principal payments due on securities issued in Greece.

GR: collective investment undertakings may invest in foreign securities up to 25 per cent of their net assets in the case of unit trusts and up to 20 per cent of their paid-up capital in the case of investment companies.

GR: residents are obliged to surrender foreign currency from exports to the domestic banking system within six months of the date of export.

GR: the following operations are subject to authorization or otherwise restricted:

- acquisition by residents abroad of foreign securities traded in the capital markets, of foreign money market securities and instruments, of units of foreign collective investment undertakings, and of foreign currency

- with certain exceptions, the issue abroad by residents in Greece of securities or other negotiable instruments and the introduction of domestic securities and other negotiable instruments in a foreign market

- operations in current and deposit accounts carried out by residents abroad

- with certain exceptions, financial loans and credits granted by non-residents to residents

- the provision by non-residents to residents of sureties, guarantees and financial back-up facilities not directly related to an international operation or where no resident participates in the underlying international operation.

5.

BANKING (cont.)

2) (cont.)

IRL *): Instructions relating to transactions between residents and non-resident brokers and dealers must, except in the case of certain institutional investors and financial service companies, be routed through an authorized resident agent. Residents are not permitted access to trust services provided abroad by non-residents.

IRL *): the operation of current and deposit accounts by residents abroad is subject to authorization.

IRL *): access by residents in Ireland to foreign exchange forwards, swaps and options is allowed only to cover known and specific future financial commitments, or for trade purposes, or where the initial impact on the Official External Reserves is positive or neutral. Irish residents are required to repatriate export receipts and convert them into domestic currency unless the Central Bank approves their retention for further trade financing.

* Ireland will abolish these restrictions by end-1992.

BANKING (cont.)

2) (cont.)

I : an establishment (a securities investment company incorporated in Italy or a bank subsidiary or branch) is needed in order to provide investment research and advice relating to securities (dealing, issue, underwriting) and asset management, securities custody, and services regarding mergers, acquisitions, corporate restructuring, management buy-outs and venture capital.

I : residents in Italy need authorization to purchase or sell abroad unrefined gold.

NL: securities denominated in guilders can be issued abroad only when the lead managing bank is under the surveillance of the Dutch Central Bank.

P : with the exception of some institutional investors, residents in Portugal only have access to cash and portfolio management services provided by non-residents abroad if they obtain authorization from the Bank of Portugal. Residents in Portugal do not have access to trust services provided by non-residents abroad.

P : open-ended investment funds are required to invest 25 per cent of their funds in Portuguese Government funds.

P : there is a requirement for a 40 per cent non-interest bearing deposit with the Central Bank of the value of foreign financial credits granted to residents, of issues of bonds or other debt instruments by resident enterprises on a foreign capital market, and of the sale to non-residents of unquoted domestic bonds.

7.

BANKING (cont.)

2) (cont.)

P: the ability of residents in Portugal to carry out the following operations abroad is restricted:

- issue or introduction on a foreign market of domestic securities and negotiable instruments
- with certain exceptions, acquisition by residents of foreign securities and other negotiable instruments and other operations in these instruments.
- acquisition of foreign collective investment securities issued by undertakings investing less than 50 per cent in securities quoted in an OECD recognised securities market
- with certain exceptions, operations in foreign exchange
- provision by non-resident institutions of financial back-up facilities to residents in Portugal.
- leasing lending by non-residents to residents
- operation of current and deposit accounts by residents abroad

UK: Sterling issues, including privately-led issues, can be lead managed only by a firm established in the United Kingdom.

BANKING (cont.)

3) None other than ***:

B : with certain exceptions (block trading), financial institutions may engage in securities trading only through stock exchange firms incorporated in Belgium.

DK: only stock-broking companies incorporated in Denmark may be authorized to trade on the Copenhagen Stock Exchange electronic trading system.

DK: Information related to payment systems such as payment cards concerning persons residing in Denmark must be registered or data processed only in Denmark.

E : foreign equity participation in securities firms is subject to prior authorization.

E : financial institutions may engage in securities trading in securities listed in an official stock exchange or in the Government securities market only through securities firms incorporated in Spain.

E, IRL, P - the establishment of non-EC banks may be subject to a test of economic need.

GR: participation by non-EC investors in the share capital of a bank established in Greece is limited in principle to 40 %.

3) None other than ***:

All member states - only firms having their registered office in the Community can act as management companies or depositories of the assets of investment funds (articles 3, 8.1 and 15.1 of the UCITS Directive, 85/611/EEC):

D: branches of foreign banks may not participate in the Federal bond consortium for the underwriting of long-term federal bonds, and are not authorised to lead manage issues denominated in Deutschmarks.

*** In France, Greece, Ireland, Netherlands, Spain and the United Kingdom the establishment of foreign banks and/or other financial companies in the form of subsidiaries or branches may be subject to reciprocity requirements; in Denmark, Germany and Italy the establishment of branches in the banking sector may be subject to a reciprocity requirement. In addition, some Member States (eg: France, Greece, Netherlands, the United Kingdom) have in their legislation provisions which enable them to impose other restrictions on the operation of foreign banks and financial companies or to deny them certain benefits such as those arising from mutual recognition of regulations and practices, if the country of origin of the firm discriminates against its firms or does not offer them competitive opportunities equivalent to those offered by these Member States to foreign banks or financial institutions. According to Community legislation, the establishment of a banking subsidiary of a bank from a third country in the Community may be subject to the condition that the third country of origin grants Community banks the right of establishment and a de facto national treatment; planned EC legislation may extend this provision to the establishment of foreign investment firms in the Community.

The Community offers as a roll-back not to apply these provisions to GATS signatories; however, this offer is conditional, and the Community may reserve the right to invoke these provisions vis-a-vis third countries which do not make adequate liberalization commitments in the financial services sector. The Community will as a general rule consider inadequate offers by third countries which do not commit to respect, under national treatment conditions, the acquired rights of Community financial institutions operating in their markets, or which, particularly in case of third countries with important financial markets, do not include a standstill for the whole financial services sector. Other factors to be taken into account in judging the adequacy of third country offers will be the actual openness of the financial services market and the roll-back of restrictions offered.

BANKING (cont.)

3) (cont.)

GR: for the establishment of a branch, a minimum amount of foreign exchange must be imported, converted into drachmas and kept in Greece as long as the foreign bank continues to operate in Greece; this minimum amount is equal to the minimum amount of share capital required for the establishment of a Greek bank.

GR: financial institutions may engage in securities trading only through stock exchange firms incorporated in Greece.

IRL: the right of establishment does not cover the establishment of representative offices of foreign banks.

I : a separate incorporation in Italy in the form of a securities investment company is required for firms other than banks (including foreign bank branches) in order to provide services related to securities dealing (including dealing for the own account or for the account of customers(2), issue and distribution of securities, acceptance of sale and purchase orders, investment advice, asset and portfolio management, and raising funds from the public by means of activities which may also be promotional(3) and carried on in a place different from the legal head office or principal administrative establishment of the issuer, offeror or person marketing the investment).

I : clearing and settlement of securities may be conducted only by the official clearing system.

I : centralized deposit, custody and administration services for Government securities can be provided only by the Bank of Italy, or by Monte Titoli SpA for dematerialized shares, securities of a participating nature and other bonds traded in an official stock exchange.

3) (cont.)

F : in addition to French credit institutions, issues denominated in French francs may be lead managed by French subsidiaries (under French law) of non-French banks which are authorised, based on sufficient means and commitments in Paris of the candidate French subsidiary of the non-French bank. These conditions apply to lead-banks running the books. A non-French bank may be, without restrictions or requirement to establish, joint-lead or co-lead manager of Eurofranc bond issue.

IRL: In the case of unit trusts and collective investment schemes constituted as variable capital companies (other than undertakings for collective investment in transferable securities, UCITS), the trustees or depository, management company or investment company may be required to be incorporated in the State or in another Member State of the Community.

I : representative offices of foreign intermediaries cannot carry out promotional activities in the area of investment in securities.

NL: branches and subsidiaries of non-EC banks need permission to lead-manage issues of guilder-denominated paper.

(2) From 1st January 1993 foreign as well as domestic banks may not provide securities dealing for its own account or for the account of customers ; however, banks, including branches of foreign banks, are allowed to deal in Treasury bonds and State-backed securities.

(3) Door-to-door dealing.

9.

BANKING (cont.)

3) (cont.)

I : factoring services may be conducted by companies
as well public or private institutions having
legal personality ; leasing services may be
provided by "societe per azioni", by "societe in
accomandita per azioni", by "societe a respon-
sabilite limitate" or "societe cooperative".

I : exercise of voting rights by foreign shareholders
in the three "banche di interesse nazionale"
(Banca Commerciale Italiana, Credito Italiano and
Banco di Roma) is restricted.

NL: only companies incorporated according to the law
and regulations of an EC Member State may become
members of the Amsterdam Stock Exchange.

P : the services of provision of venture capital,
factoring, enterprise development, pension fund
management and broker/dealer services may be
provided only by companies incorporated in
Portugal.

UK: the following categories of financial
institutions dealing in Government debt are
required to be incorporated in the United Kingdom
and be separately capitalized:

- gilt edged market makers (or GEMMs), which are
  primary dealers in gilt-edged Government debt and
  through which the Government operates in
  executing Government debt management policy;

- discount houses which are primary dealers for
  Treasury Bills and other money market
  instruments, and through which the Government
  operates in executing monetary policy;

- stock exchange money brokers (SEMBs), which act
  as intermediaries between GEMMs and lenders of
  gilt-edged stock; and

- Inter-dealer brokers (IDBs), which act as
  intermediaries between GEMMs.

4) Subject to "all sectors" limitations ; in addition :

GR : the majority of the members of the Board of Directors of a bank established in Greece must be nationals of a Member State
of the EC and residing in Greece.

IRL: EC citizenship may be required for more than half of the members of the Board of Directors of banks.

P : at least 75% of personnel of branches and subsidiaries of foreign banks must be Portuguese nationals

Sector/Sub-sector	Limitations on market access	Limitations on national treatment	Addit. Commitm.
INSURANCE AND INSURANCE RELATED SERVICES	-NOTE: Unlike foreign subsidiaries, branches established directly in a Member State by a non-Community insurance company are not, with certain limited exceptions, subject to prudential regulations harmonised at Community level which enable such subsidiaries to benefit from enhanced facilities to set up new establishments and to provide cross border services throughout the Community. Therefore, such branches receive an authorisation to operate in the territory of a Member State under conditions equivalent to those applied to domestic insurance companies of that Member State, and are required to satisfy a number of prudential requirements such as specific guarantee and deposit requirements, a separate capitalisation, and the localisation in the Member State concerned of the assets representing the technical reserves and at least one third of the solvency margin.

The relative importance of the restrictions contained in this offer needs to be assessed in the context of the functioning of the Community internal market. By virtue of Article 58 of the EEC treaty (cf. remark for "all sectors" offer, under article XVII- commercial presence), as far as a primary establishment is concerned, companies formed in accordance to the law of a Member State and having their registered office, central administration or principal place of business within the Community shall be treated as nationals of Member States; such companies benefit from the right of secondary establishment and free provision of services throughout the Community and shall be treated as Community nationals regardless of the country of ownership or control.

Thus, Member State may apply the restrictions indicated in this schedule only with regard to the direct establishment from a third country of a commercial presence or to the provision of cross-border services from a third country; consequently, a Member State may not apply these restrictions, including those concerning establishment, to third country subsidiaries established in other Member States of the Community, unless these restrictions can also be applied to companies or nationals of other Member States in conformity with Community law. | | |

* Establishment, cross-border provision of financial services and operating conditions within the Community are subject to normal prudential considerations of a non-discriminatory nature, such as capacity to provide insurance services, reporting requirements, application of various solvency and liquidity requirements such as the need to maintain a solvency margin and a guarantee fund and a requirement to localise in the Member State of activity the assets representing the technical reserves related to the insurance activities carried out in its territory, residence requirement for managers, directors, or representatives, etc.; among these conditions, the Community and its Member State require, as a general rule and in a non-discriminatory manner, that financial institutions incorporated in a Member State of the Community must adopt a specific legal form. As regards new financial services or products, their admission to the market may be subject to the existence of, and consistency with, a regulatory framework aimed at achieving the objectives indicated in Article 2.1 of the Financial Services Annex.

11.

INSURANCE (cont.)

1) No other limitation than :

DK: compulsory air transport insurance can be underwritten only by firms established in the Community.

DK: no persons or companies (including insurance companies) may for business purposes in Denmark assist in effecting direct insurance for persons resident in Denmark, for Danish ships or for property in Denmark, other than Danish companies, foreign companies registered in Denmark, or foreign insurance companies subject to the Danish Act on the provision of insurance services within Direct non-life insurance (implementing the EC second non-life Insurance Directive). The Minister of Industry may lay down rules providing for otherwise.

D: compulsory air insurance policies can be underwritten only by a subsidiary established in the Community or by a branch established in Germany.

D: if a foreign insurance company has established a branch in Germany, it may conclude insurance contracts in Germany relating to international transport only through the branch established in Germany.

E, GR : air and maritime transport insurance, covering goods, aircraft, hull and liability can be underwritten only by established firms (this restriction will be lifted on 1st January 1993).

E, IT: Access to the actuarial profession is subject to a condition of residence.

F : insurance of risks relating to ground transport may be carried out only by insurance firms established in the Community.

1) None

12.

INSURANCE (cont.)

1) (cont.)

I : insurance of risks relating to CIF exports by residents in Italy may be underwritten only by insurance firms established in Italy.

I : establishment in Italy is required for the insurance of risks related to vessels and aircraft registered in Italy ; however, authorization may be granted for the insurance of these risks with non-established insurance companies if coverage is not available with established insurance companies.

P : air and maritime transport insurance, covering goods, aircraft, hull and liability can be underwritten only by firms established in Portugal; only persons or companies established in Portugal may act as intermediaries for such insurance business in Portugal.

UK: compulsory insurance of the following risks can be underwritten only by UK authorised insurers:
- licensed conveyancers (professional indemnity)
- employers' liability
- solicitors' professional indemnity (England, Wales and Scotland only).

UK: compulsory insurance of the following risks can be underwritten only by UK or EC insurers or by UK / EC branches and agencies of third country insurers:
- credit unions (professional liability)
- insurance broking (professional indemnity)

2) No other limitation than:

DK: compulsory air transport insurance can be underwritten only by firms established in the Community.

2) None

INSURANCE (cont.)

2) (cont.)

DK: no persons or companies (including insurance companies) may for business purposes in Denmark assist in effecting direct insurance for persons resident in Denmark, for Danish ships or for property in Denmark, other than Danish companies, foreign companies registered in Denmark, or foreign insurance companies subject to the Danish Act on the provision of insurance services within Direct non-life insurance (implementing the EC second non-life insurance Directive). The Minister of Industry may lay down rules providing for otherwise.

D: compulsory air insurance policies can be underwritten only by a subsidiary established in the Community or by a branch established in Germany.

D: If a foreign insurance company has established a branch in Germany, it may conclude insurance contracts in Germany relating to international transport only through the branch established in Germany.

E, GR : air and maritime transport insurance, covering goods, aircraft, hull and liability can be underwritten only by established firms (this restriction will be lifted on 1st January 1993).

E: the provision of actuarial services in Spain is subject to a condition of residence.

F : insurance of risks relating to ground transport may be carried out only by insurance firms established in the Community.

15.

INSURANCE (cont.)

2) (cont.)

I : Insurance of risks relating to CIF exports by residents in Italy may be underwritten only by insurance firms established in Italy.

I : establishment in Italy is required for the insurance of risks related to vessels and aircraft registered in Italy ; however, authorization may be granted for the insurance of these risks with non-established insurance companies if coverage is not available with established insurance companies.

I : Companies operating in Italy are obliged to cede to the National Insurance Institute a portion of each risk covered by the life assurance in their Italian portfolios. This portion varies from 10% to 30% depending on the length of time for which the company concerned has been in business. This restriction will be eliminated by 20 November 1994.

P : air and maritime transport insurance, covering goods, aircraft, hull and liability can be underwritten only by firms established in Portugal; only persons or companies established in Portugal may act as intermediaries for such insurance business in Portugal.

UK: compulsory insurance of the following risks can be underwritten only by UK authorised insurers:
– licensed conveyancers (professional indemnity)
– employers' liability
– solicitors' professional indemnity (England, Wales and Scotland only).

UK: compulsory of the following risks can be underwritten only by UK or EC insurers or by UK / EC branches and agencies of third country insurers:
– credit unions (professional liability)
– insurance broking (professional indemnity)

INSURANCE (cont.)

3) No other limitations than ** :

D: fire insurance business and insurance against
certain other damages by natural forces for
buildings can be carried out in some parts of its
territory only by public institutions enjoying
monopoly rights.

GR, E, IRL - the right of establishment does not
cover the creation of representative offices or
other permanent presence of insurance companies,
except where such offices are established as
agencies, branches or head offices.

E : before establishing a branch or agency in Spain
to provide certain classes of insurance, a
foreign insurer must have been authorized to
operate in the same classes of insurance in its
country of origin for at least five years.

F : the establishment of branches of insurance
companies not having their head office in a
Member State of the Community is subject to a
special authorization of the representative of
the firm in France.

** In Belgium, Denmark, France, Germany (only for branches), Greece, Ireland (only for branches), Italy, Spain and the United Kingdom, the establishment of foreign insurance companies may be subject to a reciprocity requirement. According to Community legislation, the establishment of a life or non-life insurance subsidiary of an insurance company from a third country may be subject to the condition that the third country of origin grants Community insurance companies the right of establishment and a de facto national treatment.

The Community offers as a roll-back not to apply these provisions at GATS signatories; however, this offer is conditional, and the Community may reserve the right to invoke these provisions vis-a-vis third countries which do not make adequate liberalization commitments in the financial services sector. The Community will as a general rule consider inadequate offers by third countries which do not commit to respect, under national treatment conditions, the acquired rights of Community financial institutions operating in their markets, or which, in particular in case of third countries with important financial markets, do not include a standstill for the whole financial services sector. Other factors to be taken into account in judging the adequacy of third country offers will be the actual openness of the financial services market and the roll-back of restrictions offered.

16.

0172

INSURANCE (cont.)

3) (cont.)

IRL: the authorization of the establishment of branches of insurance companies not having their head office in a Member State of the Community is ultimately subject to the discretion of supervisory authorities.

IRL: schemes to provide private health insurance in competition with the State "Voluntary Health Insurance Board" can only be operated under licence granted by the Minister for Health; licences are granted on a non discriminatory basis.

I : the authorization of the establishment of branches of insurance companies not having their head office in a Member State of the Community is ultimately subject to the discretion of supervisory authorities.

P : foreign companies may carry out insurance intermediation in Portugal only through a company formed in accordance with Portuguese law, in which a majority of the capital has to be owned by Portuguese or Community nationals.

P : the establishment of agencies of foreign insurance companies is subject to a test of economic need. Before establishing a branch in Portugal, foreign insurance companies need to have operated for at least five years.

4) Subject to "all sectors" limitations; in addition :

DK: the general agent of an insurance branch shall be a national of one of the Member States of the Community or have resided in Denmark for the last two years. The Ministry of Industry may grant exemption from this requirement. Managers and the members of the board of directors of a company shall be a national of one of the Member States of the Community. However, the Minister of Industry may grant exemption from this requirement. Exemption is granted on a non-discriminatory basis.

GR: the Managers and Members of the board of directors of an insurance company shall be a national of one of the Member States of the Community.

17.

0173

외   무   부

종   별 :

번   호 : GVW-0931   일   시 : 92 0505 1800

수   신 : 장관(통기, 경기원, 체신부)

발   신 : 주제네바대사

제   목 : UR/서비스협상(기본 통신)

　　1. 5.5(화) 스웨덴의 통신분야 협상대표는 기본 통신분야 협상 타개를 위한 타협안으로서 UR이후 지속적 협상에 관한 합의 초안을 제시, 아국의 견해를 문의하여 왔는바 별첨 송부하니 지급 검토 회시 바람.

　　2. 동 초안은 미국의 제안과는 달리 기본통신분야의 MFN 일탈을 완전 배제하는 한편 UR이후 자유화 협상 시한도 정하지 않고 있다는점을 감안하여 긍정적 검토 바람.

　　첨부: 스웨덴의 제안 1부

　　(GVW(F)-0298).끝

　　(대사 박수길-국장)

통상국 　　　　　　　　　경기원

체신부

PAGE 1 　　　　　　　　　　　　　　　　　　　　　92.05.06　　07:53 DQ

외신 1과 통제관

0174

주 제 네 바 대 표 부

번 호 : GVW(F) - 0218   년월일 : 20505   시간 : 1800
수 신 : 장   관 (통기.경기원. 체신부)
발 신 : 주 제네바대사
제 목 : UR/서비스 협상 (기본통신)

총 2 매(프지프함)

브 안	
등 제	

외신과	
등 제	

체신부	전기통신		공정거래	경제기획	상공부	재무부	농수산부	동자부	경기원	공보처	안기부	청와대	외원원	문화부	동상국	경제국	국기국	중아국	우주국	미주국	북미국	신여록	영공실	기차보	차보	안보실	산경실	특특부신처
									1						0												

218-21

92. 5.5 스위스

MEMORANDUM OF UNDERSTANDING

The Signatories to this Memorandum of Understanding, which represent countries with major telecommunications markets,

recognizing that the largest potential for further liberalization of trade in telecommunications services relates to basic telecommunications services, while

acknowledging the complexity of factors and the longer-term perspective that influence domestic policy objectives and that have determined existing regulatory regimes for basic telecommunications services, and

noting the limited time available for further negotiations during the Uruguay Round,

have decided to enter into negotiations on the progressive further liberalization of trade in basic telecommunications services, with no services a priori excluded, on the assumption that such negotiations may continue under the auspices of the GATS after the conclusion of this Round in order to ensure future liberalization on a multilateral basis.

These negotiations shall be conducted in an efficient manner with the aim of Signatories agreeing to a balanced, but not necessarily symmetrical, set of commitments to liberalize measures affecting trade in as broad a range of basic telecommunications services as possible. Such commitments shall be implemented by Signatories in accordance with the GATS rules, and shall be recorded as alterations to their national schedules, without recourse to art. XXI.

During the negotiations a Signatory shall not avail itself of any exemption it might request from art. II for measures affecting trade in telecommunications services.

All Uruguay Round participants that are prepared to engage in negotiations on the further liberalization of trade in basic telecommunications services are invited to sign this Memorandum of Understanding and participate in these negotiations.

Done in Geneva 1992-05-XX.

Signed:

2/8-2-2

0176

외 무 부

종 별 :

번 호 : GVW-0979 　　　　　　　　　　 일 시 : 92 0512 1930

수 신 : 장관(통기,경기원,재무부,농수산부,상공부,법무부,문화부,건설부,교통부,

발 신 : 주 제네바 대사 　　　　　체신부,보사부,과기처,공보처,항만청,특허청)

제 목 : UR/법제화 그룹 비공식회의(개별협정문)

　　　연: 제네(정) 20644-420(1)

　　　GVW-873(2)

　　서비스 협정문 사무국 수정안(TEXT 769)에 대한 5.11 표제회의 논의 요지를 아래 보고함.

　　1. 서문

　　0 3항 5줄 및 4항 3줄의 NATIONAL POLICY OBJECTIVES 관련 당초 협상 취지가 중앙 정부의 정책뿐만 아니라 지방정부의 정책도 포함하는 것이므로 PUBLIC(또는 DOMESTIC) POLICY OBJECTIVES 로 수정하자는 카나다 제의에 대해 EC, 아르헨티나, 인도등이당초 취지보다 개념이 넓어진다는 점을 들어 이에 반대함.

　　2. 제 1조(범위 및 정의)

　　0 제 2항 및 3항은 12.20 초안의 주석에 따라 34조(개념) 논의후 검토키로 함.

　　(3P 7 항 참조)

　　3. 제 2조(MFN)

　　0 카나다는 브랏셀 TEXT 에 있었던 제 2조4항(ACQUIRED RIGHTS 에 대한 MFN 적용배제조항)이 아무런 토의없이 최종협정안에서 삭제된점에 대하여 이의를 제기한바,사무국은 통상적으로 국제협정은 현존 규제제도에 대하여 적용되는것이며 명시적 규정이 없는한 소급효과가 없기때문에 구법률하에서 주어진 혜택은 MFN적용대상은 아니므로 이를 삭제하였다고 언급함.

　　0 미국은 (사법 및 행정공조 협정에 대한 MFN적용 배제를 규정한 주석에 대하여동협정등은 사실상 서비스 무역에 별다른 영향을 미치지 않는다는 이유를 들어 삭제할 것을 제의하였으나 기타 국가들은 추가 검토가 필요한 사항이라고 반대함.

　　0 홍콩은 연호 2(2항) 소규모 비공식 회의에서 잠정합의된 COUNTRY 개념에

통상국	2차보	법무부	보사부	문화부	교통부	체신부	경기원	재무부
농수부	상공부	건설부	과기처	해항정	특허청	공보처		

대한사무국 정리문안을 배포해 줄것을 요청하면서(첨부 사무국문서 참조) 3항 4줄의 FRONTIER ZONES 의 개념이 홍콩과 같은 관세 영역에는 맞지 않으므로 BORDER ZONES 로 수정하자는 제의를 한바, EC 및 카나다가 FRONTIER 와 BORDER 개념은 차이가 없으며 FRONTIER 용어 사용에 문제가 없다는 의견 개진

4. 제 3조(공개주의)

0 카나다는 제 1항과 관련 사무국 수정안에 대하여 일반적으로 작용되는 조치만공표대상으로 하기보다는 구체적인 개별 결정, 조치들도 포함되어야한다고 하였으나EC 등 다른 나라들은 일반적으로 적용되는 조치만 공표대상으로 한정하는 것이 협상그룹의 의도였다고 반박함.

0 한편 EC 는 3항의 시장접근 약속을 한 분야에 있어서 규제 제도 변경의 통지 범위를 일반적 적용 효력을 가지는 조치로 한정하는 것은 원 협정 초안의 취지와 어긋나는 것이며, 특별한 경우에 효력이 한정되는 규제 조치의 통지 대상이 포함되어야하므로 단순히 MEASURES 라고 규정하자고 제의하였으며, 일본이 이에 동조하였으며,카나다 미국은 사무국 수정안을 지지함.

5. 제 5조 (경제통합)

0 6(B) 항의 법인 (JURIDICAL PERSON) 개념과관련, 동 개념은 제 34조에 서술되어 있으므로 CONSTITUTED 이하 PARAGRAPH 1 까지를 삭제하자는 멕시코 제의에 대해 EC는 동항의 법인개념은 34조와는 달리 모든 MTO 회원국이 아니라 경제 통합 협정 회원국내에서 영업 활동을하는 법인에 한정된다는 점을 지적하여 멕시코제의에 반대

6. 협정문 목차

0 목차(P.7-8)에 협정문의 일부인 부속서를 명기하기로 함.(부속서 리스트가 명기된 5P 의 목차는 협정문이 완성될 때까지 협상의 목적을 위해 필요한 부분임)

0 협정문 목차의 괄호안에 있는 조항은 MTO협정문에 대한 논의결과에 따라 존치여부를 결정키로 함.(3P, 9 항 참조)

첨부: COUNTRY 용어에 대한 비공식 협의결과(사무국 문서) 1부.

(GVW(F)-313)

(대사 박수길-국장)

주 제 네 바 대 표 부

번 호 : GVE(F) - 0313   년월일 : 2월5/21 /A30 시간 :

수 신 : 장   관 (동기, 경기원, 재무부, 농림수산부, 상공부, 특허청)

발 신 : 주 제 네 바 대 사   법무부, 문화부, 건설부, 교통부, 체신부,
                                              보사부, 과기처, 공보처, 항만청
제 목 :

GUW - PTA 린4

총 2 매 (표지포함)

외신관
등 제

Informal Consultations on the Term "Country" in the MTO Agreement

Informal consultations with interested delegations on the use of the term "country" in the Agreement establishing the MTO were held on 23 April 1992.

The consultations resulted in an ad referendum agreement on the following two proposals:

(a) To include an explanatory note in the text of the MTO Agreement which would read as follows:

"The terms 'country' or 'countries' as used in the Agreement establishing the MTO and the Multilateral Trade Agreements and Plurilateral Trade Agreements in the annexes to this Agreement are to be understood to include any separate customs territory Member of the MTO."

(b) The terms 'developing Member', 'developed Member' and 'least-developed Member', which are used in the current drafts of the MTO Agreement and its Annexes, would be replaced by the terms 'developing country Member', 'developed country Member' and 'least-developed country Member'.

It was understood in the consultations that the consequences of this explanatory note for the references to 'country' in the anti-dumping and subsidy agreements, in particular the references to countries member of the EEC, would need to be examined in the review of these agreements by the Legal Drafting Group.

3 /3 — 2 — 2

0180

외 무 부

종 별 :

번 호 : GVW-0988 　　　　　　　　　일 시 : 92 0513 1900

수 신 : 장 관(수신처 참조)

발 신 : 주 제네바대사

제 목 : UR/법제화그룹 비공식회의(개별협정문)

　　　서비스 협정문 사무국 수정안(TEXT 769)에 대한 5.12. 논의 요지를 아래 보고함.(이경협관,신서기관, 한경협관보 참석)

　　　1. 제 6조(국내규제)

　　　0 아국은 5항 A)... 'SPECIFIC COMMITMENTS IN ACCORDANCEWITH ARTICLE XVI AND XVII OF THIS AGREEMENT...'에 대하여 서비스 협정 제 3부의 SPECIFIC COMMITMENTS 대 상인ARTICLE XVIII(ADDITIONAL COMMITMENTS)가 누락되었을뿐만 아니라 그표현도 제8 조 1항의...'SPECIFIC COMMITMENTS UNDER PART III OF THISAGREEMENT...' 제 6조 3항의 'SPECIFIC COMMITMENT'등과 일관성이 없다고 지적한 바, EC,스웨덴, 인도등이지지하여 SPECIFIC COMMITMENTS로 통일하기로 합의함.

　　　2. 제 7조(인정)

　　　0 미국은 자격인정을 국가간에 차별적인 방법으로 하지 않도록 규정한 제 3항과관련, 자격인정을 당연히 차별적으로 이루어지므로 자의적이거나 정당화될 수 없는차별만 금지하도록 규정할 것을 제의하였으나, (DISCRIMINIATION 앞에 UNJUSTIFIABLE OR ARBITRARY 추가) EC 등 기타국가는동 사항은 이미 협상 과정에서 집중적으로 토의된바 있으며 특정 표준 또는 기준을 충족하는 경우에만 차별하지 않도록 제한적으로 규정하였으므로 당초의 표현에 문제가 없다고 함.

　　　0 서비스 협정 발효후 12개월이내에 현존인정 조치를 통지하도록 규정한 4항 A)와 관련, 사무국은 서비스 협정 단독으로 발효될 수는 없으므로 MTO 협정 발효이후 12개월이내로 통지한다는 문안으로 수정 제의하여 이를 채택함.

　　　0 2항의 PARTY 를 MEMBER 로 수정한 것은 사무국 착오임을 확인함

　　　3. 제 8조(독점)

　　　0 미국은 SPECIFIC COMMITMENT 를 한분야에 새로이 독점 기업을 지정할 경우 제21

통상국	법무부	보사부	문화부	교통부	체신부	경기원	재무부	농수부
상공부	건설부	과기처	해항정	특허청	공보처			

외신 1과 통제관 ✓

0181

조(양허수정)를 적용하도록 한 4항에 제22조(협의), 23조(분쟁해결)도 적용토록 하자고 제의하였으나 22조 23조의 적용은 당연한 것이므로 굳이 추가할 필요가 없다는다수 의견에 따라 동제의를 철회함

4. 제 12조(BOP 조항)

O MATHUR 의장은 본 조항 운영 관계기구의 기능을 MTO 협정의 구조에 비추어 다음과 같이 사무국이 정하였음을 설명함

- BOP 조항 원용국가의 협의 담당기구 : BOP위원회(5항 A 및 E)
- BOP 를 이유로한 제한조치의 통지처:일반이사회(4항)
- BOP 협의절차 제정기구 : 각료회의(5항 B)
- IMF 비회원국의 본조항 원용 절차 제정기구 :각료회의(6항 : EC는 2년에 한번씩 개최되는 각료회의 보다는 일반 이사회가 적합하다고 지적

O 이에 대해, 4항 BOP 제한 조치의 통지처는 일반이사회보다는 BOP 위원회로 하자는 EC 의 의견이 제시되었으며, 한편 E항의 IMF 조사결과는 모든 개별MTO 회원국이수용하여야 한다는 취지로 규정하기로 합의함.

5. 제 16조(시장접근)

O 1항의 OTHER MEMBERS 를 제 2조 및 제 17조 1항과 일관되게 ANY OTHER MEMBER로 통일하기로 합의함.

O 서비스의 국경간 공급에 자본이 동(유입, 유출)이필수적인 경우 당해 서비스의 국경간 공급에 시장접근 약속을 하였으면 관련 자본이동도 허용하도록 약속한 것이라고 규정한 제 16조주석(P.25 첫째 주석)을 국경간 이동 이외의 서비스공급(특히 소비자 이동에 의한 공급형태)에도 해당하도록 규정하자고 스위스가 제의(THROUGH 이하OF ARTICLE I 까지 삭제) 하였으나 대부분의 나라가 반대함.

6. 2항의 OTHER MEMBER 를 1항의 ANY OTHER MEMBER로 통일함

7. 양허협상(제 19조)

O 미국은 제3항의 후속 양허협상의 가인드라인 작성을 위한 국제 서비스 무역현황 평가담당기구로서 사무국초안의 각료회의 보다는 서비스이사회가 적합하다는 의견을 제시하였으며 인도는 가이드라인 작성 주체는 각료회의로 추정되는것인지 의문을 제시하였음.

8. 자유화약속 목록(제 20조)

O 각국의 SCHEDULE 에 기재되어야 할 요소에 대하여제 16조, 17조, 18조 본문

내용등에 따라 다음과 같이 수정(동 항목들은 각국 SCHEDULE 의 각 COLUMN 의 제목이되게 됨) 하자는 제의에 대해 다수국이 동조하였으나 인도, 홍콩, 일본등이 당초안유지를 주장함.

- 1항 A) : LIMITATION AND CONDITIONS ON MARKET ACCESS
- 1 항 B : CONDITIONS AND QUALIFICATION ON NATIONALTREATMENT
- 1항 C) : ADDITIONAL COMMITMENTS.끝

(대사　　　박수길-국장)수신처:봉기,경기원,재무부,법무부,농수부,상공부,문화부, 건설부,교통부,체신부,보사부,과기처,공보처,항만청,특허청

PAGE 3

0183

외 무 부

종 별 :

번 호 : GVW-0996   일 시 : 92 0514 1930

수 신 : 장관(통기,경기원,재무부,법무부,농수부,상공부,문화부,항만청,특허청

발 신 : 주 제네바대사   건설부,교통부,체신부,보사부,과기처 공보처)

제 목 : UR/법제화그룹 비공식회의(개별협정문)

서비스 협정문 사무국 수정안(TEXT 769)에 대한 5.13 논의 요지를 아래 보고함.(이경협관, 신서기관, 한경협관보 참석)

1. 제22조(협의), 23조(분쟁해결), 24조(공동행위)

0 통합 분쟁해결 절차 및 MTO 협정의 토의가 진전된 이후에 추후 토의키로 함.

2. 제25조(이사회)

0 제1항의 서비스 이사회의 설치 및 권능의 근거는 MTO 협정의 해당 규정과 같이 서비스협정자체에서 찾아야 한다는 것(THERE SHALL BE) 이다수 의견이었음.

0 제2항 말미의 MEMBERS OF THIS AGREEMENT 는 MTO회원국을 의미하는 MEMBERS 로 변경함.

3. 제27조(타 국제기구와의 관계)

0 뉴질랜드는 동 조문의 MTO 협정문과 중복되므로 삭제하자고 주장하였으나 EC,카나다등은 타 국제기구와의 협력은 MTO 의 전체적인 차원에서의 협력뿐만 아니라 MTO 내여러 수준의 기구에서 이루어지는 협력도 상정할수 있으므로 서비스 협정에 별도 조항이 필요하다고 함.

0 한편, EC 는 타국제기구와의 협력문제는 각료회의 보다는 일반 이사회가 취급하는 것이 보다 적합하다고 지적함.

4. 제28조(수락 및 가입)

0 사무국 초안은 본 조문을 모두 삭제하였으나SCHEDULE 을 부속서에 포함시킨 국가 및 EC 에한하여 가입자격이 있다고 규정한 제1항은 MTO협정 제11조(원가맹국의양허표 제출의무 범위 관련 조항) 논의 결과에 따라 재생시킬수도 있다는 유보의사가 제기됨.(E,C)

5. 제30조(부적용)

통상국	법무부	보사부	문화부	교통부	체신부	경기원	재무부	농수부
상공부	건설부	과기처	해항정	특허청	공보처	2시19		

O 미국은 부적용 조항 MTO 협정 보다는 개별협정별로 규정하자는 것이 자국 기본입장이며, MTO협정에 규정한다 하더라도 MTO 협정상의 규정에 서비스 협정 제 30조 2 항과 같은 특수요건(부적용 이유 명시)이 주석등의 형식을 통해 MTO협정에 반영되지 않는한, MTO 협정상의 일반 규정이 개별 협정의 규정에 우선해서는 안된다는 입장을 개진함.

O 이에 인도는 MTO 상의 부적용 조항을 일반규정, 개별협정상의 조항을 특별규정으로 하는 2중 구조를 제시하였으나, EC 는 MTO 규정에 의한 일원적인 방법이나 또는 각 개별협정에 의한 부적용 규정중 양자 택일해야 한다는 의견을 개진함.

6. 제 31조(혜택부여 거부)

O 제 34조(용어의 정의)와 관련되므로 추후 토의키로함.

7. 제 32조(개정)

O 사무국 초안은 동 조문을 모두 삭제하였으나 미국, 일본, 카나다는 32조 1,2 항은 MTO 협정과 다른요소가 있으므로 당분간 유보하고 MTO 협정결과에 따라 결정하겠다고 함.(의장은 개정관련 조항은 기본적으로 MTO 차원에서 논의할 사항이므로 개별 협정의 특수한 내용은 MTO 관련 규정에 반영되는 것이 바람직하다는 개인 의견을 피력)

8. 제 35조(부속서)

O 91.12.30 자 최종의정서안에는 없던 NATIONALSCHEDULE 양식(P.37) 이 삽입된데대하여 그 이유 및 법적 효력에 대한 의문이 제기되었는 바, 갓트법률국은 이는 최종의정서안에 누락되었던 것이며, 동 양식에 맞추어 SCHEDULE 을 제출할의무를 부과하는 것이라고 답변함.

O 이에 대하여 인도 및 EC 는 COMMITMENTS 의 명확성을 위하여 공통양식에 따라 SCHEDULE 을 제출할 필요성을 강조한 반면 스웨덴, 카나다, 호주등은 공통양식에 따를 필요성은 인정하나 SCHEDULE 양식 자체에 대해서 현재 협상이 진행중이기 때문에 이에 대한 토의는 시기상조라는 의견을 개진하면서 아무런 관련 본문없이 별도 PAGE 에 양식만 그려진 상태로법적 문서에 포함될수 있는지 의문을 표시함.

9. 제 21조(양허수정), 제34조(정의), 통신부속서,항공부속서

O 기술적 과제가 남아 있는 분야이므로 토의하지 않음.

10. MFN 일탈에 관한 부속서

PAGE 2

0185

O 3항, 4항의 MFN 일탈 재검토 기구로서 사무국초안의 각료회의 보다는 서비스이사회가 적합하다는 의견(일본, 미국: 동 항의 검토대상으로서의 MFN일탈은 2항의 워이버와 다름을 지적함)과 MTO협정의 WAIVER 결정기구와 균형을 도모하여야 한다는 의견(EC, 카나다)이 대립됨.

11. DECISION CONCERNING ARTICLE 14(B) (P.56)

O 동 DECISION 의 법적 지위와 관련, 카나다 및 스위스는 MINISTERIAL DECISION으로 하는 것이 협상그룹의 의도였다고 한 반면 기타 국가들은 그와같은 이해가 없었다고 이의를 제기하여 합의를 도출하지 못함.

2. UNDERSTANDING ON COMMITMENTS IN FINANCIAL SERVICES

O 동 UNDERSTANDING 의 법적 지위와 관련,사무국 문서 제 6항(P.3) 이 현 상황을정확히 기술한 것이라는데는 이의가 없었으나 미국, EC, 스웨덴, 카나다등은 동 UNDERSTANDING 이 영구적지위를 가져야 한다고 주장한 반면, 인도, 브라질 등 개도국들은 동 UNDERSTANDING 은 NEGOTIATION GUIDELINE 에 불과하며, 영구적 성격을 가지는 것은 SPECIFIC COMMITMENTS 뿐이라고 주장함.

O MATHUR 의장은 동 UNDERSTANDING 과 DECISIONS CONCERNING ARTICLE 14(B) 의 법적 지위에 대하여 GATS 자체도 아니고 MINISTERIAL DECISION 도 아닌제 3의 형태를법률국에서 검토하도록 하고 협의를 종결함. 끝

(대사 박수길-국장)

외 무 부

종 별 :

번 호 : GVW-1010 일 시 : 92 0515 1730

수 신 : 장관(통기, 경기원, 재무부, 법무부, 농림수산부, 상공부, 문화부, 건설부, 교통부,

발 신 : 주제네바대사 보사부, 과기처, 공보처, 항만청)

제 목 : UR/GNS 비공식협의

5.11(월)-5.13(수) 오전 법제화 그룹 서비스 협정토의에 이어 5.13(수) 오후부터 CARLISLE 사무차장주재로 20개국 비공식 협의가 개최되어 6월 협상계획과 SCHEDULING 및 조세 문제등 기술적 과제에 대하여 토의하였는바, 주요 내용 하기보고함.

1. 6월 협상 계획에 대한 토의(5.14 오전)

가. 협의결과

0 6.15 주 및 6.22 주 2주간 INITIAL COMMITMENTS 에관한 양자 협상 개최 합의

0 6.9 주간 (6.11, 12 경이 될 것으로 예상되나 구체적일자 미정)에는 SCHEDULING, 조세문제, 34조등기술적 과제 토의

나. 협의 내용

0 CARLISLE 사무차장은 6월중 양자 협상 추진에대하여 UR 전체 협상 현황을 볼때6월중 별진전이 있을 것 같지 않다는 점, 많은 나라로부터 추가 OFFER 가 나오기를기다려야 한다는점, 3월협상의 좋지 않은 경험이 되풀이 될 우려가있다는 점등 여러가지 유보적 의견이 있는 것으로알고 있으나 다음과 같은 점을 고려하여 6.9-19 간양자 협상을 추진할 것을 제의한다고 함.

- 농산물 분야 뿐만 아니라 서비스 분야에도 매우 어려운 난관이 있는바, 농산물 문제가 해결되고 난후에는 해운, 기본통신, 금융등이 주요 문제로 등장할 것이며 타결에 수개월이 소요될 것임.

- 여러가지 기술적 과제가 많이 남아 있는바,농산물 분야 타결시까지 아무작업도하지 않는다면 나중에 시간이 부족하게 됨.

0 동 제의에 대하여 미국, 일본, 아국, 이집트,스위스, EC, 헝가리, 뉴질랜드 등이 지지의사를 밝힌반면

0 인도, 브라질, 호주, 홍콩, 알제틴, 태국,말련등은 6월 협상이 단순히

통상국	2차보	외정실	분석관	법무부	보사부	문화부	교통부	경기원
재무부	농수부	상공부	건설부	과기처	해항정	공보처		

92.05.16 04:10 CJ

외신 1과 통제관 ✓

0187

기술적명료화작업에 머물것인지 실질적 협상이 될수 있을것인지 그 성격이 명확히 정해져야 한다고 전제하고 6월 협상이 실질적 협상이 되기 어려운 실정이며,그와 같은 상태에서 분야별 전문가를 협상에 참가토록 할 경우 GNS 담당자의 신뢰성이 상실된다는 점을 들어 분야별 전문가가 포함된 완전한 협상팀의 참여를 보장할수 없다고 함.

0 이에 대하여 EC 및 CARLISLE 사무차장은 협상의 마지막 단계이전에는 실질적인 양허교환이 이루어지지 않을 것이라는 점, 6월 협상이 마지막 라운드가 되지 않을 것이라는 점은 분명하나 기술적 명료화 작업보다는 한단계 높은 REQUEST와 OFFER의 격차를 줄이기 위한 작업이 될것이라고 함.

2. SCHEDULING 에 대한 토의(5.14 오후)

- 사무국에서 작성한 기술적 문제에 대하여 토의하였는바, 별첨 문서 참조 바람.

3. 조세 문제(5.13 오후 SAMPSON 서비스 국장 주재)

가. 협의 개용

0 제 14조(예외) D항 (공평하거나 효율적인조세의 부과 징수를 위한 거주자인 서비스 공급자와 비거주자인 서비스 공급자간 차별 대우에 대한 예외허용) 및 제 14조 E 항(이중과세 방지 협정에따른 국가간 차별대우에 대한 예외 허용) 에대하여 EC 및 미국이 그 포괄범위를 넓히려는 의도에서 여러문제를 제기하였으나 기타국가들은이는 TRACK 4 에 해당하는 실질적 문제이며 문제가 있는 나라는 개별적으로 자국 SCHEDULE 에 유보하여야 할것이라고 하였으며, 6월 회의시재토의키로 함.

나. 협의 내용

1) 제 14조 D 항

0 EC 는 동 조항과 관련 다음 문제들을제기함.

- 동 조항은 내국민 대우에 대한 예외만 규정하고있으나 공평하거나 효과적인 세금 부과 징수를위한 조치가 내국민 대우에 위배되는 것 뿐만아니라 MFN 문제(조세 천국 관련)를 초래하는 경우도 있음.

- 'TAXES ON INCOME' 이라는 용어가 정확한지 , 즉 자본이득세도 포괄하고 있는지 , 간접세도 포함할 필요는 없는지

- 서비스 구매자에 대한 과세 조치도 서비스 공급자간 특히 거주자인 서비스 공급자와 비거주자인 서비스공급자간 경쟁조건에 영향을 미침(예: 사금융기관에서 구입한 연금 수입에 대한 과세환급의 구입국별 차별)

- 동 조항은 비거주자에 대한 차별 조치에 대해서만 예외를 허용하고 있으나 거주자의 개념이 불명확하고 나라마다 그 기준이 다르기 때문에 실제운영에 문제가있음.

0 이에 대한 각국의 논평은 다음과 같음.

- 'TAXES ON INCOME' 이라는 용어는 자본이득세도 포함하는 개념임.(참가국간 합의 사항)

- 간접세는 포함해서는 않되며, 예외대상으로서 오직 직접세만 검토해야 함.(카나다)

- 서비스 구매자에 대한 과세조치의 차별도 결국 거주자인 서비스 공급자와 비거주자인 서비스 공급자간 차별문제임.(일본)

- 비거주자 개념은 계속 유지되어야 하며, 거주자간 차별도 포함해서는 않됨.(일본, 카나다)

0 SAMPSON 국장은 각국 조세 전문가들이 상기문제들을 검토하여 의견을 제시해 줄것을 요청하는 한편, 사무국에서 동 의견들을 취합하여 추후 재토의 하겠다고 함.

2) 제14조 E항

0 동조항의 'INTERNATIONAL AGREEMENT' 의 정의 및 범위에 대하여 다음과 같은의견이 개진됨.

- 'INTERNATIONAL AGREEMENT' 가 UNDERSTANDING 등 모든 형태의 국가간 합의 사항으로 다 포괄하므로 그범위가 너무 넓기 때문에 협정의 SIGNATORY 에 한정할 필요가 있음(EC)

- '이중 과세 방지 협정' 이라는 제목이 아닌 조세일반에 관한 협정도 많이 있는바 동 협정들도 포괄되어야 함.(미국)

- 조세 관련 협정뿐만 아니라 항공협정, 해운협정등도 조세관련 조항을 포함하고있는 경우가있음.(카나다)

0 SAMPSON 국장은 'INTERNATIONAL AGREEMENT' 의정의에 대하여 갓트 법률국의 자문을 구한뒤 추후 재토의 하겠다고 함.

3) 제11조 (지급 및 이전)

0 EC 는 제 11조 1항이 정당한 조세 조치(특히비거주자에 대한 원천세)까지도 금지하는 것으로 해석될 우려가 있다고 문제를 제기하였으나 대부분의 나라가 정당한 과세 조치는 IMF규정에서도 허용되는 것이라는 견해를 피력한바 IMF 에 동 내용을문의 추후 재토의키로 함.

4. GNS 비공식 회의(5.15 오전 CARLSILE 사무차장주재)

0 상기회의(약 40개국 참석)는 5.13-14간 20개국 비공식 협의 내용을 봉보하고곧 바로 종결됨.

5. 건의

0 5.13 토의된 조세 문제와 관련 제 14조(예외)에의하여 포괄되지 않는 과세 조치가 있는지 여부를 점검하여 이를 아국 SCHEDULE 에 기재하거나 제 14조본문에 새로이 반영할 사항이 있는지 검토 바람.

첨부: 1. WCHEDULING 에 관한 사무국 문서 1부

2. 조세 문제에 관한 사무국 문서 1부

3. 제 34조(정의)에 관한 사무국 문서 1부. 끝

(GVW(F)-0321)

(대사 박수길-국장)

PAGE 4

주 제 네 바 대 표 부

번 호 : GVR(F) - 0321   년월일 : 20515   시간 1730
수 신 : 장   관 (팀가. 경기원. 재무부. 영무부. 농수산부. 상공부. 건설부. 보사부. 노동부
고통부. 체신부. 문화부. 공보처. 과기처. 조달청)
발 신 : 주 제 네바대사
제 목 : UR/GNS회의

품 20. 벽(프지트함)

보 안 등 재	720

의신과 등 재	

321~20~1

DRAFT
14.5.92

< 5.14 회의결과 >

1. Some offers contain information for clarification purposes only, is such information suitable for a schedule? : 동정보들은 Scheduling 대상이 아님, 그러나 각국의 선택에 따라 Transparency 제고목적의 정보는 기재할 수 있으며 동정보들은 아무런 법적효력이 없음

2. If a specific commitment is made does the entry 'no limitations' in the national treatment column mean no conditions or qualifications apply other than the discriminatory measures listed in the market access column and those identified as horizontal restrictions? yes
   ○ 제한이 없는 경우 빈칸으로 남두어서는 안됨. 제한이 없을 경우인 "NONE" 으로 표기하기로 합의.

3. What degree of detail has to be given with respect to <u>legal references</u> in schedules? ○ Scheduling 대상은 제한 조치 그대로 Measure 로 간략 또한 저촉하게 기재하는 것이며 legal reference 표기는 의무사항이 아님. Measure의 기재없이 법조항만 인용해서는 안됨

4. What happens if there is no corresponding classification for a specific service <u>in the Secretariat classification of sectors</u> and the CPC classification?

5. Is it possible to exempt preferential treatment accorded to specific countries on the basis of agreements which are inconsistent with Article V of the GATS (e.g. <u>NAFTA</u>, <u>FTA</u>, association agreements between the EC and East European or Nordic countries)?
   ① GATS 5조에 합치하지 않는 FTA 등이 GATS 발효이전에 서명되었을 경우 MFN일탈 신청이 가능하며 국가간 협상에 따라 적용됨은 상관임
   ② GATS 5조에 합치하지 않는 FTA 등이 GATS 발효이후에 서명되었을 경우에는 Waiver 신청 대상임.

다음순서의 따라 분류·기재하기로 합의

1) 갓트사무국 분류표 (GNS/W/120)

2) CPC code

3) CPC Code 세세분류 구 digit (CPC code개정된 상태, UN에서 각종 통계기구에 배부되었음)

4) CPC code 구단위로도 안될경우 당해 sub-sector의 범위를 정확하게 기술

0192

321-20-2

EE4-1

12.5.92/3

RESPONSE TO TECHNICAL QUESTIONS RELATED TO
SCHEDULING AS IDENTIFIED BY PARTICIPANTS

[handwritten Korean notation]

1. Is there a need to schedule discriminatory subsidies where specific commitments are undertaken, given that there are no disciplines on subsidies in Article XV?

   Article XV merely obliges Parties to 'enter into negotiations with a view to developing the necessary multilateral disciplines' to counter the distortive effects caused by subsidies. Also, in the absence of express language, the provision cannot be interpreted to exclude subsidy measures from the scope of m.f.n. or, when taken, from the scope of national treatment commitments. Consequently, from the point of view of "scheduling" commitments, Article XVII (national treatment) covers any measure which discriminates between foreign services or service suppliers and the Party's own services or service suppliers. Therefore any subsidy which is considered to be a discriminatory measure would have to be either scheduled or brought into conformity with Article XVII. *[handwritten Korean notation]*

2. To what extent is it necessary to schedule measures covered by Articles XII (e.g. foreign exchange restrictions on repatriation of profits) and XIV?

   Measures falling under Article XIV are excepted from all obligations and commitments under the Agreement, and therefore need not be scheduled. Measures falling under Article XII are also exceptions. Exceptions from obligations under the Agreement cannot be negotiated under Part III and should not therefore be scheduled. Article XII provides separate disciplines for the measures it covers, including notification and consultation. *[handwritten Korean notation]* OK

0193

CC2-1

- 2 -

3.   Should prudential measures, such as <u>minimum capital asset requirements</u>, be scheduled if a Party undertakes a market access commitment in the financial services sector? Should a prudential measure requiring a <u>specific type of legal entity</u> (e.g. a branch and not a subsidiary) be scheduled?

Any prudential measure justifiable under paragraph 2:1 of the Annex on Financial Services constitutes a general exception to the Agreement and as such <u>should not be scheduled.</u> The scope of this Article is not defined in terms of the types of measures that it may cover but in terms of the objectives of such measures. Therefore <u>paragraph 2:1 may cover any type of measure</u>, including a requirement for <u>minimum capital assets or for specific types of legal entity, as long as the objective of such a measure is among those specified in the paragraph.</u> ʼ최소자본는 요건은 짓분야
봉안에서 모든 분야에서 국내규제 (제6조) 에 해당하는 사항으로서 Scheduling 할 필요없다
본 문제는 그 Scope를 떠나 봉능 및 답면으로 재작성 하기로 함.

4.   What is the definition of movement of consumer? Is the correct interpretation that the "consumer" is a consumer of the Party?

(a)   The mode of supply often referred to as "movement of the consumer" is more accurately referred to as "~~supply~~ ˆconsumption abroad". The essential feature of this mode is that the service is delivered abroad, i.e. outside the jurisdiction of the Party taking the measure. The actual movement of the consumer, as in tourism services, is not necessary. Activities such as ship repair abroad, where the property of the consumer "moves", or is situated overseas, are also covered.

(b)   The "service consumer of any other Party" mentioned in Article I:2(b) can be, according to a plain reading of the text, from <u>any</u> Party to the Agreement. In practice however, in applying obligations and commitments to this mode, a Party is not able to impose restrictive measures affecting consumers of <u>other</u> parties on activities taking place <u>outside</u> its jurisdiction. ː 본 사항을 차적에 이의 없다.

또, 해외소비 Mode의 경우 National Treatment Column은 "Not applicable" 이라는 해석을 추가하기로 합의 (A 체약국의 주권이 미치지 않는 B 체약국 영토내에서 B 또는 C 체약국 국민의 서비스 수매 행위에 에게서 안전한 규제도 할 수 없으므로 A체약국 국민의 해외소비에 대한 규제 라 비관할 수 없기 때문임.) A체약국이

CC2-1

0194

- 3 -

5. Should a Party be prevented from making a commitment that would cover a measure for which it also seeks an m.f.n. exemption:

- when the m.f.n. exemption is intended to allow for _less_ favourable treatment of certain Parties (reciprocity cases)?

- when the m.f.n. exemption is intended to allow for _more_ favourable treatment of certain countries (agreements on preferential treatment)?

- in both the above cases?

A Party taking a national treatment or a market access commitment in a sector under the Agreement must simply accord the stated _minimum_ standard of treatment specified in its schedule to _all_ other Parties. The m.f.n. obligation requires that the most favourable treatment _actually_ accorded must also be accorded to all other parties. However, where an m.f.n. exemption has been granted in a sector, a Party is free to deviate from its Article II obligations, but not from its Article XVI and XVII commitments. Therefore, in such cases, a Party may accord treatment in that sector more favourable than the minimum standard to some parties, as long as all other parties receive at least the minimum standard.

DRAFT
12.5.92/3

QUESTIONS FOR DISCUSSION AS IDENTIFIED BY PARTICIPANTS

\<6월부터 토의예정\>

1. To what extent do specific commitments extend to all services which
    are inputs to, or are otherwise related to, the supply of the service
    for which the specific commitment has been made?

2. Which tax measures are not covered by Articles XIV? Would such
    measures be subject to scheduling?

3. What is meant by residency; full establishment, personal presence of
    an individual, a study period, apprenticeship, simple registration, an
    address, or other? How should residency requirements be dealt with?

4. What measures of horizontal application should be scheduled?

0196

BB4-1

- 2 -

QUESTIONS FOR DISCUSSION AS IDENTIFIED BY PARTICIPANTS

M.F.N

〈6월회의시 토의 예정〉

.1. Can an exemption from the obligations of the m.f.n. provision be sought only for existing measures, or can it also be sought for future measures?

2. Is it possible to seek an m.f.n. exemption for an indefinite period without any qualification?

3. Which types of horizontal agreements, or measures taken under such agreements, require an m.f.n. exemption and which do not because they are deemed to be outside the scope of the GATS (e.g. social security agreements, investment protection agreements, labour market agreements when only relevant for the individual job seeker, visa agreements/visa exemptions)?

0197

221-20-7   BB4-1

12.05.92

Non-discrimination and Taxation: Possible Issues for Consideration

(a) Scope and definition

Prior to the issuance of the draft Final Act, it was noted that the concept of non-discrimination contained in tax conventions differs from that in the GATS. Concern was expressed that this difference could give rise to a problem wherein certain tax measures consistent with non-discrimination provisions of double taxation agreements might be inconsistent with obligations under Articles II (m.f.n.) and XVII (national treatment) of the GATS. Article XIV (d) and (e) were intended to address this concern.

However, some participants have posed the question: Should the scope of Article XIV (d) and (e) cover all instances of tax measures which may satisfy non-discrimination requirements as defined in tax conventions, but not those in the GATS?

(b) Specific questions regarding Article XIV

Specific questions have been raised about the language of Article XIV with respect to taxation. These include:

Regarding paragraphs (d) and (e) --

(i) Do double taxation agreements encompass the full range of measures to which the exceptions should apply, e.g. what about measures related to other types of tax conventions?

(ii) Should the references to "... agreements" be changed in order to cover measures relating to the avoidance of double taxation taken unilaterally or based on arrangements that do not take the form of agreements?

0198

ISS.TX

-2-

Regarding paragraph (d) --

(iii) Are the requirements in the text of paragraph (d) appropriate for
the tax measures concerned (i.e., "must be aimed at ensuring the
equitable or effective imposition or collection of taxes")?

(iv) Are "taxes on income" the full range of the types of taxes to
which paragraph (d) should apply, (e.g. does "income" include
capital gains; what about indirect taxes)?

(v) Is it only the taxes on service suppliers which need to be
covered, e.g. what about taxes on stockholders or consumers?

(vi) Is it appropriate that the exemption applies only to measures
concerning non-resident service suppliers (i.e., those "not
deemed to reside in the Party's territory")? What or whose
definition of "resident" or "non-resident" applies?

(c) Other possible means of dealing with non-discrimination   ✓

Within the context of considering whether technical clarifications to the
text would be appropriate, some participants have noted that other
possibilities, in addition to Article XIV (d) and (e), may be available for
dealing with such tax measures. These include:

(i) The coverage of certain tax measures by the Article XIV(c)
exception on measures "necessary to secure compliance with laws
or regulations which are not inconsistent with the Agreement".

(ii) The amendment of domestic legislation, rules or regulations
regarding certain tax measures to bring them into conformity with
GATS provisions on non-discrimination.

(iii) The amendment of tax conventions to clarify the relationship
between their provisions on non-discrimination and those of the
GATS.

0199

ISS.TX

-3-

(iv) The listing of certain tax measures that are not in conformity with GATS Article XVII (national treatment) in schedules of commitments.

(v) The inclusion of certain tax measures that are not in conformity with GATS Article II (m.f.n. treatment) in the lists of m.f.n. exemptions.

321-20-10

ISS.TX

0200

14.5.92

Group of Negotiations on Services

A further technical revision to definitions in the GATS
is attached. It is based on suggestions made by delegations
made to the Secretariat, as well as on recent work in the
Legal Drafting Group. No changes in the intent of the
previous version is intended. This draft will be subject to
further consultation.

0201

DRAFT
14.5.92

TECHNICAL REVISION TO GATS DEFINITIONS

FINAL ACT	PROPOSED REVISIONS	COMMENTS
Article XXXIV **Definitions** For the purpose of this Agreement:	For the purpose of this Agreement:	
(a) "measure" means any measure by a Party, whether in the form of a law, regulation, rule, procedure, decision, administrative action, or any other form;	(a) "measure" means any measure by a Member, whether in the form of a law, regulation, rule, procedure, decision, administrative action, or any other form;	Substitution of "Member".
(b) "supply of a service" includes the production, distribution, marketing, sale and delivery of a service;		
(c) "measures by Parties affecting trade in services" include measures in respect of	(c) "measures by Members affecting trade in services" include measures in respect of	Substitution of "Member".
i) the purchase, payment or use of a service,		
ii) the access to and use of, in connection with the supply of a service,		
1. distribution and transportation systems, and		

0202

3귀 - 노ㅇ - /노

0203

- 2 -

FINAL ACT	PROPOSED REVISIONS	COMMENTS
2. public telecommunications transport networks and services, and		
iii) the presence, including commercial presence, of persons of a Party for the supply of a service in the territory of another Party.	iii) the presence, including commercial presence, of persons of a Member for the supply of a service in the territory of another Member;	Clarification. Substitution of "Member".
(d) "commercial presence" means any type of business or professional establishment, including through		
i) the constitution, acquisition or maintenance of a juridical person, or		
ii) the creation or maintenance of a branch or a representative office,		
within the territory of a Party for the purpose of supplying a service.	within the territory of a Member for the purpose of supplying a service.	Substitution of "Member".
	(..) "sector" of a service means one or more, or all, sub-sectors of that service, as specified in a Member's schedule	Simplification. Avoids repeated use in the Agreement of "sectors and sub-sectors". Substitution of "Member".
	(..) "service of a Member" means a service which originates in the territory of the Member	Origin rule. Substitution of "Member".

- 3 -

FINAL ACT		PROPOSED REVISIONS		COMMENTS
(e)	"service supplier" of another Party means any person of that Party that supplies a service;	(e)	"service supplier" means any person that supplies a service;	Separates origin rule from definition.
		(...)	"monopoly supplier of a service" means any person, public or private, which in the relevant market of the territory of a Member is authorized or established formally or in effect by that Member as the sole supplier of that service.	Definition of term used in Article VIII.
(f)	"service consumer" of a Party means any person of that Party that receives or uses a service;	(f)	"service consumer" means any person that receives or uses a service;	Clarification. Separates origin rule from definition.
(g)	"person" of a Party is either a natural or a juridical person of that Party	(g)	"person" means either a natural person or a juridical person	Clarification. Separates origin rule from definition.
(h)	"natural person" of a Party means	(h)	"natural person of a Member" means a natural person who	Clarification. Substitution of "Member".
i)	a natural person who is a national of the Party under the law of that Party, or	i)	is a national of the Member or,	Clarification. Substitution of "Member".

- 4 -

FINAL ACT	PROPOSED REVISIONS	COMMENTS
ii) in the case of a Party which does not have nationals, a natural person who has the right of permanent residence under the law of that Party,	ii) in the case of a Member which does not have nationals, or a Member which makes a special declaration to the Council on Trade in Services, has the right of permanent residence in the Member	Provides option for Member of having its permanent residents included within scope of Agreement. Substitution of "Member".
and who resides in the territory of that Party or any other Party.	under the law of that Member, and who resides in the territory of that Member or any other Member.	Substitution of "Member".
(i) "juridical person" of another Party means any corporation, partnership, joint venture, sole proprietorship or association, whether constituted for profit or otherwise, and whether privately-owned or governmentally-owned, which is	(..) "juridical person" means any legal entity duly constituted or otherwise organized under applicable law, whether for profit or otherwise, and whether privately-owned or governmentally-owned, including any corporation, trust, partnership, joint venture, sole proprietorship or association.	Mention of "trust" ensures coverage of an important form of juridical person. Mention of any "legal entity" ensures that coverage of definition is not exhaustive.
	(i) "juridical person of another Member" means a juridical person which is	Origin rule. Substitution of "Member".
i) constituted under the law of that Party and is engaged in substantive business operations in the territory of that Party or any other Party, or	i) constituted or otherwise organized under the law of that other Member, and is engaged in substantive business operations in the territory of that Member or any other Member; or	Ensures that definition is comprehensive. Substitution of "Member".

0205

0900

- 5 -

FINAL ACT	PROPOSED REVISIONS	COMMENTS
ii) owned or controlled by	ii) in the case of the supply of a service through commercial presence, owned or controlled by	Clarification in order to limit the application of the ownership and control criterion to relevant cases of commercial presence.
1. natural persons of that Party, or		
2. juridical persons of that Party as defined under paragraph (i).	2. juridical persons of that other Member identified under subparagraph (i).	Clarity. Substitution of "Member".
(j) A juridical person is		
i) "owned" by persons of a Party if more than 50 per cent of the equity interest in it is beneficially owned by persons of that Party;	i) "owned" by persons of a Member if more than 50 per cent of the equity interest in it is beneficially owned by persons of that Member;	Substitution of "Member".
ii) "controlled" by persons of a Party if such persons have the power to name a majority of its directors or to otherwise legally direct its actions;	ii) "controlled" by persons of a Member if such persons have the power to name a majority of its directors or to otherwise legally direct its actions;	Substitution of "Member".

- 6 -

FINAL ACT	PROPOSED REVISIONS	COMMENTS
iii) "affiliated" with another person when it controls, or is controlled by, that other person; or when it and the other person are both controlled by the same person.		
Article I **Scope and Definition**		
1. This Agreement applies to measures by Parties affecting trade in services.	1. This Agreement applies to measures by Members affecting trade in services.	Substitution of "Member".
2. For the purposes of this Agreement, trade in services is defined as the supply of a service:		
(a) from the territory of one Party into the territory of any other Party;	(a) from the territory of one Member into the territory of any other Member;	Substitution of "Member".
(b) in the territory of one Party to the service consumer of any other Party;	(b) in the territory of one Member to the service consumer of any other Member;	Substitution of "Member".
(c) through the presence of service providing entities of one Party in the territory of any other Party;	(c) by a service supplier of one Member, through commercial presence in the territory of any other Member;	The revised wording brings Article I into accordance with Article XXXIV definitions of "commercial presence" and "juridical person". Substitution of "Member".
(d) by natural persons of one Party in the territory of any other Party.	(d) by a service supplier of one Member, through presence of natural persons of a Member in the territory of any other Member.	The revised wording brings Article I into accordance with the Article XXXIV definition of "natural person". Substitution of "Member".

0207

FINAL ACT	PROPOSED REVISION:	COMMENTS
3. For the purposes of this Agreement:	3. For the purposes of this Agreement:	Rectification. Substitution of "Member".
"measures by Parties" means measures taken by:	(a) "measures by Members" means measures taken by:	
(i) central, regional or local governments and authorities; and		
(ii) non-governmental bodies in the exercise of powers delegated by central, regional or local governments or authorities;		
In fulfilling its obligations and commitments under the Agreement, each Party shall take such reasonable measures as may be available to it to ensure their observance by regional and local governments and authorities and non-governmental bodies within its territory.	In fulfilling its obligations and commitments under the Agreement, each Member shall take such reasonable measures as may be available to it to ensure their observance by regional and local governments and authorities and non-governmental bodies within its territory.	Substitution of "Member".
(b) "services" includes any service in any sector except services supplied in the exercise of governmental functions.*	(b) "services" includes any service in any sector, except a service supplied in the exercise of governmental authority. A service supplied in the exercise of governmental authority shall not be understood to include a service supplied on a commercial basis, or in competition with one or more service suppliers.	Revision and clarification.
*The terms of the exclusion of services supplied in the exercise of governmental functions will be reviewed in the context of the work on Article XXXIV.		

0208

- 8 -

FINAL ACT	PROPOSED REVISIONS	COMMENTS
Article XXXI		
Denial of Benefits		
1. A Party may deny the benefits of this Agreement:	1. A Member may deny the benefits of this Agreement:	Substitution of "Member".
(a) to the supply of a service, if it establishes that the service originates in the territory of a country that is not a Party to this Agreement, or in the territory of a Party to which the denying Party does not apply this Agreement; and	(a) to the supply of a service, if it establishes that the service originates in the territory of a country that is not a Member to this Agreement, or in the territory of a Member to which the denying Member does not apply this Agreement; and	
(b) to a service supplier that is a juridical person, if it establishes that ultimate ownership or control of such person is held by persons of a country that is not a Party to this Agreement, or of a Party to which the denying Party does not apply this Agreement.	(b) to a service supplier that is a juridical person, if it establishes that ultimate ownership or control of such person is held by persons of a country that is not a Member to this Agreement, or of a Member to which the denying Member does not apply this Agreement.	Substitution of "Member".

ANNEX ON FINANCIAL SERVICES		
1. Scope and Definition		
1.2 For the purposes of Article I:3(b) of the Agreement, "services supplied in the exercise of governmental functions" means the following:	1.2 For the purposes of Article I:3(b) of the Agreement, "services supplied in the exercise of governmental authority" means the following:	Reflects new wording in Article I.

0209

- 5 -

FINAL ACT	PROPOSED REVISIONS	COMMENTS
1.2.1 activities conducted by a central bank or monetary authority or by any other public entity in pursuit of monetary or exchange rate policies;		
1.2.2 activities forming part of a statutory system of social security or public retirement plans; and		
1.2.3 other activities conducted by a public entity for the account or with the guarantee or using the financial resources of the Government.		
1.3 For the purposes of Article I:3(b) of the Agreement, if a Party allows any of the activities referred to in paragraph 1.2.2 or 1.2.3 to be conducted by its financial service providers in competition with a public entity or a financial service provider, "services" shall include such activities.	1.3 For the purposes of Article I:3(b) of the Agreement, if a Member allows any of the activities referred to in paragraph 1.2.2 or 1.2.3 to be conducted by its financial service providers in competition with a public entity or a financial service provider, "services" shall include such activities.	Substitution of "Member".

0210

외교문서 비밀해제: 우루과이라운드2 22
우루과이라운드 서비스 분야 양허 협상 1

초판인쇄 2024년 03월 15일
초판발행 2024년 03월 15일

지은이 한국학술정보(주)
펴낸이 채종준
펴낸곳 한국학술정보(주)
주 소 경기도 파주시 회동길 230(문발동)
전 화 031-908-3181(대표)
팩 스 031-908-3189
홈페이지 http://ebook.kstudy.com
E-mail 출판사업부 publish@kstudy.com
등 록 제일산-115호(2000. 6. 19)

ISBN 979-11-7217-124-7 94340
      979-11-7217-102-5 94340 (set)